Education in Ancient India

Reconstructing Indian History & Culture
(ISSN 0971-3824)

1. Society in Ancient India; by Sures Chandra Banerji.
2. Political Thought in Ancient India; by G.P. Singh.
3. Early Indian Historical Tradition and Archaeology; by G.P. Singh.
4. Vasantotsava: The Spring Festivals of India; by Leona M. Anderson.
5. Ecological Readings in the Veda; by M. Vannucci.
6. Vṛndāvana in Vaiṣṇava Literature; by Maura Corcoran.
7. Social History of the Tamils (1707-1947); by P. Subramanian.
8. Ancient Indian Coinage; by Rekha Jain.
9. Buddhism and Socio-Economic Life of Eastern India; by Bimal Chandra Mohapatra.
10. Chandragupta Maurya; by P.L. Bhargava.
11. Mṛtyu: Concept of Death in Indian Traditions; by Gian Giuseppe Filippi.
12. Yama: The Glorious Lord of the Other World; by Kusum P. Merh.
13. Sacred Complex of Ujjain; by D.K. Samanta.
14. Vedic View of the Earth; by S.R.N. Murthy.
15. Society in the Atharvaveda; by B.S. Kharade.
16. Orissan History, Culture and Archaeology; by S. Pradhan.
17. Education in Ancient India; by Mitali Chatterjee.
18. Surà: The Liquor and the Vedic Sacrifice; by M.B. Kolhatkar.
19. Human Ecology in the Vedas; by Marta Vannucci.
20. Governance in Ancient India; by Anupa Chandra Pandey.
21. The Cultural Glory of Ancient India: A Literary Overview; by Sures Chandra Banerji.
22. Kauṭilya's Arthaśāstra in the light of Modern Science & Technology; by Sunil Sen Sarma.
23. History of Jainism — With Special Reference to Mathurā; by V.K. Sharma.
24. Cultural Tourism in India: Museums, Monuments & Arts — Theory and Practice; by S.P. Gupta; Krishna Lal; Mahua Bhattacharya.
25. Ancient Indian Historiography — Sources and Interpretations; by G.P. Singh.
26. Republics, Kingdoms, Towns and Cities in Ancient India; by G.P. Singh.
27. Facets of Ancient Indian History and Culture — New Perception; by G.P. Singh.
28. Kamakhya — A Socio-cultural Study; by Nihar Ranjan Mishra.
29. History and Culture of Tamil Nadu as Gleaned from the Sanskrit Inscriptions Vol. 1 (up to c. AD 1310); by Chithra Madhavan.
30. Lifestyle of the Vedic People; by Pranati Ghosal.
31. History and Culture of Tamil Nadu as Gleaned from the Sanskrit Inscriptions Vol. 2 (up to c. AD 1310 - *c.* 1885 AD); by Chithra Madhavan.
32. Matrimonial Alliances and Ancient Indian Polity (*c.* 600 BCE to *c.* 650); by Preeti Prabhat.
33. Artisans and Craftsmen of Northern India; by Kuldeep Singh Thind.
34. The Evolution of Historiographical Tradition in Ancient and Medieval India; by G.P. Singh.
35. Warfare in Ancient India, Theory and Practice by Soma Basu.
36. Sanskrit Education and Literature in Ancient and Medieval Tamil Nadu by Chithra Madhavan

Reconstructing Indian History & Culture, no. 17

Education in Ancient India

(From Literary Sources of the Gupta Age)

Mitali Chatterjee

DK PRINTWORLD
Publishers of Indian Traditions

Cataloging in Publication Data — DK
[Courtesy: D.K. Agencies (P) Ltd. <docinfo@dkagencies.com>]

Chatterjee, Mitali, 1951 –
Education in ancient India.
(Reconstructing Indian history & culture ; no. 17).
Includes bibliographical references (p.).
Includes index.
ISBN 13: 9788124601136

1. Education, Ancient — India. 2. Education — India — History. 3. India — History — 324 BC – 1000 AD. I. Title. II. Series: Reconstructing Indian history & culture; no. 17.

ISBN 13: 978-81-246-0113-6

First published in India in 1999
Second impression published in 2014

Printed and published by:
D.K. Printworld (P) Ltd.
Regd. office : *'Vedaśrī,'* F-395, Sudarshan Park
(Metro Station: Ramesh Nagar)
New Delhi - 110 015
Phones: (011) 2545 3975, 2546 6019; *Fax*: (011) 2546 5926
E-mail: indology@dkprintworld.com
Web: www.dkprintworld.com

Preface

THE present work is an honest attempt to estimate highly developed educational system followed by people during the time of the Gupta monarchs (AD 319 to 550). The golden age of the Guptas sometimes has been described as the Periclean Age of India. During this period India witnessed a wonderful emergence of culture. With inscriptional and other literary records we can detect the fortunes obtained by the people of a single dynasty. India had experienced a unique political unity as well as cultural interest under the supreme banner of the Guptas. India saw the extensiveness of the Gupta civilisation. The intellectual and cultural activities that India experienced during this period continued for centuries mainly through vast literary records produced under the patronage of the Gupta monarchs.

Many aspects of political, social, religious and cultural history of the Guptas have been the topics of researches of various eminent scholars. But so far my knowledge goes scholars have not seriously taken the educational system of the Gupta Age as the subject of their study. Various literary works including Purāṇas, poems, dramas, Sanskrit inscriptions and coins belonging to this period furnish us with valuable documents relating to the history of the Guptas. In these works though details about educational system of that period have not been elaborately dealt with by any prominent author of that age, yet there remain scattered a good number of materials concerning education in innumerable works of this period. The educational system practised by people of later Gupta period sometimes helps us to imagine as to how the system of education was nurtured by the people of the Gupta age. In any case like the political and social condition religious toleration, development of art and architecture, the educational system of this age was also in a highly developed condition. For this reason an attempt has been made in this work to evaluate the educational system of the Gupta age and this would certainly help the present generation to think over the academic atmosphere created in India several centuries back.

The present study has been distributed over six chapters.

In the first chapter an account of the prominent Sanskrit works written and revised in this period, has been presented.

In the second chapter an elaborate study of the educational system revealed in the Purāṇas and Smṛti literature has been made. Though it is not possible to definitely determine the age of the Purāṇas, and Smṛti texts some of the reputed scholars of Indology have tried to place some of the principal Purāṇas in or near the time of the Guptas. Only those Purāṇas and the Upapurāṇa, *Viṣṇudharmottara* have been taken for study. Regarding the Smṛti texts their actual age cannot also be determined. But as *Manu-smṛti* and *Yājñavalkya-smṛti* had extensive influence over the social structure of ancient India and as there are several stray references to utterings of Manu and Yājñavalkya in the Sanskrit works of the Gupta age, the elements on education that are occasionally discussed by Manu and Yājñavalkya have also been incorporated in this chapter. Incidentally some of the aspects of education that have been discussed in Kauṭilya's *Arthaśāstra* and Kāmandaka's *Nītisāra* have also been dealt with.

In the third chapter classical Sanskrit works that are believed to have been composed during the Gupta age have been discussed and therefrom many elements of educational system have been detected. Among the classical authors of this period, most probably Kālidāsa was the foremost one. So his works have been given special emphasis. In this period Kumāradāsa, Viśākhadatta and some other prominent authors are believed to have been born. So these authors have been taken up for detecting educational pattern of that age. Some classical authors like Bāṇabhaṭṭa and Bhāravī who most probably flourished at the periods later than that of the Guptas, have touched some of the important points on education. Their works have been discussed in this chapter to show that they inherited a highly advanced system of education from the age of the Guptas. Some of the minor but important works like *Āryabhaṭīya* and *Bṛhat-saṁhitā* have also been included in this chapter.

Educational system revealed in the Buddhist and Jaina works has been touched upon in the next chapter. It should be noted that a good number of Buddhist works are composed in Pāli and the Jaina works in Prākṛt. So an estimate of the educational system of the Buddhist and the Jaina would be incomplete if one does not go through those Pāli and Prākṛt texts. To know the educational systems of the Buddhist, the account of the Chinese traveller Fa-hien, who visited India in the first quarter of the fifth centrury AD, is very important. His views on education have been presented and have substantiated by the accounts of other travellers who visited India in successive periods.

Education of the Gupta age as has been reflected in the Gupta inscriptions has been discussed in the fifth chapter. The inscriptions selected for this chapter are concerned mainly with the glorious reign of the Gupta monarchs and partly with the achievements of their contemporaries. Only inscriptions composed in Sanskrit have been taken here for discussion.

In the conclusion chapter, a general trend of education in Gupta India and its possible legacy or deviation in the educational system prevalent in the modern age have been taken for discussion.

In preparing this work, I have consulted the available primary sources as far as practicable. In the present study, I sincerely acknowledge the guidance and assistance that I have received from various persons and I like to record due thanks to them.

12. 10. 98 **Mitali Chatterjee**
Calcutta

Contents

Abbreviations

ABORI : *Annals of the Bhandarkar Oriental Research Institute,* Poona.

AHRS : *Andhra Historical Research Society.*

AIHT : *Ancient Indian Historical Tradition.*

AIOC : All-India Oriental Conference.

ĀpDhS : *Āpastamba Dharma-sūtra.*

ARASI : *Annual Report of the Archaelogical Survey of India.*

BauDh : *Baudhāyana Dharma-sūtra.*

BI : *Bibliotheca Indica.*

BORAS : *Bombay Branch of Royal Asiatic Society.*

BṛhUp : *Bṛhadāraṇyaka Upaniṣad.*

BS : *Bṛhat-saṁhitā.*

ChāUp : *Chāndogya Upaniṣad.*

CII : *Corpus Inscriptionum Indicarum.*

EHI : *Early History of India* by V.A. Smith.

EI : *Epigraphia Indica.*

EpEnd : *Epigraphia Indica.*

GOS : Gaekwad's Oriental Series, Baroda.

IA : *Indian Antiquary,* Bombay.

IHQ : *Indian Historical Quarterly.*

JA : *Journal Asiatique.*

JAHRS : *Journal of the Andhra Historical Research Society.*

JARS : *Journal of the Assam Research Society.*
JASB : *Journal of the Asiatic Society of Bengal.*
JBBRAS : *Journal of Bombay Branch of the Asiatic Society,* Bombay.
JBORS : *Journal of the Bihar and Orissa Research Society*, Patna.
JDLCU : *Journal of Department of Letters,*Calcutta University.
JORI : *Journal of the Oriental Research Institute,* Pune.
JPASB : *Journal and Proceedings of Asiatic Society of Bengal.*
JPTS : *Journal of the Pali Text Society.*
JRAS : *Journal of the Royal Asiatic Society.*
Kumāra. : *Kumārasambhava.*
Mahā : *Mahāvagga.*
Mālavikā.: *Mālavikāgnimitra.*
Manu : *Manu-smṛti.*
Megha. : *Meghadūtam.*
Milinda : *Milindapañho.*
Mudrā. : *Mudrārākṣasam.*
n.d. : non dated.
PAIOC : Proceedings of All India Oriental Conference.
Pāṇ : Pāṇini's *Aṣṭādhyāyī.*
PB : *Prabuddha Bharat.*
PIHC : Proceedings of Indian Historiecal Congress.
Raghu. : *Raghuvaṁśam.*
Śāk : *Śākuntalam.*
S.B.E. : Sacred Books of the East.
Sel. Ins. : *Select Inscriptions* of D.C. Sircar.
Vik. : *Vikramarvaśīyam.*

1

India in the Gupta Age

Writing and Revision of Sanskrit Works during this Period

THE reign of the Imperial Gupta kings (AD 319 -500) is popularly known as the Gupta Age. Various names attributed to Gupta age prove its speciality and importance. India under the rules of Guptas was united under one sovereign and the age reflected its supremacy in education, literature and scientific achievements. The age has been named as Golden, Classical and Periclean age of India.

The age may be called Golden Age as in Europe the Elizabethan and the Victorian Ages are used to make their specialities. The term 'Classical' refers to the literary and other artistic production of the first rate order. After the downfall of the Gupta empire, the memory of its greatness continued for centuries.

One of the sources of history of advancement of imperial Gupta Age in several Sanskrit literary works written during that period or in the following years. V.S. Smith maintains that along with the renovation of the Brāhmaṇical religion, the revival of the Sanskrit language was made a success by the Gupta emperors in the fourth and fifth centuries.[1] But it would be wrong to think that Sanskrit writings ever ceased to exist. On the contrary, the cultivation of Sanskrit writings which started several centuries preceding the Gupta era attained a finished

1. *Early History of India*, 4th edn, 1924, p. 320.

form in this period. The spacious period of the Guptas is marked by all types of Sanskrit compositions relating to *kāvya*, drama, romantic stories, philosophical and scientific literature, grammar, architecture, painting, music, etc.

The Sanskrit literary works include (1) the Purāṇas, (2) the works of Kālidāsa, Viśākhadatta, Kumāradāsa, the play called *Kaumudī-mahotsava* composed by a female dramatist Vajjika by name, (3) the works of the Buddhist scholars like Vasubandhu and Diñnāga who adopted Sanskrit as the chosen medium of their literary creations, (4) The astronomical works like Āryabhaṭiya, etc., (5) The grammatical works by Bhartṛhari — *Mahābhāṣyapradīpikā*, *Vākyapadīya*, (6) The comprehensive works of lexicon like *Amarakośa*, *Nānārthasaṁgraha*, (7) The Smṛti literature viz., *Vyāsa-smṛti*, *Hārita-saṁhitā*, *Pitāmaha-smṛti* and *Pulastya-smṛti*, (8) works on polity like *Kāmandakīya Nītisāra*. The cultivation of Sanskrit was in regular practice at this time is evident from the forceful *kāvya*-element in the Gupta inscription.

Some of the Purāṇas were re-constructed and re-arranged in this period. The word *purāṇa* occurred in the same sense of *itihāsa* or simply old narrative. A Purāṇa is supposed to deal with *pañcalakṣaṇa* or five topics namely creation, destruction, re-creation, genealogy of the gods and *ṛṣi*s, periods of Manus and history of royal dynasties. But none of the available Purāṇic texts fulfils the clauses of the definition.

It may be supposed that the available texts are revised versions and became little afar from the core of the texts. According to the definition as we find in the Purāṇa-texts themselves, the number of Mahāpurāṇas is eighteen. There are similar number of the Upapurāṇas. Though they are styled as *upa*, they are not at all minor in character. As the original authors of the Purāṇas were *sūta*s or the bards, the texts were later on preserved by the local priests. Many narratives of local origin have been interwoven in the Purāṇas. So the Purāṇas are more or less sectarian and propounds favourable incidents to highlight a particular deity or a place which is sacred to that particular deity. Still the importance of Purāṇas cannot be neglected. The picture of ancient India can be discovered by peeping through these Purāṇas. The Purāṇic literature depicts all aspects and facets of Hinduism including the daily life of the contemporary people as well as the highest philosophy. Apart from these we find in the Purāṇas some historical aspects such as the genealogies of kings and those of the sages. Some of the Dharmasūtras, viz. the *Gautama Dharmasūtra* enlisted the Purāṇas as source of law. However the importance of the Purāṇas cannot be neglected in order to study the ancient age of India. Among the eighteen Mahāpurāṇas, at least *Mārkaṇḍeya*, *Matsya*, *Vāyu* and *Viṣṇu*, as well as the *Viṣṇudharmottara Purāṇa* which has been included in the eighteen Upapurāṇas, were composed or came to be finally shaped during the rule of the Guptas. MM P.V. Kane is of the opinion that these Purāṇas were composed between AD 300-600.[2]

The extent Sanskrit literature composed during the Gupta rule bears the testimony of the spontaneous manifestation of the creative faculty of the people. The Sanskrit literature of the Gupta age obtained the esteemed position with the famous works of Kālidāsa, Viśākhadatta, Kumāradāsa and several others.

Kālidāsa may be described unanimously as the best litterateur of Sanskrit literature. His works is the fountain of joy to the readers throughout the ages. Even nowadays not only Indian scholars but foreign scholars are in the first row to instal him as the best writer. The date of Kālidāsa varies from second century BC to the seventh century AD.[3] But many of the scholars are inclined to place him in the glorious period under the rule of the Guptas.[4] The life-story of Kālidāsa shrouded in mystery. His works prove that though he believed in Śaiva faith he was liberal to other faith and well proficient in philosophical systems

---

2. P.V. Kane, *History of Dharmaśāstra*, Vol. V, Pt. II, Chronological Table, p. xiii.
3. V.V., Mirashi, 'The Rāṣṭrakūṭas of Kuntala and the date of Kālidāsa' in *Pañcāmṛta*.
4. K.P. Pathak, *Introduction to the Meghadūta*, Poona, 1916, p. vii; R.G. Basak in Proceedings of 2nd All India Oriental Conference, Calcutta, 1922, p. 327.

and other various branches of knowledge prevalent in those age. The clear and easy style of his works has universal appeal. *Abhijñāna-Śākuntalam* is the best known drama by Kālidāsa. Apart from that, the *Mālavikāgnimitra, Vikramorvaśī* are other two dramas which came down to us from the pen of Kālidāsa. He also wrote two *mahākāvya*s namely the *Raghuvaṁśa* and the *Kumārasaṁbhava* and the lyrical poems *Meghadūta* and *Ṛtusaṁhāra*.

An astronomical work entitled *Jyotirvidābharaṇam* is also ascribed to him. But there is controversy regarding the authorship.

Kālidāsa is justly regarded as the greatest of all Indian poets and dramatists. Under the patronage of the imperial Guptas, he was able to demonstrate his proficiency in a much advanced technique of poetry. His works display a very calm and prosperous state of things.

The *Kaumudī-mahotsava*[5] is a five-Act drama ascribed to Vijjaka, whose date and place are not accurately known. The drama depicts the story of the treacherous Caṇḍasena, an adopted son and the army-commander of Sundaravarman, king of Magadha; Caṇḍasena allied himself with the barbarian Licchavis and got possession of Magadha by defeating the king, his adopting father. Various dates starting from the fourth to eighth century have been ascribed to the play.

K.P. Jayaswal feels certain that the story of this drama brings into light the early Gupta history and his contention is that Caṇḍasena was no other than the historical king, Candragupta I. His satisfaction in this regard is that both Caṇḍasena and Candragupta I had alliances with the Licchavis.[6] But the relevance of this view of Jayaswal has been called into question, for, excepting the reference to the connexion with the Licchavis, there is no similarity between the contents of the *Kaumudī-mahotsava* and the historical incidents of the Gupta period. D.C. Sircar has tried to prove that the *Kaumudī-mahotsava* was

5. *Kaumudī-mahotsava*, edited by Ramakrishna Kavi and Paṇḍit Rāmanāth Śāstrī, Madras, 1929.

6. *JBORS*, Vol. XIX, p. 113.

composed about seventh or eighth century AD.[7] K.C. Chattopadhyaya also maintains the similar view.[8] But the style and diction of our dramatist show that she was very much indebted to and influenced by Kālidāsa. It appears that the drama is nearer to Kālidāsa's time.[9] From the perusal of the drama, it should be admitted that the *Kaumudī-mahotsava* does not lack the literary spirit of the Gupta age, and most probably it was written within one or two centuries after the appearance of Kālidāsa.

The famous Buddhist *vijñānavādin* of this age was Diṅnāga. He first formulated a systematic science of logic. His views have been criticised and refuted by many famous brāhmaṇa logicians. He wrote a good number of treatises. Among them *Pramāṇasamuccaya*, *Nyāyapraveśa* and *Prajñāpāramitā-piṇḍārtha* is worth mentioning.

A few astronomical works like *Āryabhaṭīya*, *Daśagītikāsūtra*, *Āryāṣṭaśata* written by famous astronomer Āryabhaṭa have come down to modern time. *Āryabhaṭīya* was composed on AD 499 and Āryabhaṭa dealt Mathematics as a distinct subject. He explained the cause of eclipse of the moon and other theories. The notation system was uniquely propounded.

Traditionally, Kumāradāsa — the author of the *mahākāvya*, *Jānakīharaṇa*, was a contemporary and a friend of Kālidāsa. According to the late Ceylonese tradition, Kumāradāsa, also known as Kumāradhātusena, was a king of Ceylon about the middle of the sixth century AD; he was a profound scholar and died after a glorious reign of nine years.[10] As the name suggests, the *Jānakīharaṇa* is based on the *Rāmāyaṇa* story, but the entire text has not yet been recovered. Paṇḍit Haridās Śāstrī's edition (Calcutta, 1893) contains fifteen cantos among which the 15th concludes with the description of the construction of the

7. *JAHRS*, Vol. XI, pp. 63-7.
8. *IHQ*, Vol. XIV, pp. 593f.
9. K.P. Jayaswal, *History of India* (AD 150-250), p. 95.
10. M. Krishnamachariar, *History of Classical Sanskrit Literature*, Delhi, 1970, p. 135.

bridge on the ocean by Rāma's party. But the poem seems to have twenty-five cantos as is indicated by the colophon of the said edition.[11] Paṇḍit Śāstrī could not perhaps collect the last ten cantos.

The *Kundamālā*,[12] a play in six Acts, is based on the concluding part of the *Rāmāyaṇa* story, beginning with the incident where Lakṣmaṇa takes Sītā into banishment and ending with the consecrating of Kuśa and Lava as Rāma's heirs. A controversy remains among scholars regarding the name of the author of this play. These are Diṅnāga, Vīranāga, Dhīranāga, and Nāgayya M. Ramakrishna Kavi and Rāmanāth Śāstrī, in their edition of the *Kundamālā* ascribe the authorship of the drama to Diṅnāga. They have identified this Diṅnāga with the great Buddhist logician of the same name and hold that he was the rival of Kālidāsa. Krishnamacariar, on the other hand, is of the opinion that[13] the drama was written by Dhīranāga who lived at Arālapura, sometime earlier than the fifth century AD, i.e., during the middle of the Gupta era.

Viśākhadatta is believed to be a dramatist belonging to the Gupta period.[14] He is the author of the famous *Mudrārākṣasa* and the long-lost drama, *Devīcandragupta* — both being based on historical incidents. The subject-matter of the *Devīcandragupta* is mainly known from the *Nāṭyadarpaṇa* of Rāmacandra and Guṇacandra. The other sources of our knowledge of this drama are the *Abhinavabhāratī* of Abhinavagupta, Bhoja's *Śṛṅgāraprakāśa* and the *Nāṭakalakṣaṇaratnakośa* of Sāgaranandin. This drama gives some light on a little-known but a

---

11. *iti siṁhalakaver atiśayabhūtasya kumāradāsasya kṛtau jānakīharaṇe mahākāvye rāmābhiṣeko nāma pañcaviṁśatitamaḥ sargaḥ* ।
12. Ed. by M. Ramakrishna Kavi and S.K. Rāmanāth Śāstrī, Madras, 1923; ed. by Jayacandra Śāstrī, Lahore, 1929; ed. by Vedavyāsa and Sarandas Bhanot, Lahore, 1932.
13. *History of Classical Sanskrit Literature*, p. 604.
14. M. Winternitz, *History of Indian Literature*, Vol. III, Pt. I, 1963, p. 233; K.P. Jayaswal, *IA*, Vol. XLM, 1913, p. 266; Sten Konow, *IA*, Vol. XLIII, 1914, pp. 66ff.

formative chapter of the history of the imperial Guptas. The *Mudrārākṣasa*, in seven Acts, portrays the artful efforts of Cāṇakya to force Rākṣasa, the hereditary minister of the Nandas, to accept the ministership of Candragupta Maurya.

The *gadya-kāvya* itself came to be produced at a later period. Sanskrit prose works, composed during the Gupta age, have not yet came to light excepting the extensive inscriptional and some Buddhist writings. The inscriptions are composed sometimes in a very forceful prose showing therein high standard of prose composition. The language in the inscriptions indicates regular practice of writing prose-*kāvya* during this period. But unfortunately no complete Sanskrit *gadya-kāvya* can be unqestionably placed in the Gupta period.

So far as the educational system is concerned, we may bring under the scope of our study the famous prose works, *Kādambarī* and *Harṣacarita* of Bāṇabhaṭṭa, *Vāsavadattā* of Subandhu and *Daśakumāracarita* of Daṇḍin. Though these works were composed about one century after the eclipse of the Gupta supremacy, they are rich with elements related with Education which are certainly the same that were in practice during the Gupta rule.

In the field of astronomical and mathematical literature of ancient India, the most prominent writer is Āryabhaṭa. His *Āryabhaṭīya*[15] is a masterpiece as a learned *jyotiṣa* work. It has been generally accepted that Āryabhaṭa was born in AD 476 and composed his work in AD 479.[16]

In the field of science of grammar Bhartṛhari is a popular name. He is said to be the disciple of Vāsurata, a contemporary of the great Buddhist philosopher Vasubandhu. Vasubandhu is ascribed to the middle of the fifth century AD.[17] Bhartṛhari is to be accepted as the

---

15. Ed. by K. Sambasiva Śāstrī, with the commentary of Nilakantha, Trivandrum, 1930.
16. A.B. Keith, *History of Sanskrit Literature*, p. 521.
17. J. Takakusu, 'A Study of Paramartha's Life of Vasubandhu and the date of Vasubandhu', *JRAS*, 1905, pp. 34f.

author belonging to the period not much later than AD 500. Bhartṛhari is the author of a commentary of Patañjali's *mahābhāṣya*, called *Mahābhāṣyapradīpikā*, he is also credited with the authorship of the illustrious work *Vākyapadīya* dealing with the doctrines of *sphoṭa* and *śabdādvaita*.

According to traditions Amarasiṁha, author of the *Nāmaliṅgānuśāsana*, usually called *Amarakośa*, was one of the nine jewels of Vikramāditya and so his date has been fixed during the fourth century AD.[18]

In the field of Legal Literature (Smṛti) the Gupta period formed an age of transition. This period is marked by the cultivation of some of the important Dharmaśāstras which bear clear evidence of a distinct and very developed branch of literature. Of the Dharmaśāstra literature belonging to this period, we may mention *Bṛhaspati-smṛti*, *Kātyāyana-smṛti*, *Hārita-smṛti* etc. P.V. Kane is of the opinion that the authors of these Smṛti texts flourished between the fourth and sixth century AD.[19]

The *Nītisāra* of Kāmandaka is ascribed by some to the period of the reign of Candragupta II.[20] The *Nītisāra* is a work on the essence of science of politics. It is based mainly on Kauṭilya's *Arthaśāstra*. In fact, the contents of the *Arthaśāstra* elaborated by Kauṭilya in 180 chapters have been made brief and simplified in the *Nītisāra*.

Among the works on Buddhism, particularly those composed by the authors belonging to the Hīnayāna Buddhism, three or four prominent works composed, or compiled or partly composed during the Gupta period. The *Mahāvastu Avadāna*, which is believed to be originally composed about second century BC, was enlarged by fresh additions and interpolations during the fourth and fifth century AD. The *Divyāvadāna*

---

18. A.B. Keith, *History of Sanskrit Literature*, p. 413.
19. *History of Dharmaśāstra*, Vol I, Pt. I, pp. 290f.
20. (i) R.N. Saletore, *Life in the Gupta Age*, p. 466.
    (ii) K.P. Jayaswal, *Hindu Polity*, Pt. I, Pl. 215, Bangalore, 1955.

seems to have followed the same fate. The *Jātakamālā* of Āryasura, *Samādhirājasūtra*, *Saddharmapuṇḍarīka*, *Laṅkāvatāra Sūtra* and similar other works were compiled or partly composed during the period under consideration. But it is generally believed by the scholars that Vasubandhu and Diñnāga, the most renowned authors on Buddhist philosophy flourished during this period. Vasubandhu's most important work is *Abhidharmakośa* and Diñnāga is reputed for his work *Pramāṇasamuccaya*. Buddhaghoṣa, the author of *Padyacūḍāmaṇi*, is according to F. Max Müller, the author who conducted his literary activities in Ceylon in the period sometime between AD 410-12.[21] The *Padyacūḍāmaṇi* is a complete *mahākāvya* in 10 cantos consisting of 600 and odd verses.

During this period some important Sanskrit works on ancient Indian culture and architecture came to light and these works sufficiently prove that fine arts including architecture, sculpture and paintings were in an astonishingly developed condition in India during the Gupta Age. The Śilpaśāstra literature of this period includes the *Mayamatam* of Mayamuni and *Pratimāmānalakṣaṇam* of an unknown author.

One of the sources of Indian history is the huge inscriptional literature composed during the rules of various kings of ancient India. The Gupta inscriptions throw considerable light on the political, social and economic and religious History of the rulers of the Gupta Age. Some of these inscriptions speak of wide cultivation and sporadic development of Sanskrit *kāvya* literature. Two prominent authors of literary insciption of the Gupta period are Hariṣeṇa, the author of Allahabad Pillar Inscription of Samudragupta, Vatsabhaṭṭi, author of the Mandasore Inscription of Kumāragupta.

Besides the Sanskrit works referred to above there were certainly many other works which were composed under the patronage of the

21. Max Müller, *Buddhaghosa's Parable*, London, 1870, Introduction, p. xii.

Gupta emperors or their officials. The literary efforts carried on by eminent scholars throw a flood of light on the cultural progress of the Gupta age. From these literature extended over more than 300 we came to know satisfactorily the trend of educational systems and similar other information that were current in the Gupta Age.

2

Education in the Purāṇa and Smṛti Literature

THE material and moral progress and advancement of knowledge of the country can be achieved only in the background of stabilized political condition. The Gupta empire was a well-organised state. It succeeded to set-up political unification of a large part of India under the extensive umbrella of its paramount sovereignty. The staunch patronage towards Sanskrit learning gave shape to the advancement of Sanskrit literature in all its branches. The ultimate development of the Purāṇas and the last phase of the Smṛti literature took place in the Gupta Age.

In the Vedic literature the word *purāṇa* usually means *itihāsa*. From the derivative meaning it means 'old narrative'. The name Purāṇa as a special branch of the sacred literature occurs in the *Atharvaveda*. Purāṇa, as a branch of the Vedic literature is as old as sacred as the Vedic *mantras*, in their Saṁhitā form. There did not exist any special feature. According to the traditional definition, a Purāṇa deals with five topics (*pañca-lakṣaṇa*).[1]

(1) *Sarga* or creation of the universe, (2) *pratisarga* or re-creation after destruction, (3) *vaṁśa* or genealogy, (4) *manvantara* or the great periods of time with Manu as the primal ancestor, (5) *vaṁśānucarita*

1. The following verse indicating the contents of a Purāṇa appears in almost all the Purāṇas —

   sargaśca pratisargaśca vaṁśo manvantarāṇi ca |
   vaṁśānucaritañcaiva purāṇam pañcalakṣaṇam ||

or the history of the dynasties both solar and lunar. But the existing Purāṇas hardly conform to this definition since they contain either something less than the limitations set by it or something more.

The Purāṇas themselves state their number to be eighteen.[2] They are in most cases as follows: *Brahma*, *Padma*, *Viṣṇu*, *Śiva* or *Vāyu*, *Bhāgavata*, *Nārada*, *Mārkaṇḍeya*, *Agni*, *Bhaviṣya*, *Brahma-vaivarta*, *Liṅga*, *Varāha*, *Skanda*, *Vāmana*, *Kūrma*, *Matsya*, *Garuḍa* and *Brahmāṇḍa*. The *Padma Purāṇa* classifies these texts according to the three *guṇas* and ascribes them to one or the other principal deity.[3] Thus the Vaiṣṇavite Purāṇas are *sāttvika* Purāṇas lead to salvation. The Purāṇas devoted to Brahmā, secure only heaven for their readers, are *rājasa* purāṇa. Lastly the Śaivite Purāṇas are *tamasa* Purāṇa, lead to hell.

Besides these eighteen Purāṇas, there exists the Upapurāṇas. The number of Upapurāṇas is also stated to be eighteen. They are more or less the outcome of local cults and different religious sects. The original authors of the Purāṇas were the *sūta*s or the bards. Thus in almost all the Purāṇas the *sūta* Lomaharṣaṇa or his son Ugraśravas appears as the narrator. In later period it was controlled by priests who were not always well educated and lived on worship. They added new materials to serve their own ends. Thus the Purāṇas became more or less sectarian carrying on propaganda in favour of a particular deity or a place sacred to that deity. According to Pargiter, Pusalkar and others the Purāṇas were originally composed in Prākṛts and later on converted into Sanskrit.[4]

The importance of Purāṇas is noteworthy for the development of later Hinduism. According to Winternitz "they afford us far greater insight into all aspects and phrases of Hinduism — its mythology, its

2. *Kūrma Purāṇa*, *Pūrvabhāga*, 1.13-15.
3. *Padma Purāṇa*
4. F.E. Pargiter, *Ancient Indian Historical Tradition,* Oxford 1922, pp. 50-1, x-xi; Pusalkar, *Acharya Druva Comm.*, *Vol.* Pt. III, pp. 101-4.

idol-worship, its theism and pantheism, its love of God, its philosophy, and its superstitions, its festivals and ceremonies, and its ethics, than any other work".[5] The *Vāyu*, *Brahmāṇḍa*, *Matsya* and *Viṣṇu Purāṇas* depict ancient royal genealogies. Besides the *Bramāṇḍa*, *Vāyu* and *Matsya* offer the genealogies of important brāhmaṇa families. As there is said to be lack of history in ancient India, these genealogies of kings and brāhmaṇas are the available ancient source of history which can be utilised in writing the history.

According to Jackson and F.E. Pargiter[6] there was originally a single Purāṇa out of which all the present texts have taken place.

Dr. Hazra has suggested probable dates for some of the important Purāṇas.[7] According to Dr. Hazra these Purāṇas may be placed like thus: (1) *Mārkaṇḍeya Purāṇa* — third to fifth century AD (some portions may be much later), (2-3) *Brahmāṇḍa* and *Vāyu Purāṇa* — third to fifth century AD, (4) *Viṣṇu Purāṇa* — third to fourth century AD, (5) *Bhāgavata Purāṇa* — sixth century AD, (6) *Matsya Purāṇa* — sixth to seventh century AD (some portion may be later). These Purāṇas may be older than others but as the *Vāyu*, *Brahmāṇḍa*, *Viṣṇu* and *Bhāgavata Purāṇas* mention the Guptas among the royal dynasties, so they are not earlier than fourth century AD. The *Vāyu Purāṇa* is mentioned in *Harṣacarita*[8] so it is earlier than the seventh century AD. Bhavabhūti's *Mālatīmādhava* and Bāṇa's *Caṇḍīśataka* may be the outcome of inspiration gathered from Caṇḍī, which is a portion of the *Mārkaṇḍeya Purāṇa*. So it may be safely concluded that the *Mārkaṇḍeya Purāṇa* is earlier than the seventh century AD.

---

5. M. Winternitz, *History of Indian Literature,* Vol. I, p. 529.
6. Jackson, *Journal of the Bombay Branch of the Royal Asiatic Society, Centenary Memorial Volume*, p. 67; Pargiter, *Ancient Indian Historical Tradition* (Oxford, 1922), pp. 33, 49.
7. Hazra, *Studies in the Puranic Records and Hindu Rites and Customs*, pp. 174-89.
8. *gītyā pavamāno-proktam purāṇam papāṭha* — *Bāṇabhaṭṭa's Harṣacarita*, ed. by P.V. Kane, Delhi, 1965, Chapter III, p. 89.

It may be noted that besides its mythological importance of *Viṣṇu Purāṇa*, here the arrangement of the Vedas and other writings are considered sacred and the authorities of religious rites and beliefs which are described in the third book of this Purāṇa bear importance for speculating the history of Indian literature and religion.

In the section seventeenth of the *Viṣṇu Purāṇa*, Parāśara, being enquired by Maitreya, described the story of Prahlāda, son of Hiraṇyakaśipu, sovereign of the *daityas*. Prahlāda was sent to the house of his preceptor.[8a] He was residing in the dwelling of his preceptor, read such readings as are studied in early year. He accompanied by his preceptor came to visit his father. While Prahlāda praised the highest soul the lord of the *daityas* became full of anger and rebuked the preceptor of Prahlāda. He told him to be a vile and vicious-minded brāhmaṇa, for he taught his son the worthless commendation of his enemy. Thus it can be assumed that dwelling of boys in the houses of their preceptors was in vogue in the Gupta Age. Here we find Prahlāda was being taught by many preceptors. It is described that Prahlāda again repaired to the abode of his preceptor.[9] There the preceptor instructed the boy daily in the science of polity, essentially necessary for the administration of the government. The science of polity was invented by Uśanas for the benefit of kings. The preceptor of Prahlāda informed Hiraṇyakaśipu that his son Prahlāda had become conversant with the principles of government as laid down by the descendant of Bhṛgu. The polity propounded by Uśanas contained the rules of the behaviour of a king towards his friends or foes and the steps to be taken at the three periods, i.e., advance, retrogression and peace. Instructions

---

8a. *tasya putro mahābhāgaḥ prahlādo nāma nāmataḥ*
papāṭha bālapāṭhyāni gurugehe gato'rbhakaḥ
ekadā'to sa dharmātmā jagāma guruṇā saha
pānāsaktasya purataḥ piturdaityapatestadā
— *Viṣṇu Purāṇa*, I, Ch. XVII, Śl. 10ff.

9. *ityukto'sau tadā daityairnīto gurugṛhaṁ punaḥ*
jagrāha vidyāmanīśam guruśuśruṣanodyataḥ
— *Ibid.*, Ch. XVII, 28

were also given there regarding the behaviour of the king towards his ministers, courtiers, the state and household officers, his emissaries, his subjects, those of doubtful allegianace and his open enemies. The science of polity included the advice about whom a king should make alliance, with whom he should enter into war, he should build what sort of fortress, how he would bring down to subjection forest and mountain tribes, how internal disturbance of his dynasty could be removed.

Four expedients, i.e., conciliation, gift, punishment and sowing dissension have been prescribed for the subjection of friends and foes.

While describing the hells below the earth and the water into which sinners fall, description is given of the cause of their falling. The moral conduct of the student is first and foremost thing to be observed. It is recorded that he who commits adultery with the wife of his preceptor, is despatched *tālā* (padlocks) hell.[10] That vile of a man who disrespects his spiritual guide or his better half, who reviles the Vedas or sells them is sent into *lavaṇa* hell.[11] The student who sleeps during day time and becomes defiled called *svabhojana* (where they feed upon dogs).[12]

While delineating the situations and dimensions of the sun and other luminaries Parāśara has described that in sooth, there is neither rising nor setting of the sun; for he always exists, the appearance and disappearance of the sun are merely called rising and setting.[13] This proves that the knowledge of astronomy was advance at that time.

---

10. . . . . *tāle tathaiva gurutalpagaḥ* ।
— *Viṣṇu Purāṇa*, Book II, Sec. VI, 10/1

11. *avamantā guruṇām yo yaścakroṣṭā narādhamaḥ* ।
vedaduṣayitā yaśca vedavikrayikaśca yaḥ ।
. . . . . *syāt te yānti lavaṇaṁ dvija* ।
— *Ibid.*, Book II, Sec.VI, 12f

12. *divāsvapne ca skandante ye nara brahmacārinaḥ* ।
. . . . . *ye ca te patanti śvabhojane* ।। — *Ibid.*, 25

13. *naivāstamānamarkasya nodayaḥ sarvadā sataḥ* ।
udayāstamanākhyam hi darśanādarśanam raveḥ ।।
— *Ibid.*, Sec. VIII, 15

While describing the fawn with Bharata, the fawn is compared with the pious lads chanting the *Sāmaveda*. It proves that teaching of Vedas was prevalent in Gupta age.[14]

After the completion of the study of a student preceptor sometimes used to visit the student to impart more advanced knowledge to the student. It is seen that Ṛbhu, the preceptor went to the abode of Nidāgha, the pupil, several times.[15] The pupil offer him *arghya* (usual present) and led him into the house. When the preceptor washed his hands and feet, Nidāgha, the pupil, requested him respectfully to eat. After finishing his meal he imparted higher knowledge to Nidāgha.

The disciple disobeying the order of the preceptor may be punished. Yājñavalkya is reported to have been punished by Vaiśampāyana.[16] Yājñavalkya accepted the punishment without any hesitation. This calm submission to the teacher's order, even if it be unjust could be expected only from an Indian student. Perhaps any objection of students against teacher might not be paid in heed at that age.

The *Viṣṇu Purāṇa* has enumerated fourteen principal kinds of knowledge — the four Vedas, the six *aṅga*s (the subsidiary portion of the Vedas, i.e., (1) *Śikṣā* (rules for reciting prayers); (2) *Kalpa* (ritual); (3) *Vyākaraṇa* (grammar); (4) *Nirukta* (glossary); (5) *Chanda*s (metre); (6) *Jyotiṣa* (astronomy); the *Mīmāṁsā* (theology), *Nyāya* (logic), *Dharma* (the institutes of law) and the Purāṇas. They are enumerated as

---

14. (i) *kuśaḥ kāśa virājante vaṭavaḥ sāmagā iva* ।
— *Viṣṇu Purāṇa*, Sec. XIII. 27, p. 367; tr. p. 157

15. (i) *ṛbhuvarṣasahasre tu samatīte nareśvara* ।
nidāghajñānadānāya tadeva nagaraṁ yāyan ॥
— *Ibid.*, Book II, Ch. XVI, 1

(ii) *jāgama sa ṛbhuḥ śiṣyam nidāghamavalokakaḥ* ।
— *Ibid.*, Pt. II, Sec. XV, 8

16. *tataḥ kruddho guruḥ prāha yājñavalkyaṁ mahāmatiḥ* ।
mucyatāṁ yat tvayādhītamatto viprāvamānaka ॥
— *Ibid.*, Book III, Sec. V, 8

eighteen[17] with the addition of these four—*Āyurveda*, medical science taught by Dhanvantari; *Dhanurveda*, the science of archery taught by Bhṛgu; *Gāndharvaveda*, the art of music, dancing, etc., of which the *muni* Bharata was the author; *Arthaśāstra*, or, the science of government, taught by Vṛhaspati.

While narrating duties of brāhmaṇas teaching as one of the duties is mentioned. The duties of kṣatriyas consist in receiving instructions from the preceptor.[18] Study, sacrifice and gift are within the duties of the vaiśyas.[19] In cases of emergency a brāhmaṇa may follow the occupation of a kṣatriya or vaiśya.[20]

When a youth is initiated with the sacred thread, he must reside in the house of his preceptor and study the Vedas with a concentrated mind and leading a life of continence. He must be possessed of pure mind, wait upon his spiritual preceptor and with the performance of religious rites acquire the knowledge of the Vedas. He must with concentration worship both in the morning and evening, the fire and the sun and after that he must bow to his spiritual guide. He must stand when his preceptor is standing, he must move when he is walking and he must sit beneath him when he is seated; he must never sit nor walk, nor stand when the teacher does the otherwise. Whatever portion of the

---

17. *aṅgāni caturo veda mīmāṁsā nyāyavistaraḥ*
purāṇaṁ dharmaśāstraṁ ca vidyā hyetāścaturdaśaḥ
āyurvedo dhanurvedo gāndharvaścaiva te trayaḥ
arthaśāstra caturthantu vidyā hyaṣṭādaśaivataḥ
—*Viṣṇu Purāṇa*, Pt. III, Sec. VI, Śl. 28, 29

18. *svādhyāyatatparaḥ* ǀǀ 22 ǀǀ 1
vṛtyartham yājayeaccānyānanyānadhyāpayet tathā ǀ
—*Ibid.*, Pt. III, Sec. VIII, 22, 23

19. .... *kṣatriyo'pi hi* ǀ
... *adhīyīta ca pārthiva* ǀǀ
—*Ibid.*, Pt. III, Sec. VIII, 26

20. *kṣatram karma dvijasyoktaṁ vaiśyam karma tathāpadi* ǀ
—*Ibid.*, Pt. III, Sec. VIII. 39

Vedas he shall be taught by his preceptor, he must read that with undivided mind before him. He must beg when permitted by his teacher and eat the food thus collected. He must bath in the water which has been first used by his preceptor and every morning he must bring for him fuel, water or anything that he may require. Having thus completed his studies, he must receive dismissal from his preceptor and then enter into the order of the householder.[21]

Brāhmaṇas were to travel all over the earth either for studying the Vedas or for beholding the holy places.[22]

After going through the initiary ceremonies, i.e., *nāmakaraṇa* and *upanayana* and being purified, the youth should acquire knowledge from his preceptor. Having acquired knowledge from the preceptor and given him presents, he should desirous of entering the order of householders, marry. If he desires to continue his life as a student, he should, taking that vow, engage in the service of his preceptor and his descendant.[23]

The gift should be offered to an educated brāhmaṇa. In *Viṣṇu Purāṇa* while describing the duty of householder it is stated that he should present to a brāhmaṇa, who is well versed in the Vedas, four handfuls of food, set apart; with the exclamation Hanta. He can also make gifts to a religious student.[24]

---

21. *bālaḥ kr̥topanayano vedāharaṇastatparaḥ* ।
gurugehe vased bhūpa brahmacārī samāhitaḥ ।।
— *Viṣṇu Purāṇa*, Pt. III, Sec. IX, 1-7

22. *vedāharanakāryāya tīrthasnānāya caprabho* ।
aṭanti vasudhāṁ vipraḥ pr̥thivīdarśanāya ca ।।
— *Ibid.*, Pt. III, Sec. IX, 12

23. *brahmacaryena vā kālam kuryāt saṁkalpa pūrvakam* ।
guroḥ śuśruṣaṇaṁ kuryāt tatputrāderathāpi vā ।।
— *Ibid.*, Pt. III, Sec. X, 14

24. *annāgraśca samuddhr̥tya hantakāropakalpitam* ।
nivāpabhūtaṁ bhūpāla ! śrotriyāyopakalpayet ।।
dadyācca bhikṣātritayaṁ paribrāṅg brahmacāriṇam ।।
— *Ibid.*, Pt. III, Sec. XI, 63

In ancestral ceremonies the description of a brāhmaṇa who would be fed, is given. He must be *trinaciketa*, *trimadhu*, and *trisuparṇa*. *Trinaciketa*, is so-called from reciting three *anuvākas* of the *Kāṭhaka* branch of the *Yajurveda*, beginning with the term *trinaciketa*, etc. *Trimadhu* is so-called from reciting three *anuvākas* of the *Sāmaveda* beginning with Madhuvātā. *Trisuprana* is so-called from a similar portion commencing *brahmavan namāmi*; or one who is versed in the six supplementary sciences of the Vedas; one who is well acquainted with the Vedas; one who practises the duties laid down in the Vedas.[25] In the *śrāddha* ceremony the wise should invite eminent teachers of Vedas and according to their instructions he must settle what is to be dedicated. This proves the dignified place of the teachers in the society.

The Saubhari who was versed in *Ṛgveda* is honoured by the king.[26]

After the initiation, the Vedas and the science of artillery was taught. We find *aurva* invested Sagara with the sacred cord, taught him the Vedas and the use of all weapons and specially those of fire called after Bhārgava.[27]

The student used to obey the order of the preceptor. So Sagara reverentially obeyed the request of his spiritual guide, Vasiṣṭha. Vasiṣṭha also withdrew from Yavaṇas, Śakas, Pāradas the privilege of studying the Vedas.

Hiraṇyanābha taught Kṛta the philosophy of *yoga* and Kṛta compiled the twenty-four Saṁhitās for the use of the eastern brāhmaṇas studying

---

25. *brāhmaṇān bhojayecchrāddhe*
trinaciketastrimadhustrisuparṇaḥ ṣaḍaṅgavit
— *Viṣṇu Purāṇa,* Book II, Pt. III, Sec. XV, 1ff.

26. *athāgamanaśravaṇasamanantaram totthāya tena rājñā samyag arghyādinā pūjitaḥ kṛtāsanaparigrahaḥ saubhariḥ.*
— *Ibid.*, Pt. IV, Sec. II

27. *kṛtopanayanañcarnām aurvo vedān śāstrāṇyaśeṣāni astraṁcāgneyam bhārgavākhyamadhyāpayāmāsa.*
— *Ibid.*, Pt. IV, Sec. IV, 111

the *Sāmaveda*. Satyadhṛti was well versed in military science.[28]

It is foretold that Śatānīka, the son of Janamejaya will study the Vedas from Yājñavalkya, and learn the use of weapons from Kṛpa.[29]

Kṛṣṇa described the four divisions of knowledge as — (1) logical, (2) spiritual, (3) practical and (4) political.

Agriculture, commerce and tending of cattle — the knowledge of these three was considered to be the practical science.[30]

Disciples submitted to teachers whole-heartedly. This ideal was followed by Kṛṣṇa and Balarāma. The two excellent Yadu youths (i.e., Kṛṣṇa and Balarāma), versed in all knowledge and possessed of all wisdom, submitted to the instructions, of their teachers.

Kṛṣṇa and Balarāma went to Sāndīpanī who resided in Avantī. So the custom of going to a far off place to learn subject of study was prevalent in that period. Kṛṣṇa and Balarāma studied from Sāndīpanī the science of arms. They were obedient and attentive to their master, exhibiting an example to all men of the observance of intellectual rules. They had gone through the elements of military science, with the knowledge of respective treatises on the use of arms; they also gathered knowledge of the directions for the mystic incantations. Sāndīpanī, astonished at the proficiency in learning of the two brothers and knowing that it exceeded human faculties imagined that the sun and

---

28. *kṛto'bhūt yaṁ hiraṇyanābhoyogamadhyāpayāmāsa,*
yaścaturviṁśati prācyāsāmagānam cakāra saṁhitāḥ || 13 ||
satyadhṛtiḥ dhanurvedāntago yajñe | 16 |
— *Viṣṇu Purāṇa*, Pt. IV, Sec. XX, 13

29. *śatānīka yājñavalkyād vedamadhītya kṛpādastrāṇya vāpya* |
— *Ibid.*, Pt. IV, Sec. XXI

30. *ānvikṣikī trayī vārtā daṇḍanītistathāparā* |
vidyācatuṣṭayam tvetat vārthāmatra śṛṇusva me ||
kṛṣirvānijyam tadvattu tṛtīyaṁ paśupālanam |
vidyā hyete mahābhāga! vārtā vṛttitrayāśrayaḥ ||
— *Ibid.*, Pt. V, Sec. X, 27

moon had became his disciples.[31] After completion of the study which was acquired from Sāndīpanī, they inquired about the fee of their preceptor. The prudent Sāndīpanī requested them to give him his dead son and they restored him in his former person to his father.[32]

We find Keśīdhvaja wanted to present gift to Khāṇḍikya, his preceptor.

We find Duryodhana taking lessons in club fighting from Balarāma when he lives in Mathurā.

The philosophy of life as conceived in ancient India laid great stress on knowledge and action both by which human mind can remain in perfect control and harness and there would be seldom any chance of violation of law and to incur lawlessness. In the *Viṣṇu Purāṇa* it has been said that "*vidyā* or learning is that by which *mukti* or liberation (the eternal bliss) is achieved".[33]

In the beginning of the *Matsya Purāṇa* it is stated that for the sake of promulgating the Vedas, Viṣṇu, in the beginning of a *kalpa*, related to Manu the story of Narasiṁha; and the events of several *kalpas*; though the *Matsya Purāṇa* is believed in fact it contains no more to contain twenty thousand stanzas, than fourteen or fifteen thousand stanzas. The subjects of the Purāṇa were communicated by Viṣṇu, in the form of fish, to Manu. It is a miscellaneous compilation. At the same time it is of too mixed a character to be considered as a genuine work of the Paurāṇic class.[34]

---

31. *sandīpanīrasaṁbhāvyam tayoḥ karmātimānuṣam* ǀ
vicintya tau tadā mene prāptau candra-divākarau ǀǀ
—*Viṣṇu Purāṇa*, Pt. V, Sec. XXI, 19-22

32. *astrgrāmamaśeṣañca proktamātramavāpya tau* ǀ
ūcetuvriyatām yā te dātavyā gurudakṣiṇā ǀǀ
— *Ibid*., Pt. V, Sec. XXI, 23-4

33. *sā vidyā yā vimuktaye*
— *Ibid.*, *Aṁśa* I, *Adhyāya* 19, verse 41

34. Wilson, *Purāṇas*, p. 84.

Although it is a Śaiva work, it is not exclusively so and it has not such sectarian absurdities. It is a composition of considerable interest. Education of that age has been reflected in *Matsya Purāṇa*.

While a person is worthy to be invited to the feast of *naimittika* (*pārvana*) *śrāddha*, it is noted that one who is acquainted with the doctrine of the five mystic fires (*pañcāgni*), a *snātaka brahmacārī* who is well versed in the Vedas with their six *aṅgas*, and the *śrotriya* brāhmaṇa, one highly proficient in the rules of *vidhi* (or laws).[35] Thus it is clear that *snātaka*s and *śrotriya* brāhmaṇa received an exalted place in the society. It is also noted that a teacher, a grammarian, a person who knows the *Sāmaveda* and the method of chanting it, one who is highly learned and respectable or eminent, their very presence may be considered to elevate and purify the people who sit to feast with him in the same row; a *brahmacārī* and a professor of Vedas, are the sort of people worthy of being invited to the *śrāddha* feast.[36]

It is noted that the Budha was master of all the *śāstra*s and was the author of a treatise on elephants. He was known as *rājaputra*, the doctor of elephants.[37]

Kaca, the son of Vṛhaspati went to Śukra, the preceptor, to be accepted as pupil. He approached Śukra, and requested him to accept him describing his lineage as his pupil. He wanted to lead a typical disciple's life and asked to keep him as his pupil for thousands of year.

---

35. *pancāgniḥ snātakaścaiva trisuparṇaḥ ṣaḍaṅgavit* ।
śrotriyaḥ śrotriyasuto vidhivākyaviśāradaḥ ॥
—*Matsya Purāṇa*, edited by Panchanana Tarkaratna, Calcutta, Nabaharat, 1989, Ch. XVI, 7f.

36. *yaśca vykurute vākyam yaśca mīmāṁsate'dhvaram* ।
sāmasvaravidhijñaśca paṁktipāvanapāranaḥ ॥
— *Matsya Purāṇa*, XVI. 9

37. *sarvārthaśāstraviddhimān hastiśāstra-pravartakaḥ* ।
nāma yadrājaputrīyam viśrutam gajavaidyakam ॥
— *Ibid.*, Ch. XXIV

Śukra welcomed him as well as his words. He said that he is worthy of being adored.[38]

Afterwards Kāca followed all the injunctions of Śukra and observed the fasts at the proper periods according to the prescribed rites, and began to serve Śukra and Devayāṇī. Śukra taught him *sañjīvanī* knowledge.

Kāca addressed Śukra in a way that Śukra was bounteous like an ocean and most generous among the givers of boons. Those who do not show due regard to such a preceptor, are sinners doomed to hell after being wrecked.[39]

When Devayāṇī, the daughter of the preceptor of Kaca offered her hand in marriage according to due rites and *mantras*, Kaca answered that she was to be honoured as a daughter of his *guru* therefore should be honoured as his *guru*.[40]

It may be inferred that the daughter of the preceptor was also highly revered. So when Śarmiṣṭhā put on the garments of Devayāṇī by mistake, Devayānī quarrelled and cursed her.[41]As a result of this quarrel Devayāṇī made Śarmiṣṭhā to be her maid and forced her to go

---

38. *kaca sukhāgatam te'stu pratigṛhṇāmi te vacaḥ* ।
arcayiṣye'hamarcyaḥ tvamarcito'stu vṛhaspatiḥ ॥
— *Matsya Purāṇa*, Ch. XXV, Śl. 24

39. *nidhiṁ nidhīnāṁ varadaṁ varāṇaṁ ye nādriyante gurumarcanīyaṁ* ।
prāleyādriprojjvala bhālasaṁsthaṁ pāpaṅlokāṅste vrajantya pratiṣṭhāṁ ॥
— *Ibid.*, Ch. XXV, 58-59

40. *yathā mama gururnityaṁ mānyaṁ śukraḥ pitā tava* ।
devayānī tathaiva tvaṁ naivam māṁ vaktumarhasi ॥
— *Ibid.*, Ch. XXVI, 8

41. *kasmād gṛhnāsi me vastraṁ śiṣya bhūtvā mamāsuri* ।
samudācarahīnayā na te śreyo bhaviṣyati ॥
— *Ibid.*, Ch. XXVIII, 8

with her wherever she would be married. So the esteemed place of the preceptor can be imagined.[42]

Yayāti stated that a student who, thinking too much of his learning, employed his knowledge to belittle others, lost his privilege of finding a place in the higher regions, and that wisdom did not bear him fruit. The acquirement of knowledge, in spite of its being good deed, is marred by indulgence in drinks and conceit. To give alms and to study the Vedas, according to the ways prescribed, should be considered to be the best of all.[43]

Yayāti further described that a student (*brahmacārī*) attained his end by diligently studying when called by his teacher to do so, by showing reverence and obedience to his preceptor, by getting up ahead of his preceptor, and by going to bed after him, by being mild, by controlling his passions, by keeping himself steady and not fickle, and by applying himself to his studies.[44] A householder who constantly studies Upaniṣadas and Purāṇas is also ideal.

It is delineated that Vṛhaspati, in disguise of Śukra became preceptor of the *daityas*.

Bali was endowed with knowledge of the past, present, future and he was a philosopher.

King Śāntanu was a very learned, physically equipped and was highly accomplished. It is laid down in the books on medicine that by his

42. *dāsīm kanyāsahasreṇa śarmiṣṭhāmabhikāmaye* ।
anuyāsyati māṁ tatra yatra dāsyati me pitā ॥
— *Matsya Purāṇa*, Ch. XXIX, verse 17

43. *na mānyamāno mudamādadīta*
na santāpaṁ prāpnuccāvamānāt ।
— *Ibid.*, Ch. XXXIX, 26

44. *āhūtādhyāyī gurukarmasu codyataḥ pūrvotthāyī caramañcātha śāyī* ।
sudurdānto dhṛtimānapramattaḥ svādhyāyaśīlaḥ sidhyati brahmacārī ॥
— *Ibid.*, Ch. XL, 2

mere touch even the patients suffering from a most dreadful disease would be instantly cured and become young.[45]

In the observance of *nakṣatra-puruṣavrate* the brāhmaṇa, versed in astronomy, should dismiss the evil by giving away the image of *nakṣatra-puruṣa*, along with clothes, garland, sandalpaste, etc. So the proficiency in astronomy is highly revered.[46]

While describing *ananta-tṛtīyā vrata* it is stated that the teacher should also be adored, with prescribed rites, because where the *guru* is left unadored, all the rites prove fruitless.[47] In *ananta-tṛtīyā vrata* a devotee and his consort should adore brāhmaṇas with their wives. While such adorning is offered *dakṣiṇā* must be given first to the *guru* to gain infinite benefit. Thus a preceptor was treated with high esteem.[48]

The measurement of altar and *maṇḍāla* of the sacrifice is described with vivid description. It shows the knowledge of the geometry was not absent in the teaching of ancient India.[49]

The gift should be offered to one acquainted with *Sāmaveda*. Only

---

45. *śāntanustvabhavadrājā vidvān sa vai mahābhiṣak* |
idañcodāharastyatra ślokam prati mahābhiṣak ||

yaṁ yaṁ karābhyāṁ spṛśati jīrṇaṁ rogiṇameva ca |
punaryuvā ca bhavati tasmāt taṁ śāntanuṁ viduḥ ||
— *Matsya Purāṇa*, Ch. L. 42-3

46. *Nakṣatra-puruṣa vrata* is worship of Viṣṇu in the star Mūla, Rohiṇī, Uttarāṣāḍha, Uttaraphālgunī, Revatī, Anurādhā, Viśākhā, etc. So the knowledge of astronomy is necessary.
— *Ibid.*, Ch. LIV, 7-21

47. *tathopadeṣṭāramapi pūjyed yatnato guruṁ* |
na pūjyate gururyatra sarvāstatraphalāḥ kriyāḥ ||
— *Ibid.*, Ch. LXII, 21

48. *pūrvaṁ datvā tu gurave śeṣānapyarcayed budhaḥ* |
uktānantatṛtīyaiṣā sadānantaphalapradā ||
— *Ibid.*, Ch. LXII, 33

49. *Ibid.*, Ch. XCIII, 7f.

he, versed in the Vedas and knowing the Vedic principles, is fit to receive such an offering.[50] Suitable things might be given to the preceptors. Thus it is clearly shown that the preceptors and educated persons were highly esteemed.

That the knowledge of georgraphy was not lacking can be easily inferred from the description of *dvīpas*.[51]

The concept of equator (*viṣava rekhā*) and poles was known to the writer of the *Matsya Purāṇa*. Astronomers were well acquainted with the position of stars like Āṣāḍha, Mūla, Puṣya, Āśleṣā and Punarvasu, Svāti, etc. and the calculations based on them were the great achievements of the astronomy.[52]

The knowledge of architecture was known to them. The Tripurā fort is described here.[53]

While describing the duties of the *varṇas*, it is stated that brāhmaṇas should enlighten the kṣatriyas and the later should educate the vaiśyas, and vaiśyas should mould up the śūdras. The sons of Brahmā framed the Saṁhitās (or books) on medicine (how their health should be kept up).[54] *Cakravartī* kings were great archers.

It is stated that there was only one Veda, having four feet (parts). Due to short lives of the people that Veda was abridged and completely divided in four Vedas. The sons of *ṛṣis*, due to their respective faulty understanding inserted *Brāhmaṇa* portions within the Saṁhitā portions of the *Ṛg*, *Yajur* and *Sāma-vedas*. They even changed the *svaras* or

---

50. *jyeṣṭhasāmavide deyam na vakavratine kvacit* |
guṇajñe śrotriye dadyādācārye tattvavedinī ||
— *Matsya Purāṇa*, Ch. XCV, 30

51. *Ibid.*, Ch. CXXII.

52. *Ibid.*, Ch. CXXIV, 50.

53. *brāhmaṇaiśca vidhīyante kṣatriyaṁ kṣatriyair-viśah* |
vaiśyaṁ śūdrānuvartante śūdrān paramanugrahāt ||
— *Ibid.*, Ch. CXXXVII, pp. 427f.

54. *Ibid.*, Ch. CXL, II, 52ff.

musical tones in the songs of the Vedas. Some parts were correctly explained. At first, the Adhvaryu's work was one, afterwards it was divided into two.[55]

While describing the duty of a *brahmacārī*, it is stated that the *brahmacārī* is given to good conduct and *ācāra* and the do good to the preceptor (*guru*) performs divine functions.[56] It is stated that who are free from avarice, self-restrained, not haughty and followers of the path of virtue are known as *ācārya*. Such brāhmaṇas versed in the doctrine of *dharma*, *śrauta* and *smārta*, have enunciated the path of virtue.[57]

The knowledge of politics was known to them. Vṛhaspati narrates that those who want to conquer the enemy having fourfold armies as chariots, horses, elephants and infantry should resort to either of the four policies beginning with *sāma* (peace), *bheda* (dissension), *dāna* (gift), *yuddha* (war). These are the four policies in the *Nītiśāstra* (war politics). These four means are to be applied after due consideration of the time, place and the strength of the enemy.[58] Persuation for peace is best in connection with the good, the wicked can never turn out good.

It is stated that the second son of Brahmā went down to the earth and began to study the Vedas from the preceptors.[59]

---

55. *eko vedaścatuṣpādaḥ saṁhṛtya tu punaḥ-punaḥ* । etc.
— *Matsya Purāṇa*, II, Ch. CXLIV, 10-5

56. *śrauta-smārto hi yo dharmo jñānadharmaḥ sa ucyate* ।
divyānāṁ sādhanāt sādhurbrahmacarı gurorhitaḥ ।।
— *Ibid.*, II, Ch. CXLIV, 10-5

57. *bṛddhaścalolopāścaiva ātmavanto hyādāmbhikāḥ* ।
samyagvinītā mṛdavastānācāryān pracakṣyate ।।
— *Ibid.*, 29-30

58. *sāmabhedastathā dānaṁ daṇḍaścāṅga-catuṣṭayaṁ* ।
nītau kramāddeśa-kāla-ripuyogakramādidaṁ ।। 66 ।।
— *Ibid.*, II, Ch. CXLVIII, p. 483

59. *brahmābhyāsantu kṛtabān bhuvaśca pṛthivīṁgataḥ* ।।
— *Ibid.*, Ch. CLXXI

The teaching of politics is scattered here and there. *Matsya* narrated that a king should pick out worthy man for his assembly as his advisors and helpers on various subjects to work on his staff in order that his rule may be prosperous, for the prosperity of his kingdom depends solely on the men in his council and in various other departments. Even the smallest function cannot be successfully performed by one single man not helped by anybody. A king should choose his ministers from a respectable family bearing good qualities, used to gentle speaking, able to give friendly advise, loyal, knowing to act in the proper time and place, and eager for a good name. Such men should be employed by a king to discharge responsible and good functions. People unsuited to particular offices should be given places according to their respective merits where they can make themselves useful, after they had been duly examined. Improper discharge of duties leads to the extinction of a sovereign. A king should appoint a brāhmaṇa or a kṣatriya to be his commander-in-chief. He should be skilled in archery, expert in examining and managing horses and elephants and having a knowledge of disposing troops in battle and of military affairs in particular. A king's spy should be conscientious enough to submit true and accurate reports, have a knowledge of dialects of many countries, to speak fluently, etc. The man with full knowledge of king's six-fold expedients in foreign politics, *sandhi* (peace), *vigraha* (war), *yāna* (morals), *āsana* (halt), *dvaidhibhāva* (duplicate) and *āśraya* (seeking shelter) and the language of the country should be employed as ministers for war.[60]

It is stated that *sabhāsadas* should be well acquainted with the writing of many countries.[61] The art of writing was known. In *Matsya Purāṇa* it is stated that the writers of a king should write neatly and legibly. The letters are to be full and placed at equal intervals. He should be clever in devising means, and in the use of stray expressions,

---

60. *Matysya Purāṇa.*, Ch. CCXV, 8-17.

61. . . . . *sabhāsadaḥ* ।
sarvadeśākṣarābhijñaḥ sarvaśāstra-viśāradaḥ ॥
—*Ibid.*, Ch. CCXV, 25

versed in all the *śāstras* and capable to express many meanings fully in short phrases.[62]

The medical science and the men proficient in the medical science are treated with high esteem. One who is skilled in the eight-fold[63] medical science by heredity, should be employed as a physician and a king should choose such a person as the preceptor for his whole life. The king is to obey the words of the physician, like an ordinary person, for he deals with welfare of the life.[64]

The art of training elephants was well advanced. It is stated that one who knows the art of training elephants and is aware of the races of wild beasts, and is accustomed to bear hardships should be made the superintendent of royal elephants.

The faculty of engineering was well advanced. It can be proved from the fact that the engineer of a king should know engineering, and be able to prepare plans and would be hardy and energetic and have a nimble hands, keen foresight.[65]

The learning of a king is described. A king should read the Vedas from those who are learned in them. He should also master in politics, logic, philosophy and temporal science.[66]

The punishment of the preceptor for not doing duties to the student

---

62. *vahvarthavaktā cālpena lekhakaḥ syānnṛpottama* ।
— *Matsya Purāṇa*, II, Ch. CCXV, 25-27

63. *Aṣṭāṅga* - eight part of medical sciences, viz., *śalyam, śālākyam, kāya, cikitsā, bhūtavidyā, kaumāratantra, agadatantra, rasāyanatantra, vājīkaraṇatantra.*

64. *prāṇācāryaḥ sa vijñeyo vacanaṁ tasya bhūbhujā* ।
rājan rājñā sadā kāryaṁ yathā kāryaṁ pṛthagjanaiḥ ॥
— *Ibid.*, Ch. CCXV, 33

65. *vāstuvidyānidhānajño laghuhasto jitaśramaḥ*
dīrghadarśī ca śūraśca sthapatiḥ parikīrtitaḥ ॥
— *Ibid.*, Ch. CCXV, 39

66. *traividyebhyastrayīṁ vidyāṁ daṇḍanītiṁ ca śāsvatīm* ।
— *Ibid.*, Ch. CCXV, 53-4

is described. One who does not impart knowledge or mechanical training to his students after having received his fee for the same should be fined the whole amount of his wages.[67]

One who is guilty of an illicit connection with his preceptor's wife should observe the ordinance prescribed for the sin committing adultery with a lady of one's own community.[68]

A rule of conduct was very severe. It is stated that a śūdra who teaches *dharma* to the twice born should also be punished by a sovereign by pouring hot oil poured into his ears and mouth.[69]

One who uses harsh words towards his preceptor and does not make room for his preceptor should be fined one *rattī* of silver (one *kṛṣṇala*).[70]

Fallen preceptor should not be abandoned, but a man doing so should be fined 600 gold pieces.[71]

A pupil who reads at forbidden times should be made to pay a fine of 3 *kāhanas* and the master should be fined twice the amount. If one quits one's *ācāra*, he would have to pay three *kāhanas* as fine. Disciples

---

67. *mūlyamādāya yo vidyāṁ śilpaṁ vā na prayacchati* ।
daṇḍyaḥ sa mūlyaṁ sakalaṁ dharmajñena mahīkṣitā ।।
— *Matsya Purāṇa*, II, Ch. CCXXVII, 6

68. *gurutalpavratam kuryād* . . . . ।
— *Ibid.*, II, Ch. CCXXVII, 50

69. *dharmopadeśam śūdrastu dvijānāmabhikurvītaḥ* ।
taptavāse cayet tailam vaktrye śrotre ca pārthivaḥ ।।
— *Ibid.*, 75

70. *ākrośayan śataṁ daṇḍyaḥ panthānacārdayam guroḥ* ।
. . . . *sa dāpyaḥ kṛṣṇalaṁ* . . . ।।
— *Ibid.*, 82

71. . . . . *patitāstyājyā tyega daṇḍyaḥ śatāni ṣaṭ* ।
patita guravastyājyā . . . . ।।
— *Ibid.*, 50-1

should be beaten on their back with a rope or a cane when they commit a fault. They should never be beaten on their heads. One who does so should be punished like a theif.[72] Those who indulge with preceptor's wife should be killed. If such a man be a brāhmaṇa he should be banished, with a mark on his body.[73] Those who indulge with preceptor's wife should be branded with a mark resembling the female privacy. Man branded with such marks should not be taken in society. None should speak, interdine or live with him.[74] One who kills his preceptor with poison or fire, etc. should be punished by his nose being clipped, ears and lips being chopped, and then killed near a cowyard.[75]

It is stated that *graha-yajña* should be performed by a king in company of his preceptor.[76]

Śukrācārya obtained the *maheśvarī mṛtasanjīvanī vidyā*, direct from the mouth of Lord Śiva.[77]

Dhanvantari, the great performer of *Āyurveda* was adored by the

---

72. *pṛṣṭhatastu śārīrasya nottamāṅgaṁ kathañcana* ।
ato'nyathā prahārataḥ prāptaṁ syāccorakilviṣam ॥
— *Matsya Purāṇa*, Ch. CCXVII. 152-55

73. . . . . *garutalpagaḥ* ॥
. . . .
mahāpātakino vadhyā brāhmaṇantu vivāsayet ।
kṛtacinhaḥ svadeśācca śṛṇu cinhākṛtiṁ tataḥ ॥
— *Ibid.*, 162-3

74. *asambhāṣya hyasambhojyā asaṁvāhyā viśeṣataḥ* ॥
— *Ibid.*, 165

75. *vikarṇanāsikāṁ vyoṣṭhīm kṛtvā gobhiḥ pramāpayet* ।
— *Ibid.*, 200, p. 813

76. *guruṇā caiva ṛtvigbhiḥ sārdhaṁ bhūmiṁ parīkṣayet* ।
— *Ibid.*, Ch. CCXXXIX, 4f., p. 826

77. *tasya tuṣṭena devena śaṅkarena mahātmanā* ।
mṛtasañjīvanī nāma vidyā dattā mahāprabhā ॥ 5 ॥
— *Ibid.*, Ch. CCXLIX, 5-6, p. 853

devas. During the time of the churning of the ocean many valuable things were taken by him.[78]

It delineated detailed instructions for the selection and examination of the ground for building.[79] Earth is divided by it into four classes according to its colour.[80] The merits of those different kinds of earth as substance for building or as materials for the brick-making are enumerated. Detailed accounts are given of *Catuḥśālās*,[81] measurements of the pillars, the dimensions of temples, the characteristics of the various *maṇḍapas* (halls attached to the temple).[82] So it is clear that the study of the science of architecture was prevalent in the age.

The *Matsya Purāṇa* also enumerates measurements of limbs of the images of the gods, characteristics of the images,[83] the forms of images, the description of pedestals of the idols, the dimensions of the phallus, conservation of the idols and such other things. So it can be safely concluded that the study of iconography was highly advanced.

Colebrook, Burnof,[84] Wilson,[85] Macdonell and Dayānanda Sarasvatī[86] consider the *Bhāgavata* to be the work of Vopadeva who belonged to the thirteenth century.

Mādhavācārya is credited with authorship of the book entitled the *Bhāgavata-tātparya-nirṇaya*.

---

78. *dhanvantariñca jagrāha lokārogyapravartakaṁ* ||
— *Matsya Purāṇa*, Ch. CCLI, 4
79. *Viṣṇu Purāṇa*, I, Ch. CCLIII, pp. 879f.
80. *Matsya Purāṇa*, Ch. CCLVI.
81. *Ibid.*, Ch. CCLIV, 1f.
82. *Ibid.*, Ch. CCLV, 1f.
83. *Ibid.*, Ch. CCLVIII-CCLXV.
84. Burnof, *History of Indian Literature,* p. 556.
85. Wilson, *Introduction to Viṣṇu Purāṇa* (L-LI).
86. Dayānanda Sarasvatī, *Annals of Bhandarkar Oriental Research Institute,* XIV, p. 182.

Dr. Hazra in his *Studies in Puranic Records on Hindu Rites and Customs* opines that a comparison of theology of *Bhāgavata* and *Kūrma Purāṇa* makes one believe that *Kūrma Purāṇa* is influenced by Śākta ideas. The date of *Kūrma Purāṇa* is between AD 550-650. The *Bhāgavata* being an earlier work cannot placed later than sixth century AD.[87]

The *Bhāgavata Purāṇa* utilized the materials of *Viṣṇu Purāṇa* and the *Harivaṁśa*. The *Harivaṁśa* is considered to be a work of the fourth century AD. Thus *Bhāgavata* belongs to the post-fourth century AD.

The *Bhāgavata Purāṇa* is the most famous among the Purāṇas and its influence is profound. Wilson remarks that "the *Bhāgavata* is a work of great celebrity in India and exercises a more direct and powerful influence upon the opinions and feelings of the people, than perhaps any other of the Purāṇas. It is book of synthesis and the narrow partisan spirit displayed by the Purāṇa literature in general is absent from it."

The *Bhāgavata Purāṇa* is divided into twelve *skandhas* and contains about 18,000 *ślokas* and narrated by Śuka.

In the *Bhāgavata Purāṇa*, Kapila, the propounder of Sāṁkhya system of philosophy is described as an *avatāra*. Dhvanantari, the promulgator of the science of Medicine is also described as an *avatāra*. Ghora Aṅgirasa is described as the instructor of Śrī Kṛṣṇa.

The education and culture of women is reflected in the *Bhāgavata Purāṇa*. That the general education and culture among women was high can be proved by passages from the *Bhāgavata Purāṇa*.[88] While conversing among themselves the women of Hastināpura commented about Vāsudeva that he is the same eternal person, who abides in his singular undifferentiated self even during the night of universal dissolution prior to the manifestation of the three *guṇas* when the individual souls retire into god, the universal spirit, and when all the forces of creation lie dormant. It was He who with the intention of

87. R.C. Hazra, *Studies in Puranic Records on Hindu Rites and Customs*, p. 55.

88. *Bhāgavata Purāṇa*, I.10. 21-30.

endowing with a form and name the spirit who is neither, then inspired His *prakṛti* — which deludes the *jīvas*, who are identical in essence with Him and which impelled by His own energy is disposed to create — and revealed the Vedas and other scriptures . . . etc. This high lavelled remark indicates the level of general education among the women of that time.

Education need not only mean bookish learning. Any instruction which upholds the body and mind is education. The elders in the house instruct children orally. Vast treasures of learning have been handed down orally and it is not rare to find that a women were as learned as men in the different fields of study.

There were two kinds of women, the *brahmavādinīs* and *sadyavadhūḥ*. Hārīta does not mention rules dividing the two. A married woman also can be a *brahmavādinī*. The learned exposition of Kuntī and Satī speaks for itself. In the *Bhāgavata Purāṇa*[89] Kuntī narrates the philosophical truth that all is one and existence of unity in this apparent diversity. She said to Kṛṣṇa that he is the soul of the universe, the universe itself. Kṛṣṇa is devoid of birth and action. His birth and actions in the subhuman species as well as among men, *ṛṣis* and aquatic creature are mere sports. All this clearly shows that Kuntī was well read and her courage to speak in an open audience in such a way is noteworthy.

Satī was also a learned lady. Besides general education she proved that she knew the science of *yoga* thoroughly and gave up her life like a true *yogī*, when insulted by her father. Her speech in the sacrificial hall is unique combining philosophical content with worldly wisdom. She remarked that a man should shut his ears and leave the place where his master is belittled. If he has the power he should forcibly cut off the vile tongue that indulges in such blasphemy and then give up one's life. *Manu-smṛti* also commented in similar manner. Satī preaches religious toleration. She remarked that the mind of a great sage

89. *Bhāgavata Purāṇa*, I.8.18-43.

revelling in his own self does not follow the utterances of the Vedas. Just as the movements of an immortal and a human being vary, even so the ways of the enlightened and the ignorant are not alike. Therefore while holding fast exclusively to one's own duty one should never cast aspersions against another. Activity in the shape of performing one's religious duties (pouring oblations into the sacred fire and so on) and that consisting of pursuits carried on in retirement are equally right both being prescribed in the Vedas for the two types of men, the one characterised by worldly attachment and the other by its absence, as will appear from the fact that the two are found incompatible in an agent practising both a time. Satī sat down on the floor facing north, sipped some water, wrapped herself with an yellow piece of linen, closed her eyes and resorted to the device of shedding the body after the manner of the *yogīs*. She gave up her body unable to bear the insult shown to her husband Śiva.

In the *Bhāgavata Purāṇa* we find, there were women who combined great wisdom and learning with their duties and to this category belonged women like Kuntī, Satī, Rukmiṇī and Satyabhāmā. Satyabhāmā was a lady possessing tremendous courage and will-power.

In the *Bhāgavata Purāṇa* the mention of *saṁskāras* or purificatory rites can be seen. It is said that Jaḍabharata's father performed all the *saṁskāras* up to the ceremony of *samāvartana* for his son. The *samāvartana* was performed at the close of the *brahmacarya* period and it marked the termination of the student life. In the 45th chapter of the tenth *skandha* the *upanayana saṁskāra*, by which the boy is invested with the sacred thread or initiated into studies is being performed to both Kṛṣṇa and Balarāma.

It is said that the king who was well-versed in the Vedas and other sacred books was competent to command armies, ruled over a kingdom, directed policies of war and exercised dominion over all the world.

The description of palaces having walls inlaid with gems and passasges is also found. "King Pṛthu planned with due regard to propriety dwelling at different places and he founded villages, towns and cities, built castles and forts of every type."[90] This reference proves that the study and practice of architecture had made great progress at that time. In the fourth *skandha*, Dhruva's palace has been described, Dhruva lived in that excellent palace built of most precious stones. It was furnished with beds of ivory and was provided with coverings of gold. In the walls of crystal and emerald, shone lights in the shape of bright gems placed in the hands of beautiful female figures carved in precious stones. The description of the palace proves the skill which the craftsman had attained at that time. Inlaying stones and carving figures had all reached a high degree of perfection.[91]

It is noteworthy that our ancestors knew the art of preserving the dead body. While Satyabhāmā's father was dead it is said that she put the dead body of her father in a jar of oil before going to Hastināpura.[92] That method would preserve the body till she came back with Kr̥ṣṇa. In the fourth *skandha* Veṇa's mother is said to have preserved the dead body of her son by means of spells and other devices.[93]

The science of medicine is very old in India and as early as in the *R̥gveda* the Aśvins are mentioned as physicians of the gods. References to medicine are found often in the *Bhāgavata Purāṇa*. In one or two places there is mention of surgical operation. In the seventh *skandha* for instance it is said that 'even an enemy (who is) beneficient as a medicine is a veritable son, while, an inimical son though begotten by one's own body should be shunned as a disease. One should ampute that

---

90. *Bhāgavata Purāṇa.*, IV.18.30f.

91. *Ibid.*, IV.9.60-4.

92. *tailadroṇyāṁ mr̥tam prāsya jagāma gajasāhvayam* |
kr̥ṣṇāya viditārthāya taptā'scakhau piturvadhaṁ ||
—*Ibid.*, X.57.8

93. *Ibid.*, IV.14. 35.

limb which is injurious to one's body and by removing which the rest of the body may survive.[94]

Preceptor is the main source of knowledge. As for the production of fire in a sacrifice, the lower piece of wood is considered to be main thing, so in acquiring knowledge preceptor is the main source.[95] He is like a pilot. But the knowledge obtained from one preceptor is not sufficient.[96]

Book XII of the *Bhāgavata* gives a detailed account of the four Vedas with their branches along with their *ṛṣis*. Upaniṣad and Vedānta have been mentioned severally.[97] The *Nirukta* is referred to.[98] The minor Vedas especially Archery[99] is mentioned with *yama*, *niyama*, etc. and the six accessory sciences have been referred to in the list of science taught to Balarāma and Kṛṣṇa.

Bhāgavata is referred to with the materials of the Dharmaśāstra. The Chapter II of book VII gives a detailed account of the duties of the different castes and stages.

The *Bhāgavata* refers to the school of Sāṁkhya system.[100] *Bhāgavata* refers to the terms like *ānvīkṣikī* and *tarka*.[101]

---

94. *paropyapatyaṁ hitakṛd yathauṣadhaṁ svadehajopyāmayavat sutohitaḥ* |
chindyāt tadaṅgaṁ yadutātmanohitaṁ śeṣam sukhaṁ jīvati yadvivarjahāt ||
— *Bhāgavata Purāṇa,* VII.5.37

95. *ācāryoraṇirādyaḥ syādante vāsyuttarāraṇiḥ* |
tatsandhānaṁ pravacam vidyāsandhiḥ sukhāvahaḥ ||
— *Ibid.*, X.12

96. *na hyekasmād gurorjñānam susthiraṁ syat supuṣkalam* |
— *Ibid.*, IX.9.31

97. *Ibid.*, V.13.3; VI.15.27; VIII.7.29; X.8.45; X.13.54; XII.6.41f

98. *jātakarṇyeśca cācchiṣyaḥ saniruktam svasaṁhitām* |
balākapaija vaitālavirājebhyo dadau muniḥ ||
— *Ibid.*, XII.6.58

99. *Ibid.*, II.8.20; VIII.21.2; X.45.34.

100. *Ibid.*, XI.22. 1-3, 7-8, 10, 16, 19, 25.

101. *Ibid.*, VIII.21.2.

The author of *Bhāgavata Purāṇa* refers to the alphabet, vowels, semi-vowels, sibilants, etc.[102] In addition to these he also uses some of the usages found in the books of Sanskrit grammar.

The *Bhāgavata Purāṇa* mentions *Āyurveda* along with other sciences and Dhanvantari as the twelfth incarnation of the Supreme Lord and propounder of the science of *Āyurveda*.[103] According to the *Bhāgavata Purāṇa* the substance which caused diseases can also cure it.[104]

This *Purāṇa* refers to magnetism.[105] It establishes the knowledge of physics.

The reference to a liquor known as *heṭaka rasa* which strengthens a person and makes him fit for coition.[106] So it shows the knowledge of chemistry.

That Purāṇa in which, commencing with the story of the birds that were acquainted with right and wrong everything is narrated fully by *Mārkaṇḍeya* as it was explained by holy sages, in reply to the question of the *muni*, is called the *Mārkaṇḍeya*, containing nine thousand verses. The *Mārkaṇḍeya Purāṇa* is so-called as being narrated by the sage Mārkaṇḍeya and by certain fabulous birds.

Among many legends and accounts of creation the long episodical narrative of the actions of the goddess Durgā, which is the special boast of this Purāṇa, is the textbook of the worshippers of Kālī, Caṇḍī, or Durgā. It is the *Caṇḍīpāṭha* or *Durgā-māhātmya* in which the victories of the goddess over different evil beings or *asuras* are detailed with considerable power and spirit.

---

102. *Bhāgavata Purāṇa*, III.12. 46-7; X.85.9.
103. *Ibid.*, III.12.38, I.3.17; II.7.21.
104. *Ibid.*, I.5.33.
105. *Ibid.*, V.18.38.
106. *puruṣaṁ rasena heṭakākhyena sādhayitvā. . . .*
— *Ibid.*, V.24.16

This Purāṇa has a character different from that of all the others. It has nothing of sectarial spirit, little of a religious tone, rarely inserting prayers and invocations to any deity. The prayers are brief and moderate. The *Mārkaṇḍeya Purāṇa* contains some stray references to the educational system of that time.

It is stated that Droṇa, the son of Mandapāla thoroughly read the Vedas and Vedāṅgas.[106a]

Common practice was to show reverence to the preceptor. In chapter III we see that the birds performed the reverential circumambulation around the *ṛṣi*. The *ṛṣi* was expounding the truths of the law in compassion for his disciples. They bowed down his feet and described him as their father and spiritual guide.[107]

The righteous birds remained on the mountain Vindhya, engaged in austerities and in the study of the Vedas with subdued minds.[108] The birds, the sons of Droṇa, became in course of time learned. They were engaged in reading like the brāhmaṇas, observing the beauties of various passages, regulating their breath, without any intermission, distinctly and without faults.[109] Jaimini remarked that Sarasvatī does never forsake these sons of the great sage. Here Jaimini also generalised that one can be forsaken by one's circle of relatives and friends but Sarasvatī does not abandon them. There the real impliction of education lies in the fact that education does not abandon one in any circumstance, even if the situation becomes unfavourable. Education only stands by one and helps to overcome the disaster fallen on the person. These birds stated that the four Vedas, Dharmaśāstra, all *aṅgas* and whatever else

---

106a. *Mārkaṇḍeya Purāṇa*, Canto II.33.

107. *ṛṣeḥ śiṣyānukampārthaṁ vadato dharmaniścayam* ।
kṛtvā pradakṣiṇam sarve caraṇāvabhyavādayan ॥
— *Ibid.*, III.5

108. *tapaḥsvādhyāyaniratāḥ samādhau kṛtaniścayaḥ* ॥
— *Ibid.*, III.85

109. *tyaktvā gacchati tat sarvam na jahāti sarasvatī* ॥
— *Matsya Purāṇa*, IV.6

is comfortable to the Vedas are their subjects of study.[110]

We find in chapter X that certain highly intelligent brāhmaṇas of Bhṛgu's line addressed his son Sumati who had undergone his initiation: As Sumati was initiated for his study his father advised him his duties to be observed then. He asked Sumati to study the Vedas from the beginning, be zealous in obedience to his *guru* or preceptor. He instructed him to make his livelihood collected by begging. After the completion of his study, he advised Sumati to observe the duties of a householder.[111]

The punishment for the blasphemy of the Vedas is death in delusion.[112] While describing the punishment for sins it is stated that those men who have given instructions in corrupt *śāstra*s and those who have advised such instructions, those who have repeated the *śāstra*s improperly, those who have given utterance to an evil word, those who have blasphemend the Vedas, or preceptor, would their tongues be torn out by the terrible birds with adamant beaks.[113] The bad-hearted men who have blasphemed their *guru*s and Vedas, would be punished by driving iron wedges into the ears by the servants of Yama.[114] The men deposing his preceptor, stubbornly pursues his learning of art—bears a rock on his head.[115] A defiler of one's *guru*'s bed

---

110. *caturṣvapi hi vedeṣu dharmaśāstreṣu caiva hi* ।
samasteṣu tathāṅgeṣu yaccānydvedasammitam ॥
— *Matsya Purāṇa*, 4.27

111. *vedānedhīṣva sumate yathākramamāditaḥ* ।
guruśuśruṣaṇe vyagro bhaikṣannakṛtabhojanaḥ ॥
— *Ibid.*, 10.9.10

112. *Ibid.*, 10.58.

113. *yaḥ śāstramanyathā proktam yairasadvāgudāhṛtaḥ* ।
vedadevadvijātīnām gurornindā ca yaiḥ kṛtā ।
haranti teṣām jihvāśca jāyamānāḥ punaḥ punaḥ ॥
— *Ibid.*, 14.44

114. *Ibid.*, 14.64.

115. *upādhyāyamadhaḥ kṛtvā stabdho yo'dhyayanaṁ naraḥ* ।
gṛhṇāti śilpamathavā so'pyevaṁ śirasā śilaṁ ॥
— *Ibid.*, 14.77

remains being burnt in blazing fire beneath, above, around for very many thousands of years. Thereafter they are reborn as men afflicted with leprosy, consumption, sickness and other diseases. When again dead they enter hell until the end of the *kalpa*.[116] The punishment of a defiler of the bed of a *guru* shows the moral behaviour is the first and foremost thing to be considered for a student. The *dvija* who has behaved towards his *upādhyāya* by coveting the latter's wife and the latter's property in his mind, undoubtedly becomes a dog.[117] The sinner who has vitiated his *guru*'s wife becomes a cock-cuckoo when released from hell. The man of lustful soul is born as a hog.[118] The fierce man who steals learning, and who falls short in his rewards to the *guru*, is tormented fiercely again and again.[119]

Veneration of *gurus*, association with the noble-minded people constitute the deeds of truth and righteousness, and these are the marks of sinless men.[120]

The son of Satrājit was sometimes resolved on investigating the whole *śāstra* literature, and at other times engrossed with poetry, dialogue, singing and the drama.[121] He enjoined himself in the discipline of all kinds of weapons; he was intent on the study of the science of

116. *vipreghnaḥ sūrapo gurutalpagaḥ* |
adhaścordhen ca dīptagnau dahyamānaḥ punaḥ punaḥ ||
— *Matsya Purāṇa*, 14.91 3

117. *upādhyāyavyalīkantu kṛtvā śvā bhavati dvijaḥ* |
tajjāyāṁ manasā vāñchena taddravyañcāpyasaṁśayam ||
— *Ibid.*, 15. 2

118. *Ibid.*, XV.11.

119. *vidyāpahāriṇaścogrā niṣkrayabhaṁśino guroḥ* ||
— *Ibid.*, 15. 36

120. *Ibid.*, 15.42-3.

121. *kadācicchāstra-sambhāra-vivekakṛtaniścayaḥ* |
kadācit kāvyasaṁlāpa-gīta-nāṭaka-sambhavaiḥ ||
— *Ibid.*, XX. 4

elephants, horses, and chariots suitable for war.[121a] These show the subjects of study generally prescribed for the princes.

In the *Mārkaṇḍeya Purāṇa* the education of a boy has been discussed with minute details through the conversation of Madālasā with Alarka. The observance of commands of *guru* (preceptor) gladden the mind of the teacher.[122] Alarka on reaching boyhood received investiture with the sacred thread and paid obeisance to his mother.[123]

After that while instructing on king's duties, Madālasā displays her knowledge in political science. It is advised that the king must in the first place conciliate his subjects, without obstructing his own duty. He would scrutinize the behaviour of the bad and good ministers; he must strenuously trace out his enemy's spies by his own spies. But a king must not always confide in friends, acquaintances, or relatives. A king must himself be conversant with the stationary, prosperous and deteriorating conditions of state polity, be familiar with the merit of the six measures of military policy, i.e., *sandhi* (peace); *vigraha* (war); *yāna* (marching); *āsana* (encamping); *dvaidhibhāva* (dividing his forces); *saṁśraya* (alliance) and not be enslaved by desire. A king must first subdue himself, and his ministers, his dependants and then citizens; then he would fight against his enemies. Desire, anger, covetousness, intoxication, pride and joy are the real enemies and these in truth tend to destroy kings.[124] A king should act like an insect against an opponent, and a king should carry out the ways of the ants at a fitting time, i.e.,

---

121a. *kadācicchāstrasaṁbhāra-vivekakr̥taniścayaḥ* ।
kadācit kāvyasaṁlāpa-gīta-nāṭakasaṁbhavaiḥ ॥

. . . . *śāstrāstravinayeṣu ca* ।
yogyāniyuddhanāgāśva-syandanābhyāstatparaḥ ॥
— *Matsya Purāṇa*, 20.4-5

122. *Ibid.*, 26.38.

123. *Ibid.*, 26.4f.

124. *kāmaḥ krodhaśca lobhaśca mado mānastathaiva ca* ।
harṣaśca śatravo hyete vināśaya mahībhr̥tam ॥
— *Ibid.*, XXVII.13

in the time of procuring treasures.[125] The king is a perfect one whose mind is attracted neither by covetousness, nor by love, nor by riches, and by other motives.

While expounding the duty of the brāhmaṇa it is stated that the duty of brāhmaṇa is threefold — liberality, study and sacrifice.[126] To perform sacrifices perfectly, to teach and to accept things from others in a righteous manner are the threefold means of livelihood of a brāhmaṇa.

While describing the brāhmaṇa's life it is stated that when duly invested with the sacred thread, he becomes a *brahmacārin* in his *guru*'s house, and he should dwell there. Among his duties are the Vedic study, attendance on holy fire, wandering about for alms, always eating food after informing his *guru* and obtaining permission from him. He should be diligent in the *guru*'s business, there should be thorough evoking of his affection; when summoned by him, he should read intently, his mind withdrawn from everything else. After acquiring knowledge in one, two or all the Vedas from his *guru*'s mouth, he is authorized to give the *guru* his fee with words of eulogy. A *brahmacārin* must pass through the period being obedient, free from self-conceit.[127]

While educating Alarka, Madālasā advised that one should offer seat to *gurus*, should received them with rising up and other respectful acts; he should accompany them in all possible places, should salute them respectfully and converse with them agreeably.[128] One should not

---

125. *kīṭasya kriyāṁ kuryād vipakṣe manujeśvaraḥ* ।
ceṣṭām pipilikānāñca kāle bhūpaḥ pradarśayet ॥
— *Matsya Purāṇa*, XXVII.18

126. *dānam adhyayanam yajño brāhmaṇasya tridhā mataḥ* ॥
— *Ibid.*, XXVIII.3

127. *kṛtopanoyanaḥ samyagbrahmacārī gurorgṛhe* ।
vaset tatra ca dharmo'sya kathyate taṁ vivodha me ॥
— *Ibid.*, 28.11-4

128. *Ibid.*, 34.32.

talk of his *guru*'s evil-doing, and he should appease him when angry. He should not listen to abuse when others utter it.[129]

A wise man should study the three Vedas, and must be continually occupied therein.[130]

In the conversation between the father and the son the nature of soul and highly advanced philosophy has been discussed.[131] Final emancipation from existence is attained through *yoga* — the means are the restraint of the breadth, mental abstraction, restraint of the senses and deep meditation.[132] Here the psychological aspect of education is discussed. Before study the mental state must be controlled and mind must be concentrated through several stages of the mind. After that one can study with concentrated mind.

Study by one who is not a *brahmacārī* is worthy to be punished. The brāhmaṇa whose mind is engrossed with sacrifice, study, discipline and alms-giving, who has made his livelihood by means of the performance of sacrifices, teaching and receiving alms is pure and praiseworthy. The kṣatriya and vaiśya who is always energetic in alms-giving, study, etc. is all pure and praiseworthy.[133] There is no fear of misfortune where the son of the householder shows reverence to his preceptor and others.[134] Reverence for preceptor was the essential quality of the pupil.

The knowledge of geography and astrology was in an advanced state can be proved from the *Mārkaṇḍeya Purāṇa*.

---

129. *duṣkṛtam na gurorvruyāt kruddhaṁ cainaṁ prasādayet* ।
parivādaṁ na śṛnuyād anyeṣām api kurvatām ।।
— *Matsya Purāṇa*, XXXIV.38

130. *adhyetavyā trayī nityam bhavitavyaṁ vipaścitā* ।
— *Ibid.*, 35.56

131. *Ibid.*, 38. 5f.

132. *Ibid.*, 39.

133. *yajanādhyāyanābhyāsa-dānāsaktiṁatiṁ sadā* ।
yājanādhyāpanādāna-kṛtavṛttim dvijam tyāja ।।
— *Ibid.*, 50.74f

134. *Ibid.*, 50, 78.

Āyurveda or Indian Medicine was also in a well-advanced stage. In chapter sixtyone the power of medicinal herbs is described.[135]

The knowledge of archery was cultivated in that age. So we find that Svarocis acquired skill in archery learnt the Vedas in due order as well as other sciences. The art of archery was also studied by women. It is found that Manoramā learnt from her father how to use this heart of all weapons, which destroys every foe.

The characteristic of Āyurveda has been described. The brāhmaṇa Brahmamitra had mastered the thirteen sections of the *Atharvaveda* and Āyurveda which is divided into eight parts. The science of *Āyurveda* was gained after a space of eight months.[136] By the favour of *Āyurveda* the friends became fresh. The *rākṣasa* bestowed on Svarocis the whole of the Āyurveda with its eight parts.[137] Satī imparted the knowledge called Padminī greatly worshipped by Mahāpadma to Kalāvatī by which she could succeed.[138] Barter at the price of knowledge is abused.[139]

The disciples of preceptor used to obey orders of the preceptor. In chapter sixtynine of the *Mārkaṇḍeya Purāṇa* an ascetic commanded his disciples to bring the *arghya* offering. But an advanced student was entitled to put questions even his preceptor. So it is stated that the prcecetor was being alerted by asking question by his student.[140]

The knowledge of astrology was well advanced. It is clear from the conversation of the *ṛṣi* and king Uttama. Thus the *ṛṣi* spoke — "When

---

135. *mahauṣadhiprabhāvena viprāpratihatā gatiḥ* ।
yoganānāṁ sahasraṁ hi dinārdhena vrajāmyaham ।।
— *Matsya Purāṇa*, 61.12

136. *gṛhītāyāntu vidyāyāṁ māsairaṣṭābhirantarāt.*
— *Ibid.*, 63.39

137. *Ibid.*, LXIII.53.

138. *Ibid.*, 64.17.

139. *vidyāpradānamūlyena vikrīto hyeṣā bhṛtyavat* ।
— *Ibid.*, 65.17

140. *Ibid.*, 69.43, 52.

thou didst take her hand in marriage, the Sun and Mars and Saturn looked on thee, and Venus and Jupiter looked on thy wife. At that moment the moon was favourable to thee, and Mercury to her. Those two groups of plants are mutually hostile; hence they have been exceedingly adverse to thee."[141]

The heritage of Medhas is delineated in a fine way. It inhabited by wild animals which were peaceful, and the hermitage was graced by the *muni*'s disciples.[142]

The disciple was entrusted with various duties in the absence of his preceptor. In the *Mārkaṇḍeya Purāṇa* in canto ninetynine Bhūti ordered his high-minded disciple Śānti to keep watch over the fire in his hermitage so that the fire might not become extinguished and having given this command Bhūti went to join his brother's sacrifice. While Śānti was fetching fuel, flowers, fruit and other things from the forest for the maintenance of order in the house of his high souled and was performing other businesses, being faithfully obedient to his *guru*, the fire died out during that interval.[143]

The knowledge of spherical astronomy was discussed with reference to the sun.[144]

Astrologers were often consulted by the kings about the best days and moments for anointing their sons in the kingdoms.[145] Astrologers were generally skilled in various scriptures.

The royal *ṛṣi*, Nīpa gave Bhananda a complete set of weapons. After acquiring skill in the weapons he went to his paternal uncle's sons.[146]

---

141. *Matsya Purāṇa*, 71.26-7.
142. *muniśiṣyopaśobhitam*. — *Ibid.*, 81.9.
143. *Ibid.*, Ch. 99, 15f.
144. *Ibid.*, Ch. 106.
145. *dinalagnānyapṛcchet* — *Ibid.*, Ch. 109, 38.
146. *prāptāstravidyāḥ sa yayau pitṛvyatanayān dvija* ।
— *Ibid.*, 114, 12

Avikṣita learnt the whole of the Vedas and the Vedāṅgas. He also acquired from Kaṇva's son perfect skill in every weapon.[147] Thus the subjects of study for the princes can be inferred from the stray reference in the *Matsya Purāṇa*. The son of Avikṣita acquired knowledge in the Vedas first from the teachers, then skill in all kinds of weapons, and afterwards the complete knowledge of archery. When he had completed his efforts in the use of the sword and bow, he next overcome toil like a hero in learning the use of other weapons also. He being intent on pleasing his *guru* obtained weapons from Bhārgava. He was accomplished in the use of weapons, skilled in the Vedas, thoroughly mastered the knowledge of archery, deeply versed in all sciences.[148] Prince Dama learnt the knowledge of the bow entirely from Vṛṣaparvan, king of men, he learnt the use of all kinds of weapons thoroughly from the noble *daitya* Dundubhi, he learnt the Vedas and all the Vedāṅgas from Śakti.[149]

The Purāṇa in which *Vāyu* has declared the laws of duty, in connection with the *Śveta kalpa*, and which comprises the *māhātmya* of Rudra is the *Vāyavīya Purāṇa*, it contains twenty-four thousand verses. The *Matsya Purāṇa* describes the *Vāyavīya Purāṇa* as characterised by its account of the greatness of the Rudra or Śiva.

The *Vāyu Purāṇa* is narrated by Śiva to the *ṛṣis* at Naimiṣāraṇya; it was formerly told by Vāyu. It is divided into four *pādas* termed severally *prakriyā*, *upodghāta*, *anuṣaṅga* and *upasaṁhāra*. This is a classification peculiar to this work. It is generally regarded as a Śaiva Purāṇa to this work. It is generally regarded as a Śaiva Purāṇa and the *Gayā-māhātmya* covering several chapters of this Purāṇa, which emphasizes Vaiṣṇavism appeared to be later edition.

---

147. *avikṣitaḥ sutastasya vedavedāṅga pāragaḥ* ।
astragrāmamaśeṣeṁ sa kaṇvaputrādathāgrahīt ॥
— *Matsya Purāṇa*, Ch. 129, 13

148. *Ibid.*, Ch. 128.12f., p. 650.

149. *Ibid.*, Canto CXXXIII, 5, p. 669.

Like other Purāṇas, the *Vāyu* also contains some references to the educational system of ancient India. The *Vāyu* says that brāhmaṇa who know the four Vedas with the *aṅga*s and Upaniṣads cannot be regarded as being attained proficiency, unless he has knowledge in the Purāṇas. It is his duty to reinforce the Veda with the *itihāsa* and Purāṇa.[150]

The knowledge of science was highly advanced. While describing the characteristic of *Vāyu* it is pointed out that his source of origin is ether, attributes are sound and touch and he was the origin of fire.[151]

The *Vāyu Purāṇa* displays enough knolwedge about the architectural and sculptural techniques and these sciences were evidently very much developed during the time of the *Vāyu Purāṇa*.

It is noteworthy that the unit of measurements of distance was set up with minute details by the mathematicians. This unit of measurement was used in building houses. A unit was termed *pradeśa* — a distance between the thumb and the forefinger. The distance between the thumb and the middle finger was *tāla* and that between the thumb and the ring finger was *gokarṇa*. *Vitasti* comprises of twelve *aṅgula*s. Twenty-one *aṅgula*s made one *ratni*, i.e., the distance between the elbow and the closed fist. Twenty-four *aṅgula*s made one *hasta* (hand). Two *ratni*s made one *kiṣku*. Four *hasta*s made one *dhanu*. Two thousand *dhanu*s made one *gavyūti*. Eight thousand *dhanu*s constituted a *yojana*.

The *Vāyu Purāṇa* speaks of a Śiva temple,[152] the pillars of which are sculptured with portraits of gods and animals. It bears testimony of the engineering skill in the temple architecture as well as skill in the art of image-making. In connexion with the description of temple construction, occasional references have been given to painting.

---

150. *yo vidyāt caturo vedān sāṅgopaniṣada dvijaḥ* |
na cet purāṇam samvidyān naiva sa syād vicakṣaṇaḥ ||
— *Vāyu Purāṇa*, I.199

151. *Ibid.*, Ch. II, 39.

152. *Ibid.*, Ch. 101. 288-92.

The art of construction of forts and town planning was also enterprising. So, the education in the field of civil engineering for acquiring knowledge in building construction in this age, was very much in practice.

The mode of construction of artificial fortress is described with minute details.[153] Huge mansions, lofty ramparts and fort-walls were built around. There was a principal gate called *svastika* and there was a *kumārīpura*. The main gate was close to a moat with flowing water. The width of the moat was eight or ten. The dimensions of hamlets, cities and villages and three types of forts are mentioned. The extent of a city shall be half or one-fourth of the maximum length. A city set-up in the form of a square with straight rows of houses in all the eight quarters was desirable. Important dwelling was constructed in a site, hundred *kiṣkus* wide. The *Vāyu Purāṇa* contains mature conception of music and dancing, the most important constituents of fine arts. It contains a lengthy discourse on the science of music (Ch. 86). Chapter 87 (*gītālaṁkāranirdeśa*) contains valuable information relating to ancient Indian music and dancing.

Teaching was assigned to brāhmaṇas as their duty. The duties common to the three classes include the srtudy of the Vedas.[154] The duties of a *brahmacārin* who wanted to acquire learning has been prescribed as bearing the staff, wearing the girdle of *muñja* grass, sleeping on the bare ground, service to the preceptor and begging alms.[155] Moral teaching considered to be the first and foremost thing.

---

153. *trividhānām ca durgānām viṣkambhamayameva ca* ।
yojanānām ca viṣkaṁbhamaṣṭabhāgārdhamāyatam ॥
— *Vāyu Purāṇa*, 8.107

154. *yājanādhyāpanam caiva tṛtīyam ca parigrahaṁ* ।
brāhmaṇānām vibhusteṣām karmānyetunyathādiśat ॥
— *Ibid.*, 8.162, p. 130

155. *daṇḍī ca mekhalī caiva hyadhaḥśāyī tathā jāṭī* ।
guruśuśruṣaṇam bhaikṣyam vidyārthe brahmacāriṇaḥ ॥
— *Ibid.*, 8.182

Begging, non-stealing, purity, non-negligence, refraining from sexual intercourse, mercy towards all beings, forbearance, absence of anger, service to preceptors and truthfulness—are the characteristics included in the code of conduct of a *sannyāsī*.[156]

The psychological training for the students was acquired through practising *yoga*. It is the steadying of the mind that is called *dhāraṇā*. The withdrawal from the sense-objects is *pratyāhāra*.[157]

That the knowledge of Physics was current is evident from the fact that the effort of *yogin* is compared with the water taken up by applying force through a pipe or mechanical device.[158]

The stages of concentration of mind, i.e., *yoga* is described as *aṇimā, laghimā, prāpti, prākāmya, īśitva, vaśitva* and *kāmavaśāyitā*.[159]

Student had to live with the preceptor. He had to remain with the preceptor for a year[160] and to engage in what is pleasing and beneficial to him. The mode of begging by a *yogī* has also been described. An intelligent *yogī* should go out (for alms) when the fires in the kitchen have become smokeless, and extinguished. He should not constantly

---

156. *āsannamusale bhaikṣamasteyaṁ śaucameva ca |*
apramādo'vyavāyaśca dayā bhūteṣu ca kṣamā ||
akrodho guruśuśruṣā satyaṁ ca daśamaṁ smr̥tam |
— *Vāyu Purāṇa*, 8.176-77

157. *mānaso dhāraṇā caiva dhāraṇeti prakīrtita |*
nivr̥tti viṣayānāntu pratyāhārastu saṁjñitaḥ ||
— *Ibid.*, 11.39

158. *nalena tu yathā toyaṁ yantreṇaiva valānvitaḥ |*
āpiveta prayatnene tathā vāyañjitaśramaḥ ||
— *Ibid.*, 11.29

159. *animā laghimā caiva mahimā prāptireva ca |*
prākāmyamcaiva sarvatra īśitvaṁ caiva sarbataḥ ||
— *Ibid.*, 13. 3-4

160. *guroḥ priyahita yuktaḥ sa tu saṁvatsaraṁ vaset |*
— *Ibid.*, 16.4

beg in the same house for it might happen that he got insulted or people to be offended.[161]

The science of uttering sounds according to the place and similarity is delineated as the groups of letters are formed by their place of utterance as the distributions.[162]

The fact that the science of archery was in an advanced stage can be proved from the information that the Pracetas[163] were the masters of the science of archery.

The idea of division of time from the beginning *nimeṣa* to day and night, fortnight, month, season and *ayaṇa* is clearly enumerated. The first year is *saṁvatsara*, the second *parivatsara*, the third *idvatsara*, the fourth is *anuvatsara* and the fifth is *vatsara* — the group is called *yuga*.[164]

The knowledge of astronomy specially regarding *dhruva* or pole star is surprisingly modern. The function of the constellation attached with *dhruva* is described.[165]

The invisibility of the luminaries and the means are described. It is stated that the movement of the luminaries among human beings cannot be precisely observed by the physical eye. These five functions are the means for ascertaining the true positions of the luminary

---

161. *vahnau vidhūme vyaṅgāre sarvasmin bhuktavajjane* ।
vicārenamatimān yogī na tu teṣveva nityaśaḥ ।।
yathaivamavamanyante yathā paribhavanti ca ।
yuktastathā cared bhaikṣam satām dharmamadūṣayat ।।
— *Vāyu Purāṇa*, 16.8-9

162. *bhaṣyanti yathāśailam varnaśca nyāyato'rthataḥ* ।
abhyāsāt sandhyāścaiva tasmājjñeyaḥ svarā iti ।।
— *Ibid.*, 26. 50

163. *sarve pracetaso nāma dhanurvedasya pāragāḥ* ।
— *Ibid.*, 30.36

164. *Ibid.*, 31.24-8.

165. *Ibid.*, 60. 8-10.

bodies, viz. the eye, scriptures, water, written documents and mathematical calculations.[166]

The science of speech (*vāgvidhiḥ*) is described in a way that when breadth touches the proper place of articulation only then the activity of speech begins.[167]

The Vedas are meant as subject of study for brāhmaṇas.[168] It is stated that the knowledge of the Vedas is firm. The Vedic texts, with ancillaries, function with uniform meaning in every age.[169]

The *Vāyu Purāṇa* was aware of the fact that there were difference of opinions in the interpretations of the *nibandhas* and the passages of the *Atharvaveda*, the *Sāmaveda* and even of the *Ṛgveda* (58.16-17).

It is stated in the *Vāyu Purāṇa* that there are variations and alterations in the sciences of *Āyurveda*, *Jyotiṣa* and the ancillaries of the Vedas. There are doubts and variations in regard to the texts on political economy and logic.[170]

The *Vāyu Purāṇa* maintains that the multiplicity of scriptures has been created by the people of different (philosophical) outlooks; single unified Veda is classified into four; the Vedas are further subdivided into *mantras* and *Brāhmaṇas* by alternations on accents, syllables, etc. in accordance with different outlooks. The Saṁhitās of the *Ṛg*, *Sāma*

---

166. *cakṣuḥ śāstraṁ jalaṁ lekhyaṁ gaṇitam buddhimattamaḥ* ।
pañcaite hetavo jñeya jyotirgaṇa vicintanā ॥
— *Vāyu Purāṇa*, 53. 123

167. *Ibid.*, LIV.13.

168. *brāhmaṇo vedam āpnoti* — *Ibid.*, 54.111.

169. *sadharmaḥ saprajāḥ saṅga yathādharmaṁ yuge yuge* ।
vikriyante sāmānārtha vedavādā yathāyugam ॥
— *Ibid.*, 57.49

170. *āyurvedavikalpaśca aṅgānāṁ jyotiṣasya ca* ।
arthaśāstravikalpaśca hetuśāstravikalpanam ॥
smṛtiśāstraprabhedaśca prasthānāni pṛthak pṛthak ।
— *Ibid.*, 58.23-4

and *Yajur-vedas* compiled by sages expert in Śrutis occasionally with general and special (known as Vedic *vikṛtis*) changes according to different standpoints. Consequently the *Brāhmaṇa* (works), *Kalpa Sūtra*, *Mantrapravacanas* (different scriptural texts) came into light.[171]

It is stated that *brahmacārin* acting in the interest of his preceptor becomes an ascetic by amassing learning.

The quality of a preceptor is given in this Purāṇa; a preceptor should teach a *dharma* that leads a person to achieve his good desires. He is called *ācārya* or preceptor: generally *ācāryas* were old persons devoid of greediness, self-possessed, non-arrogant, well disciplined and straightforward; a preceptor practised these principles himself; he used to establish a code of good conduct, he collected and mastered meanings of scriptures and was busy with practising restraints and observances.

Brahmacarya or celibacy was the first and foremost duty to be observed by a student. Abstinence from sexual acts, neither brooding nor imagining about it and complete sexual detachment was called celibacy.[172]

In the *Vāyu Purāṇa* the classification of the Vedas has as usual been attributed to Vyāsa. Vyāsa also taught the Vedas to his students. Paila, Jaimini, Vaiśampāyana and Sumantu are said to be the propounders of respective Vedas.[173]

The teaching of grammar and the disciples who learnt this science are described. It is described in the *Vāyu Purāṇa* that the renowned scholar Śākalya knew the implications of grammar and composed five Saṁhitās and had five disciples.[174] Another reputed brāhmaṇa

---

171. *eko vedaścatuṣpādāḥ vidhīyate.*

— *Vāyu Purāṇa*, 58.10

172. *Ibid.*, LIX. 23-5, 29-30, 39, 46, pp. 421-3.

173. *Ibid.*, LX.12-3, p. 430.

174. *Ibid.*, 60.63-4.

Śākapūrṇa, Rathītara compiled three Saṁhitās and composed one *Nirukta* as his fourth work. He had also four gifted students.[175]

The description of the lineage of Bahvṛcas or propagators of the Vedas is enumerated.[176] The Carakas are disciples of Vaiśampāyana. A popular etymology of Caraka is derived from ✓*car* 'to go', 'to know'. So Caraka should mean — a knower of the Vedas and the medical science. The fifteen disciples of Yājñavalkya are known as Vājins. Here the genealogy of that teachers of the different Vedas are highlighted.[177] These different recensions of the Vedas had been made by the disciples of Vyāsa and their disciples.

The traditional fourteen lores are the six *aṅgas* (ancillary subjects), the four Vedas, Mīmāṁsā, Nyāya-vistara (logic), Dharmaśāstra and Purāṇas. This enumeration of fourteen lores differs from that of *Chāndogya Upaniṣad*. If four more lores are counted in consideration, the number becomes eighteen. These are *Āyurveda* (science of medicine), *Dhanurveda* (science of archery), *Gāndharvaveda* (i.e., musicology), *Arthaśāstra* (science of economics and politics).[178]

The Sūta says that the story of the Pṛthu is not to be narrated to a brāhmṇa, without a disciple. Brāhmaṇas who were experts in the Vedas and their *aṅgas* (ancillary subjects) have been highly praised.[179]

---

175. *provāca samhitāstiśraḥ śākaparṇo-rathītaraḥ* I
niruktañca punaścakre caturthaṁ dvijasattamaḥ II
— *Vāyu Purāṇa*, 60.65

176. *ityeta vahvṛcāḥ proktaḥ saṁhitā yaiḥ pravartitāḥ* II
— *Ibid.*, 61.4

177. *Ibid.*, 61.24-6, 29.

178. *aṅgam vedaścatvāro mīmāṁsā nyāya-vistaraḥ* I
dharmaśāstram purāṇam ca vidyāstvetāścaturdaśa II

āyurvedo dhanurvedo gāndharvaścaiva te trayaḥ I
arthaśāstram caturthaṁ tu vidyāstvaṣṭādaśaiva tu II
— *Ibid.*, 61.78-9

179. *brāhmaṇaiśca mahābhāgairvedavedāṅgapāragaiḥ* I
— *Ibid.*, 63.6

The Pracetas are described as masters of the science of archery.[180]

The teaching of the Vedas along with the *pada* and *krama pāṭhas* (which were special methods of reciting Vedic texts) were in practice; this fact has been represented in allegorical way in the *Vāyu Purāṇa*. It is stated that the *Sāman mantra*, thousands of *Yajur mantra*, and the *Ṛgveda* with *pada* and *krama pāṭhas* were present there in embodied form. The details regarding the recitation of the Vedas, i.e. *lakṣaṇas* (the characterisitc topics), *svaras* (notes), *stobhas* (chanted interjections in a *Sāman*-song), *nirukta* (etymology), *svarabhaktis* (insertion of vowel sound for ease in pronunciations), *āśraya* (resting places or annexation), *vaṣaṭkāra*, *nigraha* (suppression) and *pragraha* (vowels not subject to *sandhi* rules) — have been categorically mentioned.[181] All these characteristics of the Vedic recitation testify that the authors of the *Vāyu Purāṇa* were well acquainted with the niceties of the procedure of the recitation of the Vedic *mantras*.

Śukra is mentioned as the preceptor of *devas* and *asuras*. He was the most excellent among the exponents of Vedas (*veda-vidām varam*).[182]

Education of women has also drawn the attention of the authors of the *Vāyu Purāṇa*. It is stated that Bṛhaspati's sister was an excellent woman, who had taken the vow of celebacy and perfected by means of *yoga*. Uninvolved to the worldy affairs or things, she roamed the entire universe. She had a son Viśvakarmā. He was Prajāpati of all *śilpīs* (artisans and sculptors) and maker of all arts and crafts. He was the carpenter of the *devas* and maker and caused others to make ornaments. He made the aerial chariot (*vimāna*) of all *devas*. The human craftsmen depend upon his mechanical arts.[183]

---

180. *sarva pracetaso nāma dhnurvedasya pāragāḥ* ।
— *Vāyu Purāṇa*, 63.26

181. *Ibid.*, 65.24-8.

182. *Ibid.*, 65.74-5.

183. *Ibid.*, 66.27-30.

The authors of the *Vāyu Purāṇa* were aware of the science of astronomy. The *vīthis* are described here. The constellations Mūla, Pūrvāṣāḍhā, Uttarāṣāḍhā are termed *ajavīthi*. Śravaṇa, Dhaniṣṭhā and Śatabhiṣak are the *gārgīvīthi*. Pūrva Bhādrapada, Uttara Bhādrapada and Revatī are glorified as *vaiśvanāri vīthi*.[184]

The *Vāyu Purāṇa* maintains that Vedas, Dharmaśāstras and ancient Sāṁkhya and Yoga can make one equipped to visualize the reality.[185]

The study of the Vedas, the maintenance of celebacy and other holy actions are praised.[186]

The people of this time were skilled in use of medical herbs, fruits and roots, which were used to enliven the oppressed.[187]

There is a reference to brāhmaṇas preaching principles of atheism in the holy place of Gokarṇa.[188]

In a festival, the position of the brāhmaṇa was determined by his knowledge of the Vedas. The social status of people was fixed up by the scale of education. Precedence was given to the brāhmaṇas according to their learning. Among the brāhmaṇas an ascetic was the leader. An excellent brāhmaṇa who read all the Vedas with *itihāsa* constituting their fifth Veda was highly regarded; a brāhmaṇa who studied three Vedas came next to him. Next was the place of a student of two Vedas. Then a man of a single Veda and after him came a person who studied the Nyāya (*Nyāyādhyāyī*) system.[189] It was believed that persons of

184. *Vāyu Purāṇa*, 66.51-2.

185. *sāṁkhya yogaparairvīraiḥ pṛthktvaikatvadarśibhiḥ* |
abhijātaprabhāvaṛṣibhistattvadarśibhiḥ ||
— *Ibid.*, 66.103

186. *Ibid.*, 67.28.

187. *Ibid.*, 70.82.

188. *gokarṇa varṇitaṁ viprairnāstikānāṁ nidarśanam* |
— *Ibid.*, 77.21

189. *Ibid.*, 79.52-4.

specially high character, merit, learning, etc. purified degenerate members of the society by associating with them, by sitting in their row for dining or even by their beneficient look. In this connection it is also stated that those who are firm in their sacred rites, those who are eager to acquire knowldge and are absorbed in meditations and the noble-hearted devotees of gods usually sanctified others by their mere sight.[190]

Those are called *paṅktipāvana* who sanctified the row of the diners. They are — *ṣaḍaṅgī*, i.e., person who had learnt all the six ancillary subjects of the Veda, *vinayī*, i.e., the disciplined one, *yogin*, *sarvatantrasvatantra*, i.e., he who had mastered all systems of philosophy and *yāyāvara*, i.e., a wandering mendicant saint. He who had mastered one of the eighteen lores was also sanctifier of the row. The *trinaciketas*, i.e., a brāhmaṇa who learns the three *vidyās* of Naciketas, the *traividā*, i.e., he who mastered the three *vidyās*, the brāhmaṇas who learns Dharmaśāstras, the brāhmaṇa who has mastered the Bārhaspatya scriputre — all these brāhmaṇas are said to be those who sanctificed the row.[191]

It had been prescribed that a religious gift was to be made to the guest and a *brahmacārin*, or celibate person was to be fed. An *upakurvāna*, i.e., a *brahmacāin* who completed his studies and pays his teacher and is about to be a householder, was propitiated by mere worship.[192] It is stated that those who were real brāhmaṇa, pursued knowledge and meditation. Even if they are born as brāhmaṇa, those who have false conceptions are of evil conduct.[193]

Those who made use of the Vedas as a means of employment out of covetousness and fallibility or of personal benefit were discounted as

---

190. *ye tu vrate sthita nityam jñānino dhyāninastathā* |
devabhaktā mahātāmānaḥ puniyurdarśanād api ||
— *Vāyu Purāṇa*, 79.91

191. *Ibid.*, 79.55-8.

192. *Ibid.*, 79.61-2.

193. *Ibid.*, 79.72.

the sellers of the Vedas (*brahmavikrayinaḥ*); the study of Vedas was not a profession. He who made the study of the Vedas as a profession was a sinner; this person was deprived of the enjoyment of the fruit of the Vedic study. The donor of the Vedas was also deprived of the fruit of charity. A person hired to teach the Vedas and one who was taught by such a person—both of them did not deserve invitation to a *śrāddha*, as they were disregarded as the sellers and buyers of the Vedas.[194] Those brāhmaṇas who buy and sell for the purpose of livelihood were contemptible persons, for, this was the profession of a vaiśya, but a sin for the brāhmaṇas.[195] From these statements it is clear that imparting Vedic knowledge in lieu of money by brāhmaṇas was recognised as the work of despicable people and those were never regarded with veneration. On the contrary, the actural learned persons without any monetary motif were highly esteemed and were invited with veneration to the *śrāddha* rite. A brāhmaṇa without the knowledge of the Vedas was not to be invited for participation in *śrāddha*-rites. Those who had studied all the Vedas and who had performed all religious rites, reputed brāhmaṇas who knew the *bhāṣyas* (Glosses on Aphorisms), those who regularly studied grammar, those who studied Purāṇas and Dharmaśāstras, those who were conversant with three Naciketas *vidyās*, the knowers of the six ancillary subjects of the Vedas, a master of Vedic Prosody or chanter of the Vedas, a singer of the *Jyeṣṭha Sāman*, those who strictly adhered to their own duties — all these persons might be invited in the *śrāddha* rites.[196]

The *yoga* sustains the psychological aspect of the education. The concentration of mind and other means prescribed by *yoga* trained the mind which was receptacle of the highest knowledge. A person having the knowledge of *yoga* was the knower of the Vedas. They call him the

---

194. *Vāyu Purāṇa*, 79.74-5.

195. *krayavikrayinau caiva jīvitārthaṁ vigarhitau* |
vṛttireṣām tu vaiśyasya brāhmaṇasya tu pātakam ||
— *Ibid.*, 79.76

196. *Ibid.*, 83.51-7.

knower of the Vedas and the master of Vedas. He was eligible to teach all the brāhmaṇas.[197]

The science of music or *Gāndharvaveda* is described with minute details in the *Vāyu Purāṇa*. The *Gāndharva vidyā* is included in the list of eighteen *vidyās*, viz., Vedas with Aṅgas, Mīmāṁsā, Nyāya, Dharmaśāstra, Purāṇa, *Āyurveda*, *Dhanurveda*, *Gādharvaveda* and *Arthaśāstra*.[198]

Vādya, *vāditra* or *vādanaka* appear to be the terms signifying a musical instrument in general.[199]

Śiva's connection with music as well as dance is noteworthy.

The *svara maṇḍala* or the whole musical notes are said to be comprised of seven *svaras* or notes, three *grāmas* or basic scales, twenty-one *murcchanās* or the modes of gradual ascent and descent of the seven notes and fortyone *tālas*. The names of the *svaras* are described. The *murcchanās* of the *ma*-scale of the *madhyamagrāmika* are known as Śaubiri. The *murcchanās* and *tālas* are described with minute details in chapters 86 and 87 of the *Vāyu Purāṇa*.

It is stated that Bṛhadasva had twenty-one thousand sons who were experts in *vidyās*, powerful and invincible.[200]

The science of missile was well advanced. It is described that Aurva, after post-natal holy rites of Yadavi's son, taught him Vedas and *śāstras*. Then he instructed him in the use of miraculous weapons and missiles.[201] Sagara was taught by Jāmadagnya about the use of

---

197. *Vāyu Purāṇa*, 83.98-100.
198. *Ibid.*, 61.78-9.
199. *Ibid.*, 30.248.
200. *Ibid.*, 88.30.
201. *aurvastu jātakarmādīn kṛtvā tasya mahātmanāḥ* ǀ
adhyāpya vedaśāstrāṇi tato'stram pratyapādayet ǀǀ
—*Ibid.*, 88.134

miraculous missiles of Fire-God, which could not be endured even by *asuras*.[202]

The art of the game of dice was in practice. Ṛtuparṇa was conversant with the divine *akṣahṛdaya mantra*, i.e., the *mantra* with which people became sure winners at the game of dice.[203]

Vasiṣṭha is said to have studied five hundred Vedic Saṁhitās. *Brahmāṇḍa Purāṇa* states that Pauṣyanjī was his teacher in *Sāmaveda*. Pauṣyanjī, a disciple of Sukarman, taught five branches of the *Sāmaveda*. The Yoga philosophy was taught by the intelligent Yājñavalkya Puṣya; his son was a great scholar. Manu adopted yogic practice.[204] Purūravas was described as an expounder of *Brāhmaṇa* (Vedas).[205] Paraśurāma was the most excellent of those who had mastered all lores and the science of archery as well.[206] It is described that the sage Bharadvāja created the science of *Āyurveda* along with its therapeutics.[207] *Brahmāṇḍa Purāṇa* informs us that Dhanvantari learnt *Āyurveda* along with its therapeutics from Bharadvāja.[208] Dhanvantari divided it into eight sections and taught them to different disciples.[209]

One hundred sons of Bhadraśreṇya who were master in archery were killed by king Divodāsa.[210]

Duryodhana went to Mithilā and Balabhadra imparted training in mace-fighting to him.[211]

---

202. *Vāyu Purāṇa*, 88.135
203. *Ibid.*, 88.174.
204. *Ibid.*, 88.206-07.
205. *Ibid.*, 91.2.
206. *Ibid.*, 91.91.
207. *Ibid.*, 92.22.
208. *Brahmāṇḍa Purāṇa*, II.3.67, 23-4.
209. *Vāyu Purāṇa*, 92.23.
210. *Ibid.*, 92.61.
211. *Ibid.*, 96.83.

It is described that Cārudeṣṇa and Śāmba gathered the knowledge in the use of miraculous weapons.[212]

Vidyās are mentioned as three,[213] and four *vidyās* are also enumerated as *ānvikṣikī*, *trayī*, *vārtā* and *daṇḍanīti*.[214]

Bṛhaspati asked the *daityas* that he had acquired a great *vidyā* and this would be taught to them. The *asuras* approached him for the sake of attaining the *vidyā*. When Śukra returned, Bṛhaspati asked them that he was the real preceptor and the newly arrived man is trying to conceit them in his disguise. Being misguided the *asuras* insulted Śukra and in turn Śukra cursed them. So this shows that one preceptor tried to deceive the disciples of the opposite camp to attain his personal goal.[215]

The *Vāyu Purāṇa* states that the son of Asija in his mother's womb, had learnt the Vedas with their six ancillaries and repeated the Vedic *mantras*. The unborn baby spoke to Bṛhaspati about the duty of a *snātaka*, i.e., a brāhmaṇa who just had his sacred ablution after completing the Vedic study.[216]

Two sons of Dīrghatamas studied the Vedas duly and became masters and expounders of the Vedas and became excellent ones with direct vision of Dharma.[217] The sons or disciples of Śiva are often mentioned as being brāhmaṇas learned in the Vedas and practised austerities and achieved *māheśavara-yoga*.

Kṛta was a disciple of Hiraṇyanābhi of the Kauthuma branch of Sāmavedic study. Twenty-four *Sāman Saṁhitās* were expounded by

---

212. *Vāyu Purāṇa*, 96.188.
213. *Ibid.*, 97.32.
214. *Ibid.*, 97.37.
215. *Ibid.*, 98.27-37.
216. *Ibid.*, 99.43-4.
217. *Ibid.*, 99.70-3.

him. The sons of Kṛta, the singers of *Sāman* hymns are remembered by the mame *prācyas* (easterners).[218]

The *Vāyu Purāṇa* maintains that the sellers and blasphemers of the Vedas and those who do not worship their preceptors fall into the hell named *kṛmibhakṣya.*[219]

The means of attainment of highest knowledge are enumerated in the *Vāyu Purāṇa*. It says that learned men can see the real truth manifest through inference; the *yogins* see it directly by means of yogic power and those who habitually perform holy rites observe it through *pratyāhāra*, i.e., withdrawal of physical senses, and through meditation and penance.[220] Training of mind for acquiring knowledge was considered important.

Those kings who made gifts of gold to eminent scholars, those householder brāhmaṇa who lived at home and expounded *Brahman* (*ye ca svāyatanā viprā gṛhasthā brahmavādinaḥ*), those who performed their Vedic study have been highly praised in the *Vāyu Purāṇa.*[221] It is said that philosophers used to ponder over reality, calling it by the names of *buddhi*, *manas*, *liṅga*, *mahat* and *akṣara.*[222] Preceptors should be bowed down by learned men and it is said to be conducive to wealth, fame and longevity. It has been maintained that if a disciple did not observe at least a year's student life, he would be considered to be a sinner.[223]

The six religious systems, viz., Śaiva, Vaiṣṇava, Śaura, Śākta, and Arhata (Jaina), the six traditional systems of philosophy and the

---

218. *Vāyu Purāṇa*, 99.190-1.

219. *Ibid.*, 101.157-8.

220. *vyaktam tarkena paśyanti yogāt pratyakṣadarśiṇaḥ* ।
pratyāhāreṇa dhyānena tapasā ca kriyātmānaḥ ॥
—*Ibid.*, 101.211

221. *Ibid.*, 101.282-83.

222. *Ibid.*, 102.21.

223. *Ibid.*, 103.68-70.

materialistic philosophy — have been referred to in the Purāṇa.[224] Yoga philosophy is also occasionally explained. Intelligent persons performed *dhāraṇā*, i.e., concentration of different types. Leading learned people performed the *aṣṭāṅga*, i.e., eight-limbed observance. They are as follow — *āsana* (posture), *prāṇāyāma* (concentration), *dhyāna* (meditation), *samādhi* (trance), *yama* (restraint) and *niyama* (observance).[225] The doctrine of Vedānta has been enumerated thus — just as a snake is misconceived in the rope, mirage as water in the desert, blueness in the sky is superimposed due to ignorance, so also the non-existing universe is superimposed on *Brahman* and thus it appears to exist.[226]

The science of speech is beautifully represented in an allegorical way. The mouth of the Vedas incarnate was illuminated by sixteen *svara* (vowel) sounds intermingled with *praṇava* (*oṁ*). Their hands with five fingers to each were constituted by the letters of the guttural and the palatal classes of consonants. Their right legs were formed by the labial class consonants and the left legs formed with the dental class. The sides of their belly were made with the intermediate and last consonants. The letter *na* constituted their navels. The letters ending with *ka* constituted their backs. The letter *ma* was their stomach, *ya*, *ra*, *la* and *va* were their tied up hair (tresses). Their joints consisted of the *antyastha*, i.e., semi-vowel letters. They were full of *vaikharī* speech.[227] All these statements sufficiently prove that the author or authors of the *Vāyu Purāṇa* were very much aware of the different branches of learning that were current during their times.

---

224. *Vāyu Purāṇa*, 104.16.

225. *Ibid.*, 104.24-5.

226. *rajjāvahir marau vāri nīlimā gagane yathā* ।
asadviśvam idam bhāti yasmin ajñānakalpitam ॥
— *Ibid.*, 104.39

227. *Ibid.*, 104.71-4.

There is a reference to *samiti* in the *Vāyu Purāṇa*. The three sons of Bṛhati are styled as 'Ornaments of the assembly'.[228]

The *Brahmāṇḍa Purāṇa* is so called because the god Brahmā narrated it with special emphasis on the description of the *brahmāṇḍa*, i.e., the Cosmic Egg and deals with the future *kalpa*-period.[229] It declares its main object to give the explanation of real state of affairs or the reality about the universe or the world (*loka-tattva*).[230] The term *brahmāṇḍa* itself connotes a mix of ancient Indian concepts about cosmography, cosmology and cosmogony.

Majority of Purāṇas regard *Brahmāṇḍa Purāṇa* as consisting of 12000 verses.

The Purāṇa is divided into four parts or *pāda*s:

(1) *Prakriyā Pāda* consisting of 5 chapters.

(2) *Anuṣaṅga Pāda* consisting of 33 chapters.

(3) *Upodghāta Pāda* consisting of 74 chapters.

(4) *Upasaṁhāra Pāda* consisting of 4 chapters.

It is statd that this Purāṇa emumerates the different *śākhā*s (branches) of the Vedas; the importance of the disciples; then seven types of *vākya*s, etc.[231] The importance of studying the Purāṇas is extolled here. The Purāṇa holds the view that he who knows the four Vedas with their ancillary subjects and the Upaniṣads must increase his knowledge of

---

228. *samiti-śobhanāḥ* — *Vāyu Purāṇa*, 96.246-7.

229. *brahmā brahmāṇḍa-māhātmyam adhikṛtya'bravīt punaḥ* ।
tacca dvādaśa-sahasram brahmāṇḍam dviśatādhikam ॥
bhaviṣyānām ca kalpānām śrvyate yatra vistaraḥ ।
tad brahmāṇḍa-purāṇam ca brahmaṇā samudāhṛtam ॥
— *Matsya Purāṇa*, 53.54-5

230. *loka-tattvārtham akhilam vedasammatam* ।
— *Brahmāṇḍa Purāṇa*, I.I.1.1.

231. *vedasya tadvijātyanāṁ mantrānāñca prakīrtitam* ।
śākhānām parimānañca vedavyāsātiśabditam ॥
— *Brahmāṇḍa Purāṇa*, I.I.1.112b-113a

the Vedas through *itihāsa* and Purāṇas. It is allegorically stated that the Veda is afraid of incomplete knowledge.[232]

The erudite scholar should be experts in words, meanings as well as logical arguments. Nothing was seized from them.[233] The school of linguistics was well advanced. Persons endowed with the science of sound and phonetics are mentioned. They were well aware of the power of wind which is the cause of sound or speech. It is named as Vācorani, viz., source of origin of speech which may be compared with the *araṇi*, the source of fire.[234]

While describing the Yajñavarāha, the Vedas, *yoga*, *upakarma*, i.e., extra stduy of the Veda by way of expiation, different *chanda*s (metres), the Upaniṣads with their esoteric doctrines, ancillary subjects of the Vedas, loud pitch in the *Sāman* hymns are cited as the integral parts of the Yajñavarāha.[235]

The unit of measurement is expounded with minute details. The knowledge of architecture was prevalent at that time. It is stated that they built hamlets and cities with extent and dimensions, in accordance with their knowledge. In the beginning they started measuring with

---

232. *yo vidyāccaturo vedān sāṅgopaniṣado dvijaḥ* ।
na cet purāṇām saṁvidyāyaiva sa syād-vicakṣaṇaḥ ॥
itihāsapurāṇābhyām saidaṁ samupavṛṁhayet ।
vibhetaraśrutādvedo māmayaṁ prahariṣyati ॥
— *Brahmāṇḍa Purāṇa*, I.I.1.196b-198a

233. *ṛṣayastatra vidvāṁsaḥ sāṁkyārtha-nyāyakobidaḥ* ।
na tatra dūritam kiñcid . . .
— *Ibid.*, I.I.2.32-3

234. *vācoraṇiḥ samākhyātaḥ śabdaśāstraviśāradaḥ* ॥
— *Ibid.*, I. 2. 44

235. *Ibid.*, I.5.16f.

their own fingers and they made other units.[236] Among the four types of fortresses three were natural and the fourth, which was artificial, was constituted of thick elevated rampart with cavities. The extent and specification of *pura* (city), hamlet, village are described. The *vāstu*, i.e., site of building or dwelling place is described. The specification of pathway including royal road and branch-streets is given. The architects designed the houses collecting the idea from the growth of a tree. Apartments were constructed in the same way as the branches of trees used to take place. Hence the apartments are designated as *śālās*.[237]

The importance of medicinal herbs in curing disease was known to the intelligent people of this age. Fourteen types of medicinal herbs of the villages and forests are enumerated. Some were remembered as the species of rural medicinal herbs (*grāmya-oṣadhi*).[238]

The holy duties and rites prescribed for brāhmaṇas were teaching of the Vedas and acceptance of charitable and monetary gifts.[239] The duties of the religious student were wearing the girdle of the *muñja*

---

236. 10 *aṅgulas* = *pradeśa*.
12 *aṅgulas* = *vitasti*.
21 *aṅgulas* = *ratni*.
24 *aṅgulas* = *hasta*.
1 *ratni* or 42 *aṅgulas* = *kiṣku*.
4 *hastas* = *dhanus*
2000 *dhanus* = *gavyūti*
7000 *dhanus* = *yojana*. —*Brahmāṇḍa Purāṇa*, I.2.7.93-101

237. *Ibid.*, I.8.104-14.

238. *puṣpamūlaphalinyastu oṣadhyastāḥ prajajñire* ।
—*Ibid.*, I.8.127
aphalikṛṣṭaścānupta grāmyā'raṇyāścaturdaśa ।
oṣadhyo yajñīyāścaiva grāmyāraṇyaścaturdaśa ॥
—*Ibid.*, I.8.157

239. *yājanādhyāpanaṁ caiva tṛtīyaṁ ca pratigrahaṁ* ।
—*Ibid.*, I.8.136a

grass and holding the staff. He must wear the skin of an antelope and sleep on the ground. He must serve his preceptor. He must beg for alms. He must be eager to acquire learning.[240] It is stated that descendants of Mṛkaṇḍa were masters of the Veda.[241]

The measurement of time is enumerated in the *Brahmāṇḍa Purāṇa* with minute details. The shortest unit is *nimeṣa* or moment. The period of time is termed *yuga*.[242] The divisions of time, months, seasons and the two *ayaṇas* are enumerated. The people of this age was aware of the fact that the extent of a solar *ayaṇa* is one hundred and eightythree days.

The three Vedas, the (fourteen) *vidyās*, the system of civil and criminal administration are referred to.[243]

The knowledge of astronomy was well advanced in this age. The description of the constellations and ancient names of the months are given.[244]

The Ṛtviks are described as strictly adherent to the bounds (decency) and pursuing the art of learning.[245]

The belief in the indestructibility of water is surprisingly modern.[246]

Vedic metres are compared with seven horses of the sun.[247] The

---

240. *daṇḍī ca mekhalī caiva hyadhaḥśyayı tathā jaṭī* I
guruśruśuṣaṇam bhaikṣyam vidyā vai brahmacāriṇaḥ II etc.
— *Brahmāṇḍa Purāṇa*, I.8.176f

241. *Ibid.*, I.11.8.

242. *Ibid.*, I.2.13.112-15, p. 130; 122-26, p. 131; I.2.21.131-37, p. 209.

243. *Ibid.*, I.2.19.122, p. 185.

244. *Ibid.*, I.2.21; I.2.22.

245. *Ibid.*, I.2.21, 162.

246. *na nāśa udakasyāpi tadeva parivartate* I
sanidhāranārthaṁ lokānāṁ māyaiṣā viśvanirmitā II
— *Ibid.*, I.2.22.17

247. *chandobhiraśvarūpaistairyataścakram tataḥ hitaiḥ* II
— *Ibid.*, I.2.23.46-8

Jupiter or Bṛhaspati is referred to as scholarly preceptor of the *devas*.[248] The planets are compared with the brāhmaṇas.[249] The Sun is described as the originator of all, i.e., the moon, the stars and the planets.[250]

The law regarding luminary bodies is described. It is maintained that it is impossible for all human beings to comprehend factually the movements both inward and outward of the luminary bodies by means of physical eye. The learned man should comprehend and decide anything about the luminaries by means of scripture, inference, perception and reasoning, after testing intelligently and carefully. There are five expedients to comprehend the group of luminaries, viz.: eye, scripture, water, picture and calculation.[251]

The knowledge of linguistics was well advanced. It is stated that the function of speech is dependant on *varṇa*, i.e., sound of letters and *sthāna*, i.e., place of articulation. Wind is the cause of existence of the *varṇas*.[252]

Sāṁkhya and Yoga philosophy were well read in those days.[253] The idea of three *guṇas* was prevalent and discussed in various matters.[254]

It is stated that brāhmaṇas would acquire Vedic knowledge.[255] The Saṁhitā texts were recited by the great sages differently with changes

---

248. *tataścāṅgiraso siddhau devācāryo bṛhaspatiḥ* ।
— *Brahmāṇḍa Purāṇa*, I.2.23.85; I.2.24.89

249. *Ibid.*, I.2.24.49.

250. *Ibid.*, I.24.46.

251. *cakṣuḥ śāstram jalam lekhyaṁ gaṇitam buddhivittamāḥ* ।
pañcaite pāṭavo viprā jyotirgaṇa vivecane ।।
— *Ibid.*, I.2.24.152

252. *varṇasthānagate vāyo vāgvidhiḥ sampravartate* ।
— *Ibid.*, I.2.25.9

253. *sāṁkhyāya caiva yogāya bhūtagrāmāya vai nāmaḥ* ।।
—*Ibid.*, I.2.25.66

254. *Ibid.*, I.2.25.72.

255. *brāhmano vedamāpnoti* . . . । — *Ibid.*, I.2.25.107

in the settings (arrangements) of *mantra* and *Brāhmaṇa* portions and alternations in the notes, accents and letters. Changes are brought about due to the changes in *mantras* and confusion in the viewpoints. The *Brāhmaṇas*, *Kalpa-Sūtras* and *Mantra-Pravacanas* (different scriptural texts) and other texts as well have a similar plight.[256]

A student who worked for the welfare of his preceptor was called *sādhu* because he strove for the achievement of learning.[257] The preceptor taught *dharma* which lead people to achieve what was desirable. *Ācāryas* or preceptors were old men devoid of greediness, self-possessed, devoid of arrogance, straightforward, educated and well disciplined.[258] *Ācāryas* practised *dharma*. They established the code of good behaviour and mastered the various scriptural texts.

Brahmacarya is non-indulgence in sexual intercourse as well as absence of any type of thought regarding this.[259]

While speaking about the composers of the *mantras*, kṣatriyas are cited as propounders of *mantra*. So, it is evident that the Vedic education was not confined to brāhmaṇas only. *Brahmacārins* were students who usually performed *homas*.[260] Female education was not rare in this age. So reference to ladies capable of expounding the *Brahman* can be found.[261]

Different expression used in Logic are discussed. That which mainly consists of *hetu* (reason) and *dṛṣṭānta* (example) is called

---

256. *Brahmāṇḍa Purāṇa*, I.2.31.12-14.

257. *vidyāyāḥ sādhanāt sādhur brahmacārī gurorhitaḥ* ।
— *Ibid.*, I.2.32.24

258. *Ibid.*, I.2.32.30-2.

259. *maithunasyāsamācāro na cintā nānujalpanam* ।
— *Ibid.*, I.2.32.51

260. *hotṛvad brahmacāriṇaḥ* — *Ibid.*, I.2.33.11

261. *mudgalā cātujīvaiva tārā caiva yaśasvīṁ* ।
— *Ibid.*, I.2.33.176

citraśabda, i.e., one with diverse words. The statement which has no sense, that which is not praised by anyone and that which is feeble, is *mānuṣa*.[262] Sages were composers of scriptural texts; they went everywhere, and due to their greatness they possessed the intensity of great penance.[263] Principles of *yajña* can be applied to the mode of reasoning. These are *hetu* (reason), *nirvacana* (specific explanation), *nindā* (censure), *praśasti* (praise), *saṁśaya* (doubt), *nidhi* (deposit), *purākṛti* (previous action), *purākalpa* (previous *kalpa*), *vyavadhāraṇa-kalpanā* (conception of ascertainment), *upamā* (comparison).[264]

It is stated that Vyāsa chose four disciples of preserving the continuity of the Vedas; they are respectively Paila, Jaimini, Vaiśampāyana and Sumantu. Vyāsa also accepted Lomaharṣaṇa as his fifth disciple.[265] It shows that the preceptor used to choose his disciples, according to merit, for distribution of execution of the duties. It is stated that Śākalya expounded three Saṁhitās and he had five disciples. He composed a work, called *Nirukta*.[266] The Carakas, the brāhmaṇa expounders of the Saṁhitās have been described.[267] One preceptor could accept thousand disciples; the daily time for study was fixed. It is stated that Sutvan taught his son Sukarman who studied a thousand Saṁhitās and expounded them to a thousand disciples. As they studied during those days, when the study was prohibited, Indra slew them. Being furious in rage the preceptor performed protest fast unto death (*prāyopaveśana*).[268] It is stated that intelligent and highly excellent brāhmaṇa Pauṣyanjī taught half a thousand Saṁhitās. The story of the

---

262. *Brahmāṇḍa Purāṇa*, I.2.30.31.
263. *Ibid.*, I.2.33.32.
264. *Ibid.*, I.2.33.47-8.
265. *Ibid.*, I.2.34.12-16.
266. *Ibid.*, I.2.35.3.
267. *alāmbirādiḥ prācyānāṁ trayodeśya dayastu te* |
ityete carakā proktāḥ samhitāvādino dvijaḥ ||
— *Ibid.*, I.2.35.13
268. *Ibid.*, I.2.35.32-4.

division of the *Atharvan* and to teach them to the students by the preceptor is described.[269] The *Brāhmaṇa* and *Yajuṣ* are remembered as containing *grāmya, āraṇyaka mantras*. Thus it is clear that the different schools of Vedic branches had been evolved by his disciples and the disciples of his disciples.

According to the *Brahmāṇḍa Purāṇa*, there are fourteen *vidyās* (lores). These are six Vedāṅgas (ancillary subjects), the four Vedas, the Mīmāṁsā and Nyāya-Vistara (logic), Dharmaśāstra and the Purāṇas. Four more lores, i.e., *Āyurveda* (medicine), *Dhanurveda* (science of archery), *Gāndharva* (musicology), *Arthaśāstra* (economics, political economy) constitute the eighteen lores.[270]

Study of the Vedas was prevalent among brāhmaṇas as well as kṣatriyas. It is stated as astonishing that king Veṇa was devoid of the practice of the study of the Vedas.[271]

It is stated that Pracetases were the masters of the science of archery.[272]

It is state that in the sacrifice the *Sāman mantra* and thousands of *Yajur mantras* were present in an embodied form. The *Ṛgveda* with *krama pāṭha*, i.e., the specific order of words were also present there. *Atharvaveda* with *Pratyaṅgirasas* was present. The technical details regarding the recitation of the Vedas were present. They were *lakṣaṇa*, i.e., use of a cognate word for another, *vistara*, i.e., extension, *stobha*, i.e., chanted interjection in *sāman*, *nirukta*, i.e., etymological interpretation, *svarabhakti*, i.e., phonetically inserted vowel sounds, *āśraya*, *nigraha* and *pragraha* (vowel not subject to *sandhi*-rules).[273]

---

269. *Brahmāṇḍa Purāṇa*, I.2.35.56-8.
270. *Ibid.*, I.2.35.87-89a.
271. *Ibid.*, I.2.36.130.
272. *sarvān pracetaso nāma dhanurvedasya pāragān* ||
—*Ibid.*, I.2.37.27
273. *Ibid.*, II. 3. 1. 22-3, 26, 27.

The psychological aspect of the education was cultivated through *yoga*. The training of mind and culture of inner qualities were essential parts of education, this basic fact was known to the ancient people. In this process of *yoga*, *yama*s were the first step to acquire knowledge. The famous ten qualities of restrainment of *yama*s are celibacy, non-viloence, non-stealth, etc. (*brahmacarya*, *ahiṁsā*, *asteya*, etc.).[274] It was assumed that all those born of Prajāpati would become scholars in the Vedas. All of them would be masters of speech. All of them would be holders of Vedic *mantra*s.[275]

Śukra is described as the most excellent among those who were conversant with *Brahman* (Veda). He was the preceptor of the *deva*s and the *asura*s.[276] The sons of Varatrin are described as extremely skilled in sacred knowledge.[277]

The women education was prevalent in this age. Bhuvanā, the sister of Bṛhaspati was expounder of the *Brahman* or Veda. She achived yogic power. She was never attached to the material world.[278]

The knowledge of astronomy was quite well advanced. The description of *tithi*s, i.e., lunar days and constellations and *vīthi* or orbits has been given in the *Brahmāṇḍa Purāṇa*.[279]

It is stated that the son of Praheti was endowed with great yogic power.[280]

Mention has been made to the scholars in the Vedas and Vedāṅgas. They were experts in the science of polity.[281] One Hanumān is said to be a *brahmacārin* (observer of the vow of celibacy).

---

274. *Brahmāṇḍa Purāṇa*, II.3.1.52.
275. *sarve cāpi tapasvinaḥ* —*Ibid.*, II.3.1.64
276. *Ibid.*, II. 3.1.74-6.
277. . . . . *brahmiṣṭhā daityayājakāḥ* —*Ibid.*, II. 3. 1. 79
278. *Ibid.*, II.3.3.28; II.3.59.15-6
279. *Ibid.*, II.33.32.
280. *Ibid.*, II.3.7.92.
281. *Ibid.*, II.3.7.193.

It is described that Svastyātreyas mastered the Vedas.[282] Feeding a *snātaka* (i.e., an initiated householder) was on a par with feeding many *mantrajñas*. One should feed a *brahmacārin*.

It is stated that Asita was the preceptor of the Yogic cult. Pīvarī was a *yoginī* (lady of yogic power). It is stated that Yogic cult (power) would flourish in Vyāsa. The sons of Pīvarī would be fully equipped with the yogic practice. A daughter named Kīrtimatī would be *yoginī*.[283] It is guaranteed that he who maintains the vow of celibacy and devotion to the preceptor lives for a hundred years.[284]

A person devoid of learning are condemned. These persosns could not be received as guests. A person without learning, a person who does not possess specialised knowledge could not be invited.[285] One should always feed the person who practised *yoga*.[286] The learned persons were treated with reverence. The excellent brāhmaṇa who studied the five sacred books, viz., the Vedas and the *itihāsa* should be seated after a person who is well-versed in *yoga*. A person who studied three Vedas comes after him, a person of two Vedas be seated next, after that comes the man who has studied one Veda and Upādhyāya. Those who sanctified the row of diners could be those who knew the six ancillary subjects or *aṅgas* of Vedas, who practised *yoga*, *sarvatantra*, i.e., those who had mastered all the systems of philosophy. Praises have been bestowed on those who had mastered at least one of the fourteen *vidyās*, those who were to sing the *Sāman* hymns, *traividyā*, i.e., persons who knew the three Vedas and had kindled three *naciketā* fires, the brāhmaṇas who had mastered the great scriptural texts written by Bṛhaspati.[287]

The study of the Vedas was always regarded as sacred. One who

---

282. *Brahmāṇḍa Purāṇa,* II.3.8.81.

283. *Ibid.*, II.3.10.78-82.

284. *Ibid.*, II.3.13.92-4.

285. *Ibid.*, II.3.15.14.

286. *Ibid.*, II.3.15.21.

287. *Ibid.*, II.3.15.21, 25, 26, 28-32.

neglected or tried to acquire the knowledge by other means was avoided. It is stated that there was no provision for substitutes in the study of the Vedas; he who employed any such substitute was a sinner. Those who employed others to study Vedas on their behalf and those who used to sell the copies of the Vedas were to be avoided. A person hired to teach the Vedas and a person who is taught by such a person (hired one) were not deserving for invitation in a *śrāddha* rite. Buying and selling for the sake of subsistence were despicable. He who studied the Vedas by means of hiring charges, i.e., charging tuition fees and he who made a living through the Vedas were not worthy for *śrāddha* invitation. Serving only the preceptor was prescribed for the brāhmaṇas. Serving any one except the preceptor was forbidden. The educated persons were treated with reverence. It is stated that persons endowed with perfect knowledge shall sanctify by mere sight.[288]

The education system contained in the *Brahmāṇḍa Purāṇa* is almost the same as that enumerated in other Purāṇas that were composed or compiled during the age under consideration.

It is believed that he who performs *śrāddha* on the tenth day will attain mastery over all the Vedas.[289] While depicting the performance of the *śrāddha* rites the details regarding the constellations are given. It proves the advancement of the study of the astronomy in this age. The sanctifiers of the row were learned brāhmaṇas. It is stated that those who know different languages, those who are engaged in the study of the grammar, those who study the Purāṇas and sacred scriptures, one who knows the six *aṅgas*, and one who has mastered Vedic prosody, should be invited for the *śrāddha* rite.[290]

---

288. *Brahmāṇḍa Purāṇa*, II.3.15.45.63.

289. *vedānścaivāpnyuyāt sarvān viprānāṁ samatām vrajet* |
— *Ibid.*, II.3.17.16

290. *sarvavedavratasnānān paṁktīnāṁ pāvanā dvijāḥ* |
ya ca bhāṣāvidaḥ kecid ye ca vyākaraṇe ratāḥ ||
adhīyate purāṇam vai dharmaśāstramathāpi vai |
trinaciketaḥ pañcāgniḥ sa sauparṇaḥ ṣaḍaṅgavit ||
— *Ibid.*, II.3.19.22-6

The *Brahmāṇḍa Purāṇa* mentions those who are noteworthy of being invited for the *śrāddha* rite. One who has discarded the study of the Vedas, a person who defiles the preceptor's bed, one who sells Brāhmaṇical holy rites — all these are the defilers of rows.[291]

Self-restrainment was the most important aspect intended to be attained in this age. So it is stated that a person who has mastered various subjects does not gain mastery over himself, but one who has mastered the essential features of the three Vedas is the master of academic studies. *Yoga* is the means of attainment of mental tranquillity to attain knowledge. So it is believed that the brāhmaṇa who does not take recourse to the path of *yoga* is not able to be the master of everything that comes under the purview of the system of knowledge. The knower of *yoga* receives the essence of everything that has to be comprehended in the Vedas and that which has to be realised; those who have known the Vedas call such a person the master of the Vedas.[292]

It is stated that Indra handed over the application of miraculous missiles to Paraśurāma.[293] Paraśurāma was the best perceiver of the miraculous missiles, weapons and of the sacred scriptures.

The great sage, Cyavana, is described as surrounded by the groups of his disciples in the hermitage.[294] The penance grove of the sage Jamadagni is also described. Many sages, dressed in deer skin garments and experts in the thorough study of the Vedas proceeded towards the hermitage of Jamadagni.[195]

Advancement of musicology can be proved in the description of *tārā* (high pitch) and *mandra* (low sound) in *Brahmāṇḍa Purāṇa*.[296]

291. *Brahmāṇḍa Purāṇa*, II.3.19.34-5.
292. *Ibid.*, II.3.19, 63f.
293. *Ibid.*, II.3.24.73-4.
294. *Ibid.*, II.3.25.79-80.
295. *Ibid.*, II.3.26.17-8.
296. *Ibid.*, II.3.27.3.

It is stated that Bhṛgu was the composer of the *Atharvan mantras*. He was thoroughly conversant with the Vedas and the Vedāṅgas (ancillaries to the Vedas). He knew the meaning of all scriptures.[297] He is said to have composed the treatise of politics, called after him *Auśanas* or *Śukra-nītisāra*. Even to the time of the *Brahmāṇḍa Purāṇa*, all the kings used to follow the principles contained in the work and rely on it.

Lord Śiva is described as expounding true knowledge and yogic principles to the *siddhas* by means of *tarka-mudrā*, i.e., esoteric gesture by means of fingers to indicate arguments.[298] Śiva taught Paraśurāma esoteric formula and the application of weapons.[299]

The initiation of sacred thread ceremony, was in vogue. It is stated that Śivadatta, who was an expert in all sacred lores performed the sacred thread ceremony in due order. He taught all the Vedas along with their ancillary subjects. His disciples were eagerly devoted to the study of the Vedas and were absorbed in the service of the preceptor and were enthusiastic in acquiring knowledge. Everyday the duty of a student was to go to the forest and fetch fruits, water, sacrificial twigs, *kuśa* grass and clay. After collecting them, he handed them over to his preceptor and started their study of the Vedas. Students took their bath early in the morning.[300] They offered *madhuparka*, i.e., materials for hospitable reception ready for a guest.[301]

---

297. *Brahmāṇḍa Purāṇa*, II.3.30.52-4.
298. *Ibid.*, II.3.32.21.
299. *Ibid.*, II.3.32.56-61.
300. *vedānadhyāpayāmāsa sāṅgaśca sarahasyakān* |
catvāro'pi vayaṁ tatra vedādhyayanatatparāḥ ||

guruśuśruvaṇā yuktā jātā jñānaparāyaṇāḥ |
gatvā'raṇyam phalānyambusamitkuśamṛdo'nvahaṁ ||
—*Ibid.*, II.3.35.13
301. *Ibid.*, II.3.35.52.

Student were treated by a preceptor as his own son. It is stated by Pārvatī to Śiva that Paraśurāma was at par with the sons of Śiva.[302]

Disciples were residents in the hermitage. It is depicted that Paraśurāma in his way saw that the resident disciples were joyously reciting the Vedas and Saṁhitās. The disciples were strictly adhered to the vow of celibacy.[303]

Regular self-study was prevalent at that age. It is stated that because of the cruelty of the sons of Sagara, the people could not have their regular study of the Vedas and performance of holy rites.[304]

Sadasyas, i.e., members of the holy assembly had mastered the Vedas. They knew all the prescribed injunctions. Those who were conversant with the injunctions were duly honoured even by kings.[305] Disciples used to sit surrounding the preceptor.[306]

It is stated in the *Brahmāṇḍa Purāṇa* that Viśvakarman was the creator of artisans and craftsmen. He created thousands of artistic work for the *devas*. He created the aerial chariots. Artistic creation was his contribution to the world. Maya, the son of Viśvakarman was capable of performing all creative works.[307]

Musicology had attained the highest elevation in this age. The science of music has been described with minute details. The *svara-maṇḍala* (the whole group regarding notes) with seven *svaras*, i.e., notes, three *grāmas*, i.e., basic scales, twenty-one *mūrcchanās*, i.e., gradual ascent and descent of the seven notes of the basic scale and

---

302. *Brahmāṇḍa Purāṇa*, II.3.42.11-3.

303. *yatrāntevāsibhirnityaṁ vedāḥ śāstrāṇi saṁhitāḥ* |
abhyāsante mudā yuktairbrahmacaryavrate sthitaiḥ ||
— *Ibid.*, II.3.44.7

304. *Ibid.*, II.3.52.6.

305. *Ibid.*, II.3.55.

306. *Ibid.*, II.3.57.

307. *Ibid.*, II.3.59.17-21.

forty-nine *tānas*, i.e., *mūrcchanā* in which one or two specific notes are dropped, are described.[308] It may be mentioned that according to the *Nāṭyaśāstra* of Bharata the total number of two *grāmas* is eightyfour in number.[309] These are depicted as *śuddha tānas* by later *ācāryas*. The *Vāyu Purāṇa* has also depicted the science of music with details.

It is described that king Sagara, being born in the hermitage of Aurva learnt the *āgneya astra* (a missile, the deity of which is the fire-God) from Aurva.[310] Aurva taught Sagara the Vedas and the sacred scriptures. Thereafter, he taught him how to discharge missiles and miraculous weapons.[311]

It was believed that a disciple would help the preceptor and even the son of the preceptor at the time of danger. It is stated that Śiva took up Bṛhaspati's side as Śiva was the disciple of the father of Bṛhaspati.[312]

Paraśurāma mastered all lores and the science of archery.[313]

Viṣṇu granted the boon to Dhanvantari that he would reproduce the *Āyurveda*, i.e., the science of medicine. Later on Dhanvantari learnt the *Āyurveda* along with its therapeutics from Bhāradvāja and classified it into eight sections. Afterwards he taught the subject to different disciples.[314]

The science of weapon was advanced in this age. The sons of Kārtavīrya were well-versed in wielding weapons.[315] It is stated that

---

308. *Brahmāṇḍa Purāṇa*, II. 3.61.29.
309. Bharata, *Nāṭyaśāstra*, Baroda.
310. *Brahmāṇḍa Purāṇa*, II.3.63.122-3.
311. *aurvastu jātakarmādīn kṛtvā tasya mahātmanaḥ* |
adhyāpya vedāñchāstrāṇi tato'straṁ pratyāpādayat ||
— *Ibid.*, II.3.63.133
312. *Ibid.*, II.3.65.31-3.
313. *Ibid.*, II.3.66.60b-4.
314. *Ibid.*, II.3.67.19, 23-4.
315. *Ibid.*, II.3.69.49-50.

Jara was the foremost archer.[316]

Students, specially princes, used to travel to far off countries for attaining higher learning. It is stated that king Duryodhana went to Mithilā and had undergone a training in mace-fighting under Balabhadra. The training was usually of a divine nature.[317]

The units of time have been described. The three kinds of *pramāṇa*s, i.e., means of valid knowledge have been described. The ability to comprehend holy texts and three *vidyā*s (lores) have been enumerated.[318] Four types of *vidyā*s, viz., *ānvīkṣikī*, *trayī*, *vārtā* and *daṇḍanīti* are enumerated.[319] The Vedas along with the *aṅga*s, i.e., ancillary adjuncts and *rahasya*, i.e., esoteric secret are mentioned as the subjects of study.[320]

It is depicted that the preceptor of *devatā*s took the disguise of the Śukra, the preceptor of *dānava*s in order to mislead the *asura*s and succeeded to distract the *asura*s.[321] So it is clear from this story that the preceptors also tried their best for the welfare of the disciples.

It is apprehended that Yājñavalkya will be the preceptor of Kalki.[322]

The two sons of Kaksivan and Cakṣus were learned in the Vedas in accordance with the injunctions, masters of everything and expounder to Vedic lore.[323]

---

316. *prathamaṁ Dhanurdharaḥ*
— *Brahmāṇḍa Purāṇa*, II.3.71.187

317. *atha duryodhano rājā gatvā'tha mithilāṁ prabhuḥ* |
gadāśikṣāṁ tato divyam balabhadrādavāptavān ||
— *Ibid.*, II.3.71.84

318. *Ibid.*, II.3.72.29b-33.

319. *Ibid.*, II.3.72.36.

320. *Ibid.*, II.3.72.160.

321. *Ibid.*, II.3.73.22-5.

322. *Ibid.*, II.3.73.105.

323. *Ibid.*, II.3.74.71-3.

Pravādins were the exponent of the Vedas who used to argue and expound the critical points of the Vedic texts. It is stated that three Vedas were competent in this respect.[324]

The units of time has been enumerated in the *Brahmāṇḍa Purāṇa*. Here units of time are stated to give the idea of the time of *abhūta-samplava*. Starting from *nimeṣa* or winking of the eye the units of time have been described. The measurement of time has been described with unit of *nimeṣa*s. It is also described in connection with *Nālikoccaya*, i.e., four *prastha*s filled with water and so on. So it is clear that the astronomer of this age succeeded in discovering water-clock.[325]

The arithmetic calculation was highly advanced at that age. It is found that starting from one number to *parārdha* has been enumerated. Thus numbers up to eighteen digits have been named for the purpose of counting.

The countable and uncountable are always based on Tantras, i.e., scientific treatises. The countable is observed through numbers, i.e., starting from one up to *parārdha*. When a heap is observed no specific number is available. This is the characteristic feature and quality of the countlessness.[326]

Atom is the minute particle of a matter which cannot be broken further and also it possesses the properties of the original one. The theory of atom is amazingly modern. It has described *paramāṇu* or atom as very subtle. What cannot be further broken up in the world should be known as *paramāṇu*. When the rays of the sun come through the window, minute dust particle are seen. The learned men call that particle a *paramāṇu*. It is the first and foremost in the series of units

---

324. *bhūtabhavādīnaḥ śaktastrayo vedāḥ pravādinām* ।
agnīdhraḥ kāśyapaścaiva paulstyo māgaścayaḥ ।।
— *Brahmāṇḍa Purāṇa*, III.4.1.112

325. *Ibid.*, III.4.1.211-24.

326. *Ibid.*, III.4.2.92-110.

of measurement. The time measurement starting from *paramāṇu* up to *yojana* is enumerated with details.[327] The knowledge of astronomy is also enumerated in the *Brahmāṇḍa Purāṇa*.

The person who committed grave sins would be fell into the hell. The defiler of the preceptor's bed, those who sell the Vedas, those who censure the Vedas, and those who hit the preceptors with wounding words, a person who does not honour elders and preceptors, fall into the hell.[328]

The moral constraint is the first and foremost vow to be kept by the students. It is stated that if the religious students under a vow of celibacy have seminal discharge during day-dreams pass on to the hell.[329]

The Sāṁkhya philosophy was known to that period. The mention of Kapila, Āsuri, Pañcaśikha and others can be found in the *Brahmāṇḍa Purāṇa*.[330]

The scholarly brāhmaṇa who listens to or recites or teaches this ancient *itihāsa* are highly esteemed in this age.[331]

Gurus or preceptors are to be bowed by learned men. The Purāṇa texts should not be given to a student unless he has served and studied for at least a year. It should not be given to the unlettered or to one who is antagonistic.[332]

It is stated that Agastya mastered the Vedas and Vedāṅgas and

---

327. *Brahmāṇḍa Purāṇa*, III.4.2.117ff.
328. *Ibid.*, III.4.2.155ff.
329. *Ibid.*, III.4.2.176.
330. *Ibid.*, III.4.2.273.
331. *Ibid.*, II.4.4.47-8.
332. *Ibid.*, III.4.4.70.

was conversant with the essence of the established doctrines of all schools of philosophy (*darśanas*).[333]

Yamas, i.e., restraints and *niyamas*, i.e., holy observances are the means for mental preparation for attainment of proper education.[334] The knowledge of the affairs of the three units of time, i.e., past, present and future are treated as one of the supreme knowledge.[335] Discipline was the first and foremost duty to be observed. Transgressing the preceptor's order results in sin. The theologians or philosophers are treated with high esteem.[336]

Learned persons were treated with high esteem. It was believed that the sin committed by a king was not so severe for the protection of brāhmaṇas proficient in the Vedas and one who was conversant with the Vedas as well as Vedānta.[337]

Ācārya was one who imparted *brahmopadeśa* and *deśika* is the person who imparted the teachings of the Vedas and Śāstras.[338]

The knowledge of architecture and engineering was well advanced in this age. It is believed that Maya was the original architect, engineer and artisan of the race of *daityas*.[339]

It is depicted that *Ṛg*, *Yajuṣ* and *Sāman mantras* were frequently chanted in all the houses of *daityas*. Mīmāṁsā, Nyāya and other systems of philosophy were studied in every house.[340] Science of archery was practised and skill in archery was attained by the learner.[341] It is

333. *Brahmāṇḍa Purāṇa*, V.3-4.
334. *Ibid.*, V.23.
335. *Ibid.*, VI.33.
336. *Ibid.*, VI.40.
337. *Ibid.*, VI.48.
338. *Ibid.*, VIII.6.
339. *Ibid.*, XII.4.6.
340. *Ibid.*, XII.17.
341. *Ibid.*, XVII.38.

stated that the nephews of Bhaṇḍa learnt the use of weapons from Bhaṇḍa.[342]

It is believed that Viśvakarman, the carpenter of the *deva*s who was skilled in all mechanical arts and crafts as well as Maya, the architect of *asura* were invited to build a mansion for Kāmeśvara and Lalitā.[343] By conception and imagination they could evolve constructions of great artistry. There was a description of Śrīpura, built by them with the help of their expertise in the building up temples, in the *Brahmāṇḍa Purāṇa.*

While describing the *kālacakra* or circle of *mahākāla*, the knowledge of geometry has been revealed. The reference to triangle, pentagon, radii are found in the *Brahmāṇḍa Purāṇa*.[344] There are references to hexagon, octagon, decagon, duodecagon (twelve-sided figure).[345]

The knowledge of gems was highly advanced in this age. Chapter 33 describes the seven chambers built of precious stones, viz. Topaz, Rubies, Gomeds. Diamonds, Lapis-Lazuli, Sapphire and Pearls.[346]

The Śaivite philosophy attained its development in this age. It is stated that the twenty-eight Śaiva *āgama*s (scriptural texts of Śaivite philosophy) were present there. It is not clear whether the *advaita* or *dvaita* theory was advocated by them.[347]

It is allegorically represented that thousands of *vidyā*s were seated in Rudra's boats.[348] The abode of Cintāmaṇi was made of the philosophers' stones. The crowns were constituted by *icchā*, i.e., 'Will', *kriyā*, i.e., action and *jñāna* i.e., knowledge.[349]

---

342. *Brahmāṇḍa Purāṇa*, XXVIII.6-8.
343. *Ibid*., XXXI.6-7ff.
344. *Ibid*., XXXII.8.
345. *Ibid*., XXXIV.9b-11a.
346. *Ibid*., XXXIII.
347. *Ibid*., XXXIV.89.
348. *Ibid*., XXXV.100.
349. *Ibid*., XXXIV.34-7.

The science of speech has been described in an allegorical form. *ka-varga* (gutturals), *ca-varga* (palatals), *ta-varga* (cerebrals), *ṭa-varga* (dentals), *pa-varga* (labials), the square of letters beginning with *ya*, the six letters beginning with *sa* are delineated. Reference to sweet lyrics and dramas are found here.[350]

Reference to *Yogaśāstra* is found in the *Lalitā-māhātmya* of the *Brahmāṇḍa Purāṇa*.[351]

The art of writing was prevalent in this age. There are references to pen, ink-pot, and paper.[352] It is assumed that the verbal product or the word was greater than all other objects.[353]

It is prescribed that one who aspired to attain true knowledge should get up early in the morning and meditate upon his preceptor. Thus the spiritual side of the attaining knowledge is described.

The persons who used to bear hatred for systems of philosophy are criticised and the person who are conversant with Vedas and Vedāntas are praised.

According to R.C. Hazra,[354] the *Viṣṇudharmottara Purāṇa* dated earlier than AD 400 and not later than AD 500 . Bühler also is of opinion that the date of its composition cannot be placed later than about AD 500.[355] Stella Kramrisch is of opinion that this work cannot be placed earlier than the fifth century AD.[356] This early date is fully supported by its non-tāntric character. So it can be easily assumed that this Upa-purāṇa is a work of the Gupta age.

---

350. *Brahmāṇḍa Purāṇa*, XXXVII.3ff.
351. *Ibid.*, XXXVII.28.
352. *Ibid.*, XXXVII.89-90.
353. *Ibid.*, XXXVIII.3.
354. R.C. Hazra, *Puranic Records on Hindu Rites and Customs*, pp. 41-2.
355. *Indian Antiquary*, XIX, 1890, Bühler, p. 408.
356. Stella Kramrisch, *Journal of the Department of Letters*, XI, p. 3.

The *Viṣṇudharmottara Upapurāṇa*[357] is an encyclopaedic work consisting of three *khaṇḍa*s dealing not only with stories, myths and legends, but also with varied subjects. It deals with geography, astronomy and astrology, division of time, law and politics, anatomy, medicine, treatment of the diseases of human beings and lower animals, grammar, lexicography, metrics, rhetorics, dramaturgy, dancing, vocal and instrumental music, sculpture, painting, architecture, etc.

In chapter 4 there is a description of the different measurements of space, such as *trasareṇu*, *likṣā*, *rāja-sarṣapa*, *gaura-sarṣapa*, *yava*, *aṅguli*, *hasta*, *dhanuḥ*, *krośa*, *gavyūti* and *yojana*.[358]

Chapters 6 to 11 deal with the geography of the earth.

Chapters 72 and 73 give the divisions of time according to *saura*, *cāndra*, *sāvana* and *nakṣatra*, *māna*, measurement of time — duration of a *nimeṣa* to *kalpa*.[359]

Chapters 82 to 105 deal with astrology and astronomy. Chapter 106 delineates the stories of the birth of Dhruva and the different planets.

According to the chapter 203, Rāma sent with Bharata a retinue consisting of actors, musicians, poison-doctors, physicians, surgeons,[360]

---

357. R.C. Hazra, *Studies in the Upapurāṇas*, Vol. 1, Calcutta, Sanskrit College, 1958, pp. 151-218.

358. *jālāntaragate bhānau yatsūkṣmaṁ dṛśyate rajaḥ* ।
prathamamanu tat pramāṇānām trasareṇuṁ pracakṣate ।।
— *Viṣṇudharmottara Purāṇa*, 4/ff

359. *laghvakṣarasamā mātrā nimeṣaḥ parikīrtitaḥ* ।
— *Ibid.*, 72/1f

360. *viṣa-vaidyāḥ śalya-vaidyāstathā kāya-cikitsakāḥ* ।
— *Ibid.*, 203.9

dentists (*dantakārāḥ, dantopajīvinaḥ*), engineers,[361] scribes, astrologers,[362] painters,[363] etc.

Khaṇḍa II deals with the duties of kings. Here we find the qualifications of the state-astrologer; qualifications of the *purohita*, i.e., who was to be an *Atharvan* versed in the *Yajurveda* and the *Atharvaveda* and to have thorough knowledge of the five *kalpas*, viz., *nakṣatra-kalpa, vaitāna-kapla, saṁhitā-kalpa, aṅgīraḥ-kalpa* and *śānti-kalpa*; qualifications of ministers, who were to be brāhmaṇa versed in the Vedas and the *Nītiśāstras* of Bṛhaspati and Uśanas.[364]

Chapters 16-17 deal with the construction of bows with metals, viz. gold, silver, copper and steel,[365] construction of arrows and of swords with steel of different countries, viz. Vaṅga, Śūrapāraka, Videha, Aṅga, etc. This proves that the science of metal was well advanced in this age.

In chapter 22, mention is made of the *Ṛgveda, Yajurveda, Sāmaveda, Atharvaveda*,[366] *Itihāsa, Dhanurveda, Gāndharvaveda, Āyurveda*, the six *aṅgas* (viz., *śikṣā, kalpa*, etc.), Mīmāṁsā, Dharmaśāstra, Purāṇa,

---

361. *karmāntikā sthapatayo — Viṣṇdharmottara Purāṇa,* 203.9b

362. *lekhakā gaṇakā — Ibid.*, 203/17b

363. *citrakarmavido — Ibid.*, 203/19a

364. *vṛhaspatyuśanaḥ proktāṁ nītiṁ jānāti sarvatḥ* ।
— *Ibid.*, II.6.2

365. *dhanurdravya trayaṁ lohaṁ śṛṅgaṁ cāruca bhārgava* ।
jyādravyatritayaṁ carma vaṁśabhaṅgaṁ tvacaathā ।।
— *Ibid.*, II.16.1; II.74.29, 30

366. *ṛgvedo'tha yajurvedaḥ sāmavedāstathaiva ca* ।
atharvavedo vedastvā . . . ।।
— *Ibid.*, II.22, 129-34

Sāṁkhya, Yoga, Pañcarātra and Pāśupata as the subjects of study.[367]

Chapters 28-33 — science of house-building (*vāstu-vidyā*), building of temples — is delineated.

Medical treatment of various diseases of cows, horses and elephants are found.[368]

Medical treatment of females so that they might give birth to numerous healthy sons, nursing and medical treatment of children from their very birth, use of herbs are described. In chapter 52, *vidyārambha*[369] ceremony is described.

Chapter 65 is devoted to education and protection of princes.[370]

The science of politics is discussed with elaborate details. The men who was devoted to reading the Vedas, is said to have entitled to go to the heaven.[371]

---

367. *ṛgvedamatha pailaṁ tu sāmavedaṁ to jaiminim* |
ātharvaṇaṁ sumantuṁ tu yajurvedaṁ mahāmunim || 30
aṅgāni vedāścatvāro mīmāṁsā nyāyavistaraḥ |
dharmaśāstraṁ purāṇam ca vidyāstvetāścaturdaśaḥ || 32
śikṣā kalpo vyākaraṇaṁ niruktaṁ jyotiṣāṁgatim |
chandoviśeṣaṁ ṣaṣṭhaśca ṣaḍaṅgo veda ucyate || 33
sāṁkhyaṁ yogaṁ pañcarātraṁ śaivaṁ pāśupataṅ tathā | 34
— *Viṣṇudharmottara Purāṇa,* I.74.30-4

368. *Ibid.*, II.42-50.

369. *evaṁ suniścite kāle vidyārambhaṁ ca kārayet* | 126
......
prāṅmukhaḥ sumukhāsīno vārūnāśāmukhaṁ śiśum |
adhyāpayettu prathamaṁ kuryādvālo'pi vandanam ||
— *Ibid.*, II.52.126ff

370. *traividyebhastrayīṁ vidyā daṇḍanītiṁ ca śāśvatīm* |
āṇvīkṣikīṁ cātmvidyām vārtārambhaṁ ca lokataḥ ||
— *Ibid.*, II.65.46

371. *svādhyāyaśaktā dhīmanto guruśuśruṣaṇe ratāḥ* ||
— *Ibid.*, II.117.14

Khaṇḍa III is devoted to the art of painting, dancing, science of instrumental music and vocal music. Reference to the composition of songs in Sanskrit, Prākṛt and Apabhraṁśa and various local dialects in prose and verse,[372] classification of verse into *vṛtta* and *mātrā*, some points on grammar, viz. use of *śabda-vibhaktis*, are to be found in the Purāṇas.

Definition[373] and classification of *sūtras*, different kinds of *pramāṇa*,[374] meaning of *āpta* and *āpta-vacanābhāsa* are described. Explanation of the terms *adhikaraṇa*, *yoga*, *padārtha*, *hetvartha*, *uddeśa*, *arthāpatti*, etc. are found.

Characteristics of Prākṛt and Sanskrit vocabulary, definition of *itihāsa*, *kāvya* and *mahākāvya*, defects in poetical composition, delineation of nine *rasas* in *mahākāvya*, *prahelikās*, dramaturgy, origin of dramas, general form of dramas,[375] classification of dramas into 12 varieties, etc. are found.

Chapter 18 describes the characteristics of different kinds of vocal music, appropriateness to the nine *rasas*. Style of literature is described in the 20th chapter.[375a]

---

372. *saṁskṛtaṁ prākṛtaṁ caiva gītaṁ dvividharmucyate* ।
— *Viṣṇudharmottara Purāṇa*, III.2.9

373. *alpākṣaram asaṁdigdhaṃ sāravat viśvato mukhaṃ* ।
astobham anavadyaṃ ca sūtram sūtravido viduḥ ॥
— *Ibid.*, III.5.1

374. *pratyakṣamanumānaṁ ca tathāptavacanaṁ bhavet* ॥
— *Ibid.*, III.5.12

375. *Ibid.*, III.17.

375a. *bhāratī sātvatī caiva kauśikyārabhaṭī tathā* ।
catasro vṛttayaḥ proktā ॥ *Ibid.*, III. 20. 56

Art of dancing[376] and acting[377] has also been described. Art of painting, iconography has been vividly described.

Duties of students are described in chapter 227 of 3rd *khaṇḍa*.[378] The time of *upanayana* is prescribed.[379] Chapters 254 to 259 are devoted to the benefits of acquiring of knowledge,[380] study of the sacred books, viz., the Vedas, Vedāṅgas, Upavedas, Sāṁkhya, Yoga, practising of *brahmacarya*, etc.

Vidyādāna has been highly praised and in this connection special mention has been made of the teaching of the Vedas, Upavedas, Vedāṅgas, Dharmāśastras, Siddhāntas and other *śāstras*, the different kinds of arts (*śilpa*) and *Dhanurveda*.[381]

In the chapters on astronomy and astrology, the Purāṇa has verses from the works of Garga, Vṛddha Garga, Parāśara and Bṛhaspati. Some

---

376. *udveṣṭam samaveṣṭam ca viceṣṭitavivartite* ।
karmedaṁ nṛttahastānām vijñeyam ca caturvidham ॥
— *Viṣṇudharmottara Purāṇa*, III.26.94

377. *vācikaśca tathā hāryastvāṅgikasātvikastathā* ।
catuṣprakāro'bhinayaḥ kīrtito nāṭyakovidaiḥ ॥
— *Ibid.*, III.27.1
hāsyaśṛṅgārakaruṇaraudravīrabhayānakāḥ ।
bibhatsādbhutaśāntākhyā nava nāṭye rasaḥ smṛtāḥ ॥
— *Ibid.*, III.30.1

378. *upanīya guruḥ śiṣyam śikṣāyecchaucamāditaḥ* ।
ācāramagnikāryam ca sandhyopāsanameva ca ॥
— *Ibid.*, III.228.1
mekhalāmjinam daṇḍam dhārayet prayataḥ sadā ।
— *Ibid.*, III.228.6

379. *garbhāṣṭamabde kurvīta brāhmaṇāsyopanayaṁ* ।
garbhādekādaśe rājño garbhāttu dvādaśe viśaḥ ॥
— *Ibid.*, III.233.70

380. *jñānam sukhāvaham loke jñānam cakṣuḥ param mataṁ* ॥
— *Ibid.*, III.254.1f

381. *vidyā dānāt paraṁ dānam na bhūtam na bhaviṣyati* ॥
— *Ibid.*, III.303.1

of the chapters of this Purāṇa are very much influenced by Bharata's *Nāṭyaśāstra*.

It may be concluded here that verious fields of knowledge were cultivated during the time of *Viṣṇudharmottara*.

Kāmandaka was a great *nīti* writer. He wrote the *Nītisāra*[382] or Essence of Politics. The *Nītisāra* is fundamentally based on Kauṭilya's *Arthaśāstra*. The information about the author of the *Nītisāra* is very scarce. The commentary of the *Nītisāra* states that he was a disciple of the celebrated politician Cāṇakya. The style of the *Nītisāra* is similar in nature, but simple and practical with the older Smṛtis. Its gravity and sententiousness are two main characteristic features. It deals with the various matters of politics, constitution, judicial administration and international law. Kāmandaka has shown his genius in initiating the evolution of the *nīti* literature. Kāmandaka has given some improved thoughts than Kauṭilya though he has based his work on the *Arthaśāstra*. Śukra has borrowed several verses of Kāmandaka in the same form. Several verses of Kāmandaka are also found in *Agni Purāṇa* and *Matsya Purāṇa*. Kāmandaka's *Nītisāra* has a great modern perspective.[383]

The knowledge is said to be the means of controlling sense-organs. The mind is compared with the elephant. It runs here and there under the influence of sense-organs in the dense forest of sensual pleasure. It should be brought under control by means of the goad of knowledge.[384] Perfect knowledge, the heart and the soul are the seats of consciousness, and the mind, and intellect are synonymous. If any of these is surcharged

---

382. Kāmandaka, *Nītisāra or Elements of Polity,* Calcutta: A.S.B., 1982, Introduction.

383. Chakradhar Jha, *History and Sources of Law in Ancient India,* p. 102.

384. *prakīrṇaviṣayāraṇye dhāvantam vipramathinam* |
jñānāṅkuśena kurvīta vaśyamindriyadantinaṁ ||
— *Nītisāra*, Śl. 27, p. 14

by the soul, it uses to discriminate what should be done and what should not be done.[385]

In the second chapter, i.e., *vidyāvṛddhasaṁyogaprakaraṇa* the necessity of association with the learned people is described with minute details. The association will help men and specially a king to attain success in the life. A man of good conduct and self-restraint is always devoted to his preceptor, as it is believed that the respectful attitude to the wise produces increased knowledge of *dharma* and *artha* in this world.[386] Preceptor is the essential feature for the attainment of knowledge. The importance of a teacher in the process of education is invariably noteworthy. Association with the preceptor is essential for acquiring the knowledge of the Śāstras. This knowledge leads to the development of discipline. A king, disciplined through knowledge of science, never became depressed in the time of troubles.[387] Showing honour to the wise educated person was the characteristic feature of this age. The kings of this age were not exceptions in showing honour and regards to the worthy and educated person. It is stated that the king who was devoted to the wise, is held in high esteem by the honest people. He never yielded to inducements of dishonest men in committing wrongful acts.[388] The king taking proper lessons regularly

---

385. *vijñānam hṛdayam cittam mano buddhiśca tatsamam*
anenātmā karotīha pravartana nivartane ।
Nītisāra, Śl. 30, p. 16

386. *varddhanniha dharmārthau sevitau ṣaḍbhiḥ*
nigṛhītendriyaḥ sādhu kurvīt gurusevanam ।
— *Ibid.*, Śl. 61, p. 29

387. *śāstrāya gurusaṁyogaḥ śāstraṁ vinayavṛddhaye*
vidyāvīnito nṛpatīrṇa kṛccheṣu nāvasīdati ।
— *Ibid.*, Śl. 62, p. 29

388. *vṛddhopasevī nṛpatiḥ śatām bhavati sammataḥ* ।
preryamāno'pyaṣaḍvṛttairnākāryeṣu pravartate ॥
— *Ibid.*, Śl. 63, p. 30

in different arts, i.e., 64 *kalās*, attained increased prosperity.[389] The science of polity guided a king in the way of success. He could attain predominance in the inter-state circle, i.e., *maṇḍala*. A well disciplined ruler following the prescriptions of the science of polity spoke resplendently by achieving his desired goal, i.e., predominance in the inter-state circle of *maṇḍala*. His fame or glory, i.e., *kīrtti* extended widely so as to reach the horizon or the ends of the earth.[390] Following the law of polity the king could attain the illustrious position of lord among kings. He was attended by other rulers.

The place of discipline and self-restrainment in the life of the king was very high. Discipline was the most important requirement for learning the laws of polity. Self-restraint was the real ornament of the king. He received spontaneous service from all.

The preceptor was always respected and treated with high esteem for imparting *vidyā*, i.e., the science of polity. Learning only was able to sharpen the intellect. The intelligent application of the prescribed maxims lead invariably to prosperity.[391] A skilful and learned preceptor should be respectfully served by the king for the purpose of acquiring material prosperity. Thereby a disciplined king became worthy for his position and able to maintain equilibrium.[392]

---

389. *ādadhānaḥ pratidinam kalāḥ samyam mahīpatiḥ* ।
— *Nītisāra*, Śl. 64, p. 30

390. *jitendriyasya nr̥paternītiḥ mārgānusāriṇaḥ* ।
bhavanti jvalita lakṣmyaḥ kīrtayaśca nabhaspr̥śaḥ ॥
— *Ibid.*, Śl. 65, p. 30

391. *gurustu vidyādhigamāya sevyate śruta ca vidyā mataye mahātmanām* ।
śrutānubandhinī matāni vedhasāmasaṁśayaṁ sādhu bhavanti bhūtaye ॥
— *Ibid.*, Śl., 79, p. 32

392. *sunipunamupasevya sadguruṁ śucirānuvr̥ttiparo vibhūtaye*
bhavati hi vinayopavr̥ṁhito nr̥patipadāya śamayā ca kṣamaḥ
— *Ibid*, Śl. 70, p. 33

The branches of learning prevalent in this age are described with minute details. *Ānvikṣikī*, i.e., science of reasoning, *trayī*, i.e., the three Vedas, *vārtā*, i.e., agriculture, cattle rearing and trade, and *daṇḍanīti*, i.e., laws of government, were the essential sciences to be learnt by a disciplined ruler from those well versed in theories and practical applications of these. He should also deliberate on them. *Ānvikṣikī*, *trayī*, *vārtā* and *daṇḍanīti* are the four traditional divisions of knowledge which are essential for the preservation and development of the state or society.[393] According to the school of Manu, *trayī*, *vārtā* and *daṇḍanīti* were three branches of knowledge. *Vārtā* and *daṇḍanīti* were the two branches of learning for their importance in the matter of acquisition of material wealth. According to the school of Uśanas, there was only one branch of learning and that was the *daṇḍanīti*. According to them, all other branches of learning were originated from *daṇḍanīti*. According to the Kāmandaka, all the four *vidyās* or branches of learning were essential for the purpose of the achievement of the different objects in the society. *Ānvikṣikī* was the branch of knowledge which developed mental faculties. Realising the real nature of mental faculties, a ruler renounced both joy and sorrow and in this way he could maintain the equilibrium of the state of mind. He never became elated with joy or depressed with sorrow. *Trayī* is the collective name of the three Vedas, i.e., the *Ṛg*, *Yajur* and *Sāma*. It is believed that he who was well conversant with the three Vedas secured merit in this world and the next.[394] Vedāṅgas attached to each of the four Vedas are four in number Mīmāṁsā, Nyāya, Dharmaśāstra (legal codes) and Purāṇas, these are

---

393. *ānvīkṣikīm trayīm vārtām daṇḍanītim ca pārthivaḥ* ।
tadvidaistatkriyopataiścintayed vinayānvitāḥ ॥

ānvīkṣikī trayī vārtā daṇḍanītiśca śāśvati ।
vidyāścatasra evaita yogakṣemāya dehināṁ ॥
— *Nītisāra*, II. Śl. 2, p. 25

394. *ṛgyajuḥ sāmanāmānastrayo vedāstrayī matā* ।
ubhau lokavamāpnoti trayayyam tiṣṭhan yathāvidhi ॥
— *Ibid*., II.12, p. 40

all related and collectively known as *trayī*.[395] But it may be commented that the Vedāṅgas consist of six sections — they are *Śikṣā*, *Vyākaraṇa*, *Kalpa*, *Chanda*, *Jyotiṣa* and *Nirukta*.

The root ✓*vid* implies 'to know'. A king who was well versed in the *vidyās*, i.e., the four branches of learning and realised the merit of *caturvarga*, i.e., *dharma*, *artha*, *kāma* and *mokṣa*, was considered proficient in learning.[396]

The customary and obligatory duties prescribed for the brāhmaṇas, kṣatriyas and the vaiśyas were performance of sacrifice, study of the Vedas and offering of gifts prescribed in the traditional *śāstras*. Teaching was the holy function of the brāhmaṇas. Arts and crafts, i.e., *kārukarma*, fine arts were considered accepted occupation for the śūdras.

The obligatory duties of a student is described in the *Nītisāra* of Kāmandaka. The *brahmacārī* student had to live with the family of the *guru*, i.e., preceptor. Duties of student included studying of the Vedas, offering ablutions for three times, begging for alms. A *naiṣṭhika brahmacārī*, i.e., a life-long student may live with the preceptor till death. Even in the absence of his *guru*, he may live with the son of a preceptor or with fellow *brahmacārīs*. If he wished after the death of his preceptor he can be a householder. The dress of the student is prescribed in the Dharmaśāstra. While living with his *guru* for study, a student should put on *mekhalā* (which may vary according to caste), wear matted hair and carry a *daṇḍa* or staff in his hand.[397] After the

---

395. *aṅgāni vedāścatvāro mīmāṁsā nyāya vistaraḥ* ।
dharmaśāstram purāṇaṁ ca trayīdam sarvamucyate ।।
— *Nītisāra*, II.13, p. 40

396. *vidirjñane niruccayate.* — *Ibid.*, II.17.p. 41

397. *gurau vāsau'gniśuśruṣā svādhyāyo vratadhāraṇam* ।
trikālasnāyinā bhaikṣyaṁ gurau prānāntikī sthitiḥ ।।
tadabhāve gurusute tathā sabrahmacāriṇi ।
kāmato vāśramānyatvaṁ svadharmo brahmacāriṇaḥ ।।
samekhalī jaṭī daṇḍī muṇḍī cāgurusaṁśrayaḥ ।
āvidyāgrahaṇāt gacchet kāmato vāśramāntaram ।।
— *Ibid.*, II.22ff., p. 43

completion of his study, he might take recourse to next stage of life, i.e., life of a householder.

The duty of the preceptor was to guide the student in what was right or wrong. The preceptor should prevent the student from taking wrong action. In *Kāmandakīya Nītisāra*, it is said that the minister who prevented the king from taking wrong actions were compared with the preceptor.[398] Advisers who dissuaded the king from unjustifiable actions were not mere friends, they might be ranked as the greatest of his teachers.[399] Discipline was first and foremost thing to be attained for success in politics.

The king who was well acquainted with the laws and customs of the people and well versed in the injunctions of the Vedas, should apply himself to the governance of the kingdom with the assistance of experts.[400] The action which was commended by those well versed in the legal codes, i.e., *āgamas* is justice (*dharma*) and the contrary to it was injustice (*adharma*).[401]

The king should have arranged for proper training of princes. If untrained, princes soon became instrumental in bringing about the ruin of the royal family. A prince thoroughly trained and disciplined was consecrated as the crown prince.[402]

---

398. *gurūṇāmiva caiteṣām śṛṇuyādvacanaṁ nṛpaḥ* ।
— *Nītisāra*, Śl. IV.41, p. 81

399. *satyam te naiva suhṛdo guravo guravo hi te* ।
— *Ibid*., Śl. IV.45, p. 82

400. *loke vede ca kuśalaḥ kuśalaiḥ parivāritaḥ* ।
— *Ibid*., Śl. VI.1, p. 127

401. *yamāryāh kriyamānaṁ hi śaṁsntyāgamavedinaḥ* ।
sa dharmo yaṁ vigarhanti tamadharmaṁ pracakṣate ।।
—*Ibid*., VI.7, p. 129

402. *vinayopagrāhan bhṛtaih kurvīta nṛpati sutān*
avinītakumāraṁ hi kulamāśu vinaśyati ।। 5
binītamaurasaṁ putraṁ yauvarājye'bhiṣecayet ।। 6
— *Ibid*., VII.5-6, p. 133

The Gupta period is marked as an age of transition in the field of legal literature. Some of the important Dharmaśāstras which bear clear evidence of a distinct and very developed branch of literature emerged in this period. The beginning of the Dharmaśāstra, also called Smṛti[403] can be found in the Vedas.[404] The word *dharma* is most comprehensive in its sense. Four principal aspects, namely *ācāra*, i.e., duties of people according to individual capacity, *vyavahāra*, i.e., law and legal instructions; *prāyaścitta*, i.e., expiatory rules, and *karmaphala*, i.e., consequence of the acts done previously — all these constitutes *dharma*. These four aspects specially law, custom and religious functions and attitudes are core of the term *dharma* and the literature based on it is the Dharmaśāstra. Law being an integral part of religion and ethics has been freely consulted in the Dharmaśāstras in connection with litigation, debt, partition, etc. and they are broadly called law-books. So the Dharmaśāstras dealing with *vyavahāra* section are huge in number. The Dharmaśāstra literature generally deals with multifarious subjects including those dealing with the sources of law, duties of the four castes, observances prescribed in various *āśramas*, rites concerning physical and mental purification; laws of inheritence and marriage, criminal procedure, laws of evidence and of judical administration; duties of the king's sin and its expiation, penance and so on.[405]

According to Weber, the cause of swelling of the bulk of Dharmaśāstra literature is for the purpose of obstructing the growth of Buddhism "with the view of rigidity and securely fixing the system

---

403. *srutistu vedo vijñeyo dharmaśāstram tu vai smṛtiḥ* ।
— *Manu,* II.10

404. *vedo dharmamūlam.* — *Gautama Dharmasūtra*, I.1
dharmajñāsamayaḥ pramāṇaṁ vedesća
— *Āpastamba Dharmasūtra*, I.I.2
vedo'khilo dharmamūlam . . . — *Manu*, II.6

405. *Ibid.*, I.111-18.

of caste distinctions rejected by the new faith, and of shielding the Brāhmaṇical polity generally from invocation or decay".[406] This view may have a strong ground. Literature cannot be absolutely indifferent from the Society. The extensive Smṛti and Purāṇic works based certainly on a social and political background. Historical records show that when Smṛti and Purāṇic literature were in the state of formation, north and central India faced the trouble of frequent disturbance infringed by the invasions of foreign hordes, such as the Greeks, Śakas, Hūṇas and other tribes. At the same time the religious performances of Vedic sacrifices had become greatly affected by the growing strength of Buddhism, Jainism and other dissentient sects. The intellectual personnel of the Hindu society was aware of the facts and took the responsibility of undermining the power and prestige of Buddhism and Jainism as well as of dispersing large sections of the masses from the new and attractive features of Buddhist religion. The Hindu leaders had to convince and project the faith to the people that "they could recure in the re-oriented Hindu faith the same benefits, social and spiritual, as Buddhism promised".[407]

Hence, the Purāṇas, in which a remarkable improvement on Manu and Yājñavalkya regarding varieties of Smṛti topics can be noticed, influenced the later Dharmaśāstras. The rigidity of the Vedic religion became relaxed to an earlier method of attaining *dharma*. The Smṛti chapters of the Purāṇas declare that little effort would bring great

---

406. A.Weber, *The History of Indian Literature*, Chowkhamba Sanskrit Series, Varanasi, 1961, p . 276.

407. P.V. Kane, *History of Dharmaśāstra,* Vol. V, Pt. II (revised), Poona, 1962, p. 912.

rewards.[408] Though the eagerness for uplifting the Hindu religion helped in the quick advancement of the Purāṇic and Smṛti literature, its preparation started in a far-off period. The real works of the Dharmaśāstras started with the *sūtras* composed on matters of ritual. It became the practice of including in these texts "instructions on matters closely akin to ritual, the daily life of the people, their duties of all kinds, including matters which more advanced civilisation would classify as questions of etiquette and social usage, moral, legal or religious".[409] Thus, while the Dharmaśātras had natural origin and gradual development, the Buddhist and Jaina religions became the causes for their multiplicity and peculiarity of their contents.

The earlier treatises are the *Dharmasūtras* of Gautama, Baudhāyana and Āpastamba who certainly belonged to the period between 600 and 800 BC. Other ancient works on Dharmaśāstras are of Vasiṣṭha, Viṣṇu, Śaṅkha-Likhita, Kāśyapa and many other undiscovered texts.

Though acceptance fees by the preceptor from the pupil is

---

408. *alpenaiva prayatnena dharmaḥ siddhyanti vai kalau* |
— *Viṣṇu Purāṇa*, VI.2.24

and

pravartte dvāpare yajño dānaṁ kaliyuge varaṃ |
— *Vāyu Purāṇa*, 8.66

and

Restoring to an easier process is not at all a new feature. Owing to same socio-religious problems this course have been adopted many times and philosophically also this has been justified by the sacred scriptures as the Upaniṣads and the *Brāhmaṇas*. For example we may cite — *sarvam pāpmānaṁ tarati brahmahatyām yo'śvamedhena yajate ya cainam evam veda iti* — *Tait Sam*, V.3.12.

Also compare the concept of *saṁpad upāsanā* of the *Bṛhadarāṇyakopaniṣad* which says — *atimokṣa atha sampadaḥ*

409. A.B., Keith, *History of Sanskrit Literature*, p. 487.

condemned in the *Varāha Purāṇa*,[410] but it is allowed tacitly or conditionally in the commentaries of Medhātithi[411] and Aparārka[412] and Vijñāneśvara[413] as well as in the *Smṛti-candrikā*.[414] A special title of law meaning 'non-rendition of service after entering into a contract' (*abhyupetyaśuśruṣā*) deals in their works with the duties of the student towards his teacher. Under the general heading of attendants (*śuśrukas*) are included the Vedic students as well as the craftsman's apprentice.[415] The high standard of the scholar-kings of this period can be proved such as Samudragupta, Harṣavardhana, Mahendravarman and Yaśovarman.

The course of studies laid down for the Vedic student in the Smṛti works of this period follows the traditional lines. According to Medhātithi the student should study one to three recensions of a sinlge Veda,[416] while, according to *Smṛti-candrikā* only one recension of the Veda after going through the student's own would be enough. Regarding primary education Smṛti authorities mention a sacrament called *vidyārambha* or *akṣara-svīkṛti* which was started in the boy's sixth year before his

---

410. *abhiśaptastathā ....*
bhṛtakadhyāpakaścaiva bhṛtakādhyāpitaśca yaḥ ||
— *Varāha Purāṇa*, XIV.6

411. Medhātithi on *Manu*, III.156.

412. Trivandram Edition, I, p. 50.

413. *vittado'rpanapūrvakamarthapradātā* | *ete gunāḥ samasta vyāstāścu yathāsaṁbhavaṁ draṣṭyāḥ* | *ete ca dharmataḥ śāstrānusāreṇa adhyāpyaḥ* ||
— on *Vājñavalkya*, I.28

414. *arthado gurvarthapradātā* | *ime dharmataḥ dharmānātirekenādhyāpyaḥ* | . . . *bhṛtisaṁ pratipattipūrvakamevādhyāpanaṁ pratisiddha-mitarasya vṛttihetutva-nāvirodhāt* |
— *Smṛt-Candrikā*, Vol. I, p. 140

415. R.K. Mukherjee, *Ancient Indian Education in the Cultural Heritage of India*, V. 2, p. 651.

416. On *Manu*, III.2.

upanayana. The boy read a primer called *mātṛkā-nyāsa* as also arithmetic.

Indian legal literature, which had a remote origin and had its perfection in the works of the writers like Manu and Yājñavalkya, maintained its natural flow in the Gupta age also. That the Gupta emperors followed the instructions made by Manu and perhaps by Yājñavalkya is proved by Kālidāsa in his *Raghuvaṁśa*, Canto I, verses 11 and 17.[417] It may be presumed therefore that the educational system contained in the *Manu-smṛti* and also in the other Smṛti works of that time continued up to the time of the Gupta rule. Though some minor works on the Dharmaśāstras are said to have been composed during the Gupta age, as we have referred to earlier, they do not contain any remarkable information regarding the educational system of the contemporary period. So we have to be satisfied only with the materials supplied mainly by the *Manu-smṛti* and *Yājñavalkya-smṛti*. The Smṛti-works, composed during the time of the Guptas, also contain same remarks on educational systems, these are not very different from those instructed by Manu and Yājñavalkya. It will be fair, therefore, to collect the views on education of the Smṛti writers who appeared before and during the Gupta rule. We will notice from these works the methods of educational system, courses of study, teacher-student relation and such other materials.

It is undoubted that the study of the Vedas was also of special importance in the Gupta period as it was in the earlier times. The central point of the whole educational system was the teacher who was called by the names of *ācārya*, *guru* and *upādhyāya*. The Smṛtis have always accepted the greatness of the teacher. The *Manu-smṛti* states that both father and teacher called *pitā*, but the father who teaches the

---

417. *vaivasvato manurnāma mānānīyo manīṣiṇām* |
āsīnamahīkṣitamādyaḥ praṇavaśchandasāmiva || 11

rekhāmātramapi kṣunnādā manorvartmanāḥ param |
na vyatīyuḥ prajāstasya niyenturnemivṛttayaḥ || 17

— *Raghuvaṁśa*, Canto I, Verses 11, 17

sacred Veda is superior to the father that gives physical birth.[418] The *Gautama Dharmaśāstra* expresses the view that the *ācārya* is the highest among all *gurus*. Manu has defined the *ācārya* as one who performs the *upanayana* of the student and teaches him the whole Veda.[419] Manu again states that the teacher, after conducting the *upanayana* ceremony of the student, teaches his pupil the rules of *śauca*, *ācāra*, etc. *Ācārya*, *guru* and *upādhyāya* do not contain the same meaning, for Manu is the opinion that an *upādhyāya* teaches a portion of the Veda or the Vedāṅgas to the student.[420] But a *guru* is one who performs the *saṁskāras* of a student. In this sense a father also might be a *guru*. *Ācārya* is to perform the *upanayana* of a person and to teach him the Vedas. An *ācārya* should be a brāhmaṇa, who is solely devoted to the Vedas, who is conversant with *dharma*, who has come from a noble family, who is pure and has studied all the branches of the Veda and who is not fond of laziness.[421] The instruction imparted to a student by a teacher was most probably oral.[422]

---

418. *utpādakabrahmadātrorgarīyān brahmadaḥ pitā* |
brahmajanma hi viprasya pretya ceha ca śāsvatam ||
— *Manu-smṛti*, II.146

419. *upanīya tu yaḥ śiṣyam vedamadhyāpayed dvijaḥ* |
sakalpaṁ sarahasya ca tamācāryam pracakṣate ||
— *Ibid.*, II.140

420. *ekadeśantu vedasya vedāṅgānyapi vā punaḥ* |
yo'dhyāpayati vṛttyarthamupādhyāyaḥ sa ucyate ||
niṣekādīn karmāṇi yaḥ karoti yathāvidhi |
sambhāvayati cānena sa vipro gururucyate ||
— *Ibid.*, II.140-2

421. *vedaikaniṣṭham dharmajñaṁ kulīnaṁ śrotriyaṁ śuciṁ* |
svaśākhājñamanālasyaṁ vipraṁ kartāramīpsitam ||
— Vyāsa in *Sam Pra*, p. 408

422. *ekādhyāyī dakṣiṇām bahum prtyupasīdet* |
yathāvākaśambhavaḥ ||
— *ĀpaDhS*, I.2.6. 24-5; *History of Dharmaśāstra*, Vol. II.1, p. 325

The study of the Veda was the first duty of every brāhmaṇa. The Manu has prescribed that every *dvijāti* should learn the whole Veda together with the Upaniṣads.[423] In this connection we may refer to the sense of the *Mahābhāṣya*[424] and the *Mahābhārata*[425] where it has been suggested that a brāhmaṇa will do justice to his birth by studying the Vedas with the six *aṅgas*.

Generally a teacher liked to stay in one place but there are references to the fact that even in ancient times there were teachers who wandered from one country to another. Students generally were attached to one teacher but sometimes they went to other renowned teachers who earned fame by their teaching capacity.[426] The *Mahābhāṣya* has called one type of students as *tīrthakāka*, which suggests that the students used to roam from one teacher to another's.[427]

As the study of the Veda was essential duty of the brāhmaṇa so also his duty was to teach Veda to another. The commentator Medhātithi quotes a Vedic text in this connection while commenting a *śloka* of *Manu-smṛti* (II.113) where it is said that if a brāhmaṇa after having studied the Veda do not teach it to a person who requests him to do so,

---

423. *tapaviśeṣyarvividhairvrataiśca vidhicoditaiḥ* |
vedaḥ kṛtsno'dhigantavyaḥ sarahasyo dvijātmanā ||
— *Manu*, II.165

424. *brāhmeṇena niṣkāraṇo dharmaḥ ṣaḍaṅgo vedo'dhyeo jñeya iti* |
— *Mahābhāṣya*, Vol. I, p. 1, ed. by Kielhorn, Bombay, 1880

425. *yo vidyāccaturo vedān sāṅgopaniṣadān dvijaḥ* |
na cākhyanamidaṁ vidyānnaiva sa syādvicakṣaṇaḥ ||
— I.38.17; 2.235
sāṅgopanisadān-vedān viprāscādhīyate tadā || I.58.17
— *Mahābhārata*, I.2.235; I.58.17; I.121.5; VII.8.29.XII. 224.7; 227.1-2

426. *Taittirīya*, I.4.3.

427. *yathā tīrthe kākā na ciraṁ sthātāro bhavanti evaṁ yo gurukulāni gatvā na ciraṁ tiṣṭhati sa ucyate tīrthakāka iti* |
— *Mahābhāṣya*, I, p. 38 on *Pā*, II.1.41

would certainly destroy all of his good deeds and would shut the door of his happiness.[428]

Smṛtis have prescribed some rules about the qualifications of a student. According to *Manu-smṛti* ten types of persons are to be taught by their teachers.

According to the sacred law the (following) persons viz. the teacher's son, one who desires to do service, one who imparts knowledge, one who is instant on fulfilling the law, one who is pure, a person connected by marriage or friendship, one who possesses (mental) ability, one who makes presents of money, one who is honest and a relative, may be instructed (in the Veda).

Where merit and wealth are not (obtained by teaching) nor (at least) due obedience in such (soil) sacred knowledge must not be sown, just as good seed (must) not (be thrown) on barren land.[429]

Yājñavalkya-smṛti (I.28) also supports the view of Manu and farther tells that a student must be grateful to his teacher, should not show hatred to him, should try to keep himself healthy and should not be engaged in finding faults of others.[430] According to the *Nārada-smṛti* a student should always be dependant on and under the control of his teacher.[431] The

---

428. *adhyāpanamapyadhītavedenāvaśyam kartavyam* |
atyantadurgatenāpi neṛiṇe vaptavyeti ||
— Medhātithi on *Manu-smṛti*, II.113

429. *Manu-smṛti*, II, Śl. 109, 112.
The Laws of Manu, translated by G. Bühler, Oxford, 1886, S.B.E. No. 25.

430. *kṛtajñādrohimedhāviśucikalyāṇasūyakāḥ* |
adhyāpyā dharmataḥ sādhuśaktāprajñānavittadā ||
— *Yajñavalkya-smṛti*, I. 28

431. *asvatantra-smṛta śiṣyaḥ ācārye tu svatantratā* |
— *Nārada-smṛti*, Ch. Ṛnadāna, Verse 33

Smṛti works including *Manu-smṛti*, *Yājñavalkya-smṛti*, *Āpastambha Dharmasūtra*, *Baudhāyana Dharmasūtra* and such other works deal elaborately with the conduct of a student to his teacher and teacher's wife, the method of salutation and showing respects to his elders, the food, drinks and actions that are allowed and prohibited for a student and such other numerous prescriptions.[432]

The vast Sanskrit and Prākṛt literature in ancient India, particularly during the time of the Guptas perhaps suggest that the teacher taught his students through the medium of Sanskrit or Prākṛt or by using the current languages of the locality. Thus a verse quoted from *Viṣṇudharma* says that —

saṃskṛtaiḥ prākṛtairvākyairyaḥ śiṣyamanurūpataḥ ।
deśabhāṣādyupaviśca bodhayet sa guruḥ smṛtaḥ ।। [433]

During the Upaniṣadic time usual duration of the *brahmacarya* was twelve years.[434] But this method has not been always followed. During the time of Gṛhyasūtras and Dharmasūtras the period of *brahmacarya* is said to be sometimes fortyeight years sometimes twenty-four years, sometimes twelve years, nine years and eighteen years. According to *Manu* it appears that everyone must observe *brahmacarya* for three years at least for each Veda. In this connection one point may be remembered that the study of Veda has not been recommended by every Smṛti-writer as essential. But it is said that for those who want

---

432. *upānaho chātram yānamiti varjayet* — *ĀpaDhs*, I. 2. 7. 5, but when on a journey the student may sit on a cart, if ordered by the teacher.

yānamukto'dhvanyanvāropet — *ĀpaDhs*; *History of Dharmasūtra*, Vol. II, pt. I. pp. 331-2.

433. Quoted from the *Vīramitraodaya* in the *Vyavahāra adhyāya;* edited by Jīvānanda Vidyāsāgara, p. 72.

434. *upakośala ha vai kāmalāyanaḥ satyakāme jābāle brahmacaryamuvāsa* ।
tasya hi dvādaśa varṣāṇyagnīn paricacāra ।
sa hi smānyānantevāsinaḥ samāvartayaṅsta ha smaiva na samāvartayati ।। — *ChānUpa*, IV.10.1

to perform Vedic sacrifices, the Vedic study is absolutely necessary.

The subjects of study for a student are not always confined to some limited topics only. The Sanskrit literature composed during the Gupta rule gives us the impression that there was not any fixed regulations regarding the subjects to be studied by a student. Generally fourteen *vidyās* are recommended by the Smṛtis and also by the Purāṇas.[435] These fourteen *vidyās* are — four Vedas, six *aṅgas*, Purāṇas, Nyāya, Mīmāṁsā and Dharmaśāstra. Four more *vidyās* were, however, added to these fourteen, viz., *Āyurveda*, *Dhanurveda*, *Gāndharvaveda* and *Arthaśāstra*. According to them the *vidyās* were eighteen in number.[436] Kālidāsa in his *Raghuvaṁśa*[437] openly states that Varatantu taught his pupil fourteen *vidyās*. An inscription of the time Mahārāja Saṁkṣobha, dated 199 Gupta year, says that king Suśarman 'knew the highest truth because of his proficiency in the fourteen *vidyāsthānas*'.[438]

In the *Manu-smṛti* (II.168) and *Vasiṣṭha Dharmasūtra* it has been emphasised that a brāhmaṇa, without studying the Veda goes to

---

435. *purāṇanyāyamīmāṁsādharmaśāstrāṅgamiśritāḥ* ।
vedāḥ sthānāni vidyānāṁ dharmasya caturdaśa ।
— *Yājñavalkya-smṛti*, I.3

aṅgāni caturo vedānpurānaṁ nyāyavistaraṁ ।
mīmāṁsā dharmaśāstram ca parigṛhya mayā kṛtam ।
— *Matsya Purāṇa*, LIII. 5b, 6a

aṅgāni vedaścatvāro mīmāṁsā nyāyavistaraḥ ।
dharmaśāstram purāṇam ca vidyāstvetaścaturdaśa ।
— *Vāyu Purāṇa*, Vol. I, Ch. 61, Śl. 78

436. *āyurvedo dhanurvedo gāndharvaścaiva te trayaḥ* ।
arthaśāstraṁ caturthaṁ tu vidyāstvaṣṭādaśaive tu ।।
— *Ibid.*, Vol. I, Ch. 61, Śl. 79

437. *nirbandhasanjātarūṣārthakārśyamacintayitvā gurunāhamuktaḥ* ।
vittasya vidyāparisaṁkhyayā me koṭiścatasro daśa cāhareti ।।
— *Raghuvaṁśa*, Canto V, verse 21

438. *Epigraphia Indica*, Vol. VIII, p. 287.

acquire knowledge in other subjects is to be considered as a śūdra. The study of the Veda was not confined of the utterance of the *mantras* only but knowledge of the meaning of the *mantras* was also deemed necessary. The *Mitākṣarā* commentary on the *Yājñavalkya-smṛti* (III. 300) quotes a verse of Vyāsa where it is said that a brāhmaṇa who reads the Vedic *mantra* but does not know their meanings is sure to face severe difficulty. Manu has spoken of the highly meritorious nature of the knowledge of the Vedic *mantras* and application of those *mantras* in the sacrifices (XII.103). Commentators like Viśvarūpa and Aparārka, when commenting upon relevant sections of the Smṛti texts have quoted verses from the authorities to establish that mere memorizing of the Veda was not good for the scholars.[439]

One interesting feature of the ancient educational system was perhaps the total absence of any prior agreement about fees for teaching students. Thus *Gautama Dharmasūtra* says that a student, after the end of his studies should request the teacher to accept wealth or what the teacher wants as the remuneration for the teaching. The *Manu-smṛti* also has the same spirit when it states when a student returns from his teacher's house after the end of his study, he may offer to his *guru* some wealth (II.245). But it was generally held that teaching was the main factor between a student and a teacher and lessons imparted by a teacher to his students could not be purchased by any amount of money. According to the Smṛtis, if the *guru* teaches single letter to a student, there is nothing in this world by the exchange of which the people can be get rid of the debt.[440] Yājñavalkya, however, says that a student should give to his teacher what the latter asked him

---

439. *vedasya pāranayayamarthato granthataśca svīkaraṇaṁ na granthata eva* ।
tathā ca vaktāro bhavanti vedādhyayanaṁ na vedapāraga iti ।।
— Viśvarūpa on *Yājñavalkya*, I. 51

440. *ekamapyakṣaram yastu guruḥ śiṣye nivedayet* ।
pṛthivyāṁ nāsti tad dravyaṁ yad datvā tvaṛṇī bhavet ।।
— Laghuhārīta according to *Smṛti-Candrikā*, I, p. 66

to give (*Yāj*, I. 51). Kātyāyana prescribes that a brāhmaṇa student may give to his teacher a cow, a kṣatriya student a village and a vaiśya student a horse.[441]

It was a general practice in earlier days that a king supported learned men and students and noticed that no brāhmaṇa teacher or a student died of hunger (*Manu*, VII.82, *Yāj*, I.315). Reference has been made to the fact that when a teacher demanded a heavy fee from his student the latter could approach the king for the fee. Thus in Kālidāsa's *Raghuvaṁśa* (Canto V) we see that Varatantu demanded fees amounting to fourteen crores from his pupil Kautsya and latter approached king Raghu for that amount and did not take more than his requirements.

About corporal punishment of a student Gautama says that if required pupils are to be punished without beating but if it is not possible to control the pupil by words or any other means then he may strike the student with a slender rope or a split bamboo. If a teacher struck the pupil with any hard material or by hand, the teacher should be punished by the king himself.[442]

About the education of the kṣatriyas, vaiśyas and śūdras there are various views of the *smṛtikāras*. Thus a king should be well versed in three Vedas, Dharmaśāstras, the Upavedas and the Purāṇas. Generally ksatriya prince had not to go to the teacher's house, but teachers were employed to teach them in the royal palace. This system was current from the time of the *Mahābhārata*. In Bāṇa's *Kādambarī* also we see that prince Caṇḍapīḍa had not to go to his teacher's house. But a school was built for him outside the capital. About various processes, subjects of study and other allied information regarding the education of the kṣatriyas and vaiśyas, the Smṛtis do not contain many directions. It seems that kṣatriyas and vaiśyas acquired their knowledge through

---

441. *gaurbrāhmaṇasya varo grāmo rājanyasyāśvo vaiśyasya* ।
— Kātyāyana quoted by Aparārka, p. 76

442. *śiṣyasiṣṭiravadhena* । *aśaktau rajjuveṇuvidalābhyāṁ tanubhyāṁ anyena ghan rājñā śāsyah* ।।
— *Gautama Dharmasūtra*, II.48-50

their *gurus* in almost the same way, with however some exceptions as the brāhmaṇas learnt from their teachers. About the education of the śūdras there is no remarkable rules in the Dharmaśāstras. Women however were entitled to acquire the education from the time of the Vedas. A good number of women are stated to have been composers of Vedic hymn. In Sanskrit poems and dramas we have occasionally seen that women were entitled to the higher education just like the men. In the Dharmasūtras and particularly the *Manu-smṛti*, a woman is assigned a position of dependence and even woman of higher classes were considered to be equal to śūdras so far as the Vedic study and other matters were concerned (*Manu*, IX.3). But in spite of this tendency of the *smṛtikāras*, women of the Gupta age were entitled to all branches of higher education. The works of Kālidāsa, the inscriptions issued during the Gupta rule and the entire Sanskrit literature of the later Gupta period will certainly testify to the fact that in no way women were treated or neglected to be enlightened through proper education.

The Dharmaśāstra literature in general does not however present to us an over-all picture of the educational system prevalent in contemporary India. The aim of the Dharmaśāstras was not to focus on the educational system but on the sociological rules and regulations of the time concerned. But in spite of that here and there we find in the Dharmaśāstras some remarks on education which help us to form an idea about the picture of various aspects of ancient Indian education. From the contents of the Dharmaśāstras we can draw the conclusion that the teacher had a high and honourable position. There was a close personal contact of the teacher and the student, the student's stay at the house of the teacher as his family member, the high regards towards the study of the Vedas, the oral instruction, punishment of the students and such other things. We can also draw the idea that the students in ancient India were liable to enter into all branches of Sanskrit learning. The educational system as we know from the Dharmaśāstras cannot be strictly speaking the system that was current in the Gupta age for no prominent Smṛti was cannot be definitely placed in that period. If we compare the instructions made in the Dharmśāstras with the social and cultural aspects of the poems and dramas composed during the Gupta

The most important Dharmaśāstra is of Kātyāyana. The work, which may be dated between AD 400 and 600, is known mainly from quotations. The Smṛti of Devala has the same fate.

The work of Vyāsa (AD 400-600) comprises about 250 verses divided into four chapters. He deals the topics in a very systematic way.

According to Vyāsa the year of initiation, i.e., *upanayana* of a brāhmaṇa is eighth year; for a kṣatriya it is eleventh and a vaiśya boy may be initiated in the twelfth year.[446]

The initiated student used to live in the house of his preceptor and read Śruti, Smṛti and Purāṇas. He used *daṇḍa*, *kaupīna*, *upavīta* and *mekhalā*. He would follow the path of purity and *ācāra* as prescribed by the Dharmaśāstra. He would read the texts from his preceptor and follow his instructions. He would salute his preceptor and other elderly persons. He would take care in doing welfare to others and for reading Vedas.

The *brahmacārī* would not roam here and there unnecessarily. He would take rest when instructed by his preceptor. He would beg alms without greed. He would give the rice gathered by begging to his preceptor. He would gather *samidh* and attend to the preceptor. He would stay at the house of the preceptor abiding by the rules of studenthood.

The *upakurvāṇaka* brāhmaṇa would stay for twenty-six years in the house of the preceptor. The student would return to the home after completion of the study of the four Vedas, or two Vedas or one Veda.[446a]

Only the learned brāhmaṇa were praised and though well fed

446. *vipro garbhāṣṭame varṣe kṣatra ekādaśe tathā* ।
dvādaśe vaiśyajātiṣu vratopanayamarhati ॥

— Vyāsa, *Adhyaya* I

446a. *śrutismṛtipurāṇānām bhavedadhyanakṣamaḥ* ॥

upānīto gurukule vaset nityaṁ samāhitaḥ ।
vibhṛyād daṇḍakaupīnājināmekalāḥ ॥

śaucācāravicārārthaṁ dharmaśāstramapi dvijaḥ ।
paṭheta gurutaḥ samyak karma taddiṣṭamacaret ॥ →

learned were alone worthy to be invited but a foolish brāhmaṇa who was on fast even for six nights, were not worthy to be invited.[447]

The sellers of Veda were considered to be charged with the sin of killing a brāhmaṇa.

Parāśara-smṛti (c. 100 BC to AD 200) is of distinguished merit. In his time law was essentially progressive in nature and it echoed the social needs and sentiments of the people.

It is stated that the duty of a student was bathing, uttering *japas* and performance of *homas* in the evening. Worshipping of deities and learning the Vedas were also the prescribed duties.[448]

Charity to a *yati* and *brahmacārī* yielded great *puṇya*. The gift of water and rice is compared with ocean and mountain.[449]

→ *tato'bhivādya sthavirān gurun caiva samāśrayet* ।
svādhyāyārthaṁ tadā yatnaḥ sarvadā hitamācaret ।।

bṛthāṭanamasantoṣaṁ brahmacārī vivarjayet ।
īṣaccalita madhyāhnanujñāto gurunā svayaṁ ।।

ālolupaścared bhaikṣam vratiṣuttamavṛttiṣu ।
sadyo bhikṣānnamādāya vittavattadupaspṛśet ।।

bhuktvā gurumupāsīta kṛtvā sandhukṣaṇādikaṁ ।
samidho'gnāvādadhīta tataḥ paricarad guruṁ ।।

nityamārādhyedenamāsamāpteḥ śrutigrahāt ।
upakurvāṇako yastu dvijaḥ ṣaḍvimśvārṣikaḥ ।।

samāpya vedān vedau vā vedaṁ vā prasabhaṁ, dvijaḥ ।।

447. *naṣṭaśauce vratabhraṣṭe vipra vedavivarjite* ।
vedapūrṇamukhaṁ vipram subhaktamapi bhojayet ।।

na ca mūrkhaṁ nirāhāraṁ ṣaḍrātranupavāsinam ।
vedavikretā pañcaite brahmaghātakāḥ ।। —Vyāsa, Ch. IV

448. *sandhyāsnānaṁ japo homaḥ svādhyāyo devatārcanam* ।
— *Parāśara-smṛti*

449. *yatī ca brahmacārī ca pakvānnasvāminavubhau* ।
yati haste jalaṁ dadyād bhaikṣam dadyāt punarjalam ।।

tad bhaikṣam meruṇā tulyaṁ tajjalaṁ sāgaropamaṁ ।।
— *Ibid.*

Vṛhat Parāśara, dated AD 500-600 is a comparatively later work. In the first chapter of *Vṛhatparāśara-smṛti* the *avaras* of the different Vedas were described.[450]

The principal duties of a brāhmaṇa were learning and teaching. Among the six principal duties these two were essential.[451]

The kṣatriyas should worship, and learn and be devoid of attachment on worldly things.[452]

The duty of vaiśya was worshipping, learning and charity.[453]

Pulastya and Pitāmaha wrote their works between AD 400 and 700.[454] Pulastya had dealt with the topics of education in the first chapter of the *Smṛti*. According to the scriptures learning is the obligatory duty. By the term scripture, Vedas, Purāṇas, Dharmaśāstras were to be understood.[455]

It is stated that the *vrata* (duties) of a student was to dwell with the preceptor and took care of the preceptor and the kindled fire.[456] It is prescribed that a student should bath thrice, beg alms and stay

---

450. *ṛgvedaḥ svaritodātta udāttastu yajuḥ śrutam* ।
sāmavedaḥ sa vijñeyo dīrghaḥ sa pluta eva ca ॥
— *Vṛhatparāśara-smṛti*

451. *yajanayājane vipre tathādānapratigrahe* ।
adhyāpanamadhyayanaṁ karmānyetāni ṣaṭ tathā ॥
—*Ibid.*, II

452. *yajanādhyayane rājñī viṣayāsaktivarjanam* । — *Ibid.*

453. *yajanādhyane dānam . . . kṛṣi* । — *Ibid.*

454. G.V. Devasthali, *History and Culture of the Indian People* (Classical Age), p. 299.

455. *ijyādhyāyanadānam yathāśāstraṁ sanātanam* ।
yajanādhyāpane . . . — *Pulastya-smṛti*, I/10

456. *gurau vāsogni śuśruṣvādhyāyo vratadhāraṇaṁ* ।

with the preceptor as long as he would live. If a preceptor was not alive, the student would stay with the son of the preceptor or with co-students.[457]

The *brāhmacārī*, i.e., a student living under celibacy would wear *mekhalā*, and would have matted hair, staff, shaven head and be a dweller in the house of his preceptor.[458]

After the completion of the study, a student might embrace the life of second *āśrama*, i.e., *gṛhasthāśrama*.

Pitāmaha was a writer on Smṛti. His writings are very scattered and are found in the commentaries and *nibandhas* only. According to him in the court of law, there should be the following constituents :

(1) scribe (*lekhaka*), (2) accountant (*gaṇaka*), (3) law-book (*śāstra*), (4) *sadhyapāla* and (5) *sabhāsad* (members of the judicial assembly).[459] From this statement it is clear that the study of accountancy and the art of writing were prevalent in this age. The scripture was also considered as the essential factor of the judicial matter.

Hārīta is dated AD 400-600.[460] His verses are found quoted in the later commentaries and *nibandhas*. In the first chapter of *Hārīta-smṛti*, it is stated that teaching, learning, worshipping — are the

---

457. *trikālasnāpitā bhaikṣam gurau prānāntike sthitiḥ* ||
tadabhāve gurūsakte tathā saṁbrahmacārinī
— *Pulastya-smṛti*, I. 12

458. *kāmato vā samānantvaṁ svadharmo brahmacāriṇaḥ*
samekhalā jaṭī daṇḍī gurugṛhāśrayaḥ |
āvidyā grahaṇād gacchet kāmato vāsramānantaraṁ ||

459. *lekhako gaṇakaḥ śāstraṁ sadhyapālaḥ sabhāsadaḥ* |
— Pitāmaha, quoted in the *Smṛti-Candrikā*; P.V. Kane, *History of Dharmśāstra*, Vol. I, Pt. I, p. 515.

460. P.V. Kane, *Ibid*., p. 543.

prescribed duties of a brāhmaṇa. It is stated that the scripture or Śruti and Smṛti were compared with the eyes of a brāhmaṇa.[461]

The boy should stay with his preceptor. The student who would learn the Vedas, should be controlled in his senses. He would lie in the bed placed on the ground. He would take care of the kindled fire in the house of the preceptor.[462]

A *brahmacārī* would learn purity, *ācāra* and wear deerskin, wooden staff and *mekhalā*. He who was restrained in mind would beg alms in day and evening. Having learnt all this Vedas, or two Vedas or one Veda from the preceptor and after giving the fee with reverence, the student would get the good result of the education.[463] If any student wished he could stay in the house of the preceptor up to the time of his death, but others could accept the second stage of life, i.e., the *gārhasthāśrama*.

---

461. *adhyāpanam adhyayanam yājanaṁ yājanam tathā* |
dharmaśāstraṁ tathā pāṭhyaṁ brāhmaṇaiḥ
śuddhamānasaiḥ ||

vedavit paṭhitavyam ca śrotavyaṁ ca divā niśi |
śrutismṛti ca viprāṇām cakṣusi devanirmite ||

— *Laghuhārīta-smṛti*, Ch. I

462. *upanīto mānavako vased gurukleṣu ca* |
brahmacaryamadhaḥ śayyā tathā vahnerupāsanā ||

kuryādadhyanaṁ caiva brahmacārī yathāvidhi |
vidhiṁ tyaktvā prakurvāṇo na svādhyāyyaphalam labhet ||

— *Ibid*., Ch. III

463. *śaucācūramaśeṣam tu śikṣayed gurusannidham* |
ajinam daṇḍa kāṣṭhañca mekhalāñcopavītakam ||

dhārayedapramattaśca brahmacārī samāhitaḥ |
sāyam prātaścared bhaikṣam bhojyārthaṁ saṁyatendriyaḥ ||

adhītya ca gurorvedān vedau vā vedameva vā |
gurave dakṣiṇāṁ dadyāt saṁyamī |
nayet kālamācāryaiḥ yāvadāyuṣam |
samprāpya vidyāmatidurlabham phalaṁ ca ||

— *Ibid*., Ch. III

3

Education in Sanskrit Kāvyas, Dramas and Some other Minor Works

THE relationship of Sanskrit with most of the languages of Europe, with the exception of Finnish, Estonian, Hungarian, Turkish and Basque is well established. The similarity and common features have established the theory of Indo-European language group. The relationship of Sanskrit to the languages of the West can be shown by specific resemblances, such as *pitṛ* in Sanskrit Latin *pater*; German *vater*; English father. *Mātṛ* in Sanskrit; Latin *mātár*; German *müter*, English *mother*, etc. The relationship between Sanskrit, Latin and Greek can be established by their common features of verbal systems also.

A striking feature of Vedic Sanskrit is the tonic accent which is common in Greek.

The voluminous work on Sanskrit grammar *Aṣṭādhyāyī* composed by Pāṇini was written probably in fourth century BC. It effectively stabilized the Sanskrit language. As the language was fixed, it could only develop within the framework of his rules. The language was termed as *saṁskṛta*, literally meaning perfected or refined. The medium of higher instruction and the language of the cultured classes must have been Sanskrit in Gupta age. The evidence of inscriptions written in Sanskrit proves the popularity of this language among the public also, while in the earlier days the medium of inscription was Pāli or Prākṛt.

The Sanskrit literature attained its highest perfection and subtlety during the age of the Guptas. The political unity, peace, prosperity of India under the Guptas created an atmosphere in which the Sanskrit learning and literature flourished in all its branches. The Gupta emperors extended their staunch patronage towards the literature. It may be commented that the Gupta age produced the best authors in almost all the branches of literature. The literature made the Gupta age the golden age of literature in the literary history of India. There were Hindu, Jaina and Buddhist literary figures. In the Gupta age, great poets, playwrights, composers, chroniclers, grammarians and philosophers flourished.

The account of secular literature can be started with Kālidāsa who is credited with having written the first ranked works in the first three classes of literature. His epics or *kāvya* as for example, the *Raghuvaṁśa* and *Kumārasaṁbhava*, dramas such as, *Śākuntalam* and *Vikramorvaśī* and lyric poems like *Meghadūta*, *Ṛtusaṁhāra* are considered as the first rate works in the world literature.

The date of Kālidāsa has been considered as a subject of keen controversy during two hundred years ever since the publication of English translation of *Śākuntalan* by Sir William Jones, in 1789. No less than six theories have been put forward by scholars. As scholars hold variant views regarding the date of this eminent poet, his time generally varies from the second century BC to sixth century AD. According to majority of scholars, Kālidāsa flourished during the age of the Guptas.[1]

Kālidāsa strikingly in his work is totally silent about his personal life. He had guarded all facts with much care and did not comment

---

1. R.G. Basak, *Proceedings of Second all India Oriental Conference,* Calcutta, 1922, pp. 325f.; F.W. Thomas, *JRAS*, 1909, pp. 740-2; C. Kunhan Raja, "The Historical Background of the Works of Kālidāsa", *Indian Historical Quarterly*, XIII, Calcutta, 1942, pp. 128f.; *Introduction to Raghuvaṁśa,* Delhi 1971, p. 201; T.S. Narayana, *Age of Sankara,* Madras, Pt. I, Ch. II, p. 24.

anything about the age when he flourished. Numerous legends, therefore, have gathered round his name but these dates possess little value.

Since Kālidāsa has incorporated in his works some principles of Vātsyāyana, the author of *Kāmasūtra*, he must have come after the third century AD which is generally accepted as Vātsyāyana's date. Therefore the poet must have lived about AD 400. The works of the poet delineate a very calm and prosperous state of things. Throughout his work, the life of luxury, pursuit of art and literature, peace in social and economic life is reflected. This state of life is possible only in a well protected state like that of the Guptas. The description of Śiva's *samādhi* in *Kumārasaṁbhava* resembles with the images of the Buddha in the Kuṣāṇa times. It may be assumed that Kālidāsa may have been born during the reign of Samudragupta and lived during the whole of Candragupta II's reign and the major part of Kumāragupta's rule.

According to Sri Aurobindo,[2] (Kālidāsa) gathered up in himself its present tendencies while he foreshadowed many of its future developments. He himself must have been a man gifted with all the learning of his age, rich, aristocratic, moving wholly in high society, familiar with and fond of life in the most luxurious metropolis of his time, passionately attached to the arts, acquired with the sciences, deep in law and learning, versed in the formalised philosophies. He has some notable resemblances to Shakespeare, to sum up the immediate past in the terms of present, at the same time he occasionally informed the present with hints of the future. He was Vedāntist in creed and a Śiva-worshipper but these were recommended to him by his intellectual preference and aesthetic affinities. His writings show indeed a keen appreciation of high ideal and lofty thought; but the appreciation is aesthetic in its nature. He has also the natural high, aristocratic feeling. He has exaltation and sublimity; but aesthetic grace and beauty and symmetry sphere in the sublime and prevent it from standing out with the bareness and boldness which is the sublimer's

2. Sri Aurobindo, *Kālidāsa*, Pondicherry 1964, p. 13.

natural presentation. In all this he represented the highly vital and material civilisation to which he belonged. Its characteristic features of style are a compact but never abrupt brevity, a soft gravity and smooth majesty, a noble harmony of verse, an epic precision of phrase, weighty, sparing and yet full of colour and sweetness.

Kālidāsa has depicted in his work directly and indirectly the subjects of study, student life, life in hermitage and other aspects of education. The description is traditional as it was not the practice of ancient India to change the education system frequently. But we may assume safely that the picture depicted in the works of Kālidāsa is a picture of the age in which the poet breathed.

The span of life of a man was divided into four stages. The first was that of a pupil-bachelor. Ceremony took a vital role of the people of the Gupta period. Human life from the start had to be purified by a number of practices which were called *saṁskāras*. The wearing the sacred thread cermeony was called the *upanayana*, by which the boy was initiated into the studies of the Vedas, between the age of eight to sixteen years. The first shaving of the chins was styled as *godāna* between the twenty-second and twenty-fourth years.[3]

Kālidāsa chose the term *vidyā* as the subject of study. In the *Raghuvaṁśa* (Canto I, Śl. 8) the childhood, scheduled for practising *vidyā*, is mentioned. Raghu passed the end of *vidyā*,[4] only by practising

---

3. *athāsya godānavidheranantaram vivāhadīksaṁ nivartayad guruḥ* ।
— *Raghu*, III.33

4. *kramāccatasraśca turarnavopamāḥ* । *tatāra vidyāḥ* ।
— *Ibid.*, 3.30

It means by and by he passed four subjects like four oceans.
anākrṣṭasya viṣyayair vidyānām pāradṛśvanaḥ ।।
— *Ibid.*, I/23

vidyā, than one can please others.[5] After completion of *vidyā*, fee or *guru-dakṣiṇā* should be rendered. *Vidyā*, as properly training is referred to in the context of birth of Bharata and Śatrughna. In *Śākuntalam*,[6] *Mālavikāgnimitra*,[7] and *Vikromarvaśī*, *vidyā* is used. At another place in the *Raghuvaṁśa*, three types of *vidyās* are enumerated and compared with *trivarga*,[8] while commenting upon this *śloka* (XVIII.50) of the *Raghuvaṁśa* Mallinātha quotes Kauṭilya[9] and Kāmandaka.[10] Here Kāmandaka quotes three *vidyās* approved by Manu. Yet in another place of the *Raghuvaṁśa* mention of 14 *vidyās* can be found.[11] In the *kāvyas*, *vidyās* are not enumerated specifically. *Nītisāra* also presses this enumeration. The commentator has quoted from *Nītisāra* — the course of study contained the following four, namely — (1) *ānvikṣikī*: logic: systems of philosophy and metaphysics; (2) *trayī*: the 3 Vedas along with their sections, subsections and appendices; (3) *vārtā*: agriculture, trade, commerce, pasture and rearing of the cattle, (4) *daṇḍanīti*: statecraft, science of government and administration. According to the school of Manu there are only 3 sciences, *ānvikṣikī*

---

5. *vidyāmabhyāsanenaiva prasādayitum arhasi* ।
— *Raghu*, I/88

samāptavidyena mayā . . . . gurudakṣiṇāyaiḥ ।
— *Ibid.*, V.20

samyāgāradhīta vidyā . . . — *Ibid.*, X.71

6. *parātiśaṁghatāmdhīyate yair*
vidyeti, te santu kīlāptavācaḥ । — *Śāk*. V.25

7. *athopanītam vidhivad vipaścita vininyurenam guruva gurupriyam. . .*
Raghu, III.29

8. *tisrastrivargādhigamasya mūlaṁ jagrāha vidyāḥ* ।
— *Raghu*, XVIII.50

9. *dharmādharmau trayamarthau vārtāyam*
nayānayau daṇḍanītyām । — Kauṭilya's *Arthaśāstra*

10. *trayīvārtādaṇḍanītistisro vidyā manormatā* ।
— *Kāmandaka*

11. *vidyāparisaṁkhyayā me koṭiścatasro daśa cāhareti* ।
— *Raghu*, V.21

being included in the Vedas.[12] According to Bṛhaspati, there are only two sciences, namely, *vārtā* and *daṇḍanīti*.[13] Kauṭilya agreed with Kālidāsa in his enumeration of *vidyās* as he propounded only four are the sciences.

According to Kauṭilya, *āṇvikṣikī* comprises the systems of Sāṁkhya, Yoga and Lokāyata.[14] The poet Kālidāsa in his phrase *vāgarthāvivasampṛktau*[15] refers to the direct influence of the Mīmāṁsakas, whose aphorism is *nityaḥ śabdārthasambandhaḥ*. Again the reference to the *Yogasūtras* of Patañjali can be traced while delineating the scene of undisturbed contemplation of Śiva in the *Kumārasaṁbhava*.[16] References to *Yogasamādhi* are scattered in the various palces. In the *Kumārasaṁbhava* (first canto) Girīśa is allowing Umā to serve Śiva who is absorbed in *samādhi*;[17] stages of *samādhi* are alluded in the third Canto.[18] Nine stages of *yoga* is enumerated in the 8th canto of the *Raghuvaṁśa*.[19] In *Kumārasaṁbhava* the *jīvanmukta samādhi* is mentioned.[20] In the works of Kālidāsa, philosophies of Kapila, Kaṇāda and Gautama have made their places. Kālidāsa has touched all types of branches of learning in his works.

Trayī includes the Śruti or the revealed literature. It includes the

---

12. *Arthaśāstra;* edited by R. Śamaśāstrī, translation p. 5.
13. *Ibid.*, p. 6.
14. *Ibid.*, p. 1.
15. *Raghuvaṁśa*, I.1.
16. *Kumārasṁbhava*, III.47-50.
17. *pratyārthibhūtamapi taṁ samādhiḥ śuśrumāṇā gīriśo' numene.*
— *Kumāra*, I.59
18. *samādhibhedaprabhavo bhavanti.* । — *Ibid.*, III.40
19. *na ca yogavidhernavetaraḥ*, etc.
tamasaḥ paramapadamavyayaṁ puruṣaṁ yogasamādhinā raghuḥ ।
— *Raghu*, VIII. 22. 24
20. *Kumārasaṁbhava,* III.18.

four Vedas, i.e., *Ṛg*, *Sāma*, *Yajur* and *Atharva-veda* comprising the *Brāhmaṇas*, *Āraṇyakas* and the *Upaniṣad* portions. The Vedāṅgas (limbs of the Vedas) which were useful for studying the Vedas, are six in number, namely, *śikṣā* (pronunciation), *kalpa* (rules of rituals), *nirukta* (etymology), *vyākaraṇa* (grammar), *jyotiṣa* (astronomy and astrology), *chandas* (prosody). Upavedas are again six in number, e.g., *Dhanurveda, Āyurveda*, Smṛti-Śāstras or the Dharmaśāstra like the code of Manu; *itihāsa* comprising the epics like the *Rāmāyaṇa* and *Mahābhārata*, Purāṇas dealing with the genealogies of Gods and kings. According the Kalīdāsa, Smṛti follows the Śruti.[21] In the *Raghuvaṁśa* (Canto I.19) Kalidāsa refers to spontaneous intelligence in *śāstra* and also proficiency in *Dhanurveda*.[22] The Vedas along with *aṅgas* or limbs were taught.[23] The sweet story of lord Rāma was sung.[24] In *Abhijñānaśākuntalam, itihāsa-nibandha* is alluded. In the *Raghumvaṁśa*, the historians are delineatimg the old story.[25] Purāvid is referred to in the *Raghuvaṁśa*, (XVIII.23).[26] The works of Kālidāsa shows Kālidāsa's knowledge of grammar. In the *Raghuvaṁśa* the allusion of special rule and general rule is used.[27] The united beauty of Rāma and Sītā is compared with the unity of the declension and augment.[28] In other places the roots, suffixes, prefixes, nominal and

---

21. *śruterivārtham smṛtiranavagacchat* । —*Raghu*, II.2
śrutasya yāyād, etc. —*Ibid.*, III.21
śrutaprakāśam yaśasā prakāśam —*Ibid.*, V.2
22. *śāstrasvakuṇṭhita buddhimaurvī dhanuṣi cātatā* । —*Ibid.*, I.19
23. *sāṅgam ca vedaṁ adhyāpya* । —*Ibid.*, XV.33
24. *rāmasya madhuraṁ vṛttam* । —*Ibid.*, XV.34
25. *pūrvavṛttakathitai purāvidaḥ* । —*Ibid.*, XI.10
26. *purāvido yaṁ vyuṣitasvamāhuḥ* । —*Ibid.*, XVIII.23
27. *apavāda iva utsarga* । —*Ibid.*, XV.7
28. *so'abhavad varabadhusamāgama pratyaya-prakṛti-yogasannibhah* । —*Ibid.*, XI.56

verbal bases are alluded.[29]

Vārtā means agriculture, rearing of the cattle, trade and commerce.

Daṇḍanīti or the art of government was a necessary subject of study for a king and it might comprise the sections of Dharmaśāstras which deal with vivid details the duties of a king. Kālidāsa was acquainted with the treatise on statecraft like the *Arthaśāstra* of Kauṭilya or *Nītisāra* of Kāmandaka and *sūtra* of Uśanas. *Daṇḍanīti* is referred in the *Raghuvaṁśa* (XVIII.46).[30] Thus *sūtra* of Uśaṇas is referred in the *Kumārasaṁbhava*.[31] The policy of *sāmadānavidhi* of politics is alluded in the *Raghuvaṁśa*.[32] Thus the curriculum for a king includes subjects bearing on the administration of kingdom. The proficiency in knowledge of *śāstras* is necessary.

Following the view of Manu mention of fourteen kinds of *vidyās* is also available in the *Raghuvaṁśa*.[33] The commentator on *Manu-smṛti* enumerates the fourteen kinds of *vidyās*, i.e., the four Vedas, six *aṅgas*, Mīmāṁsā, Nyāya, Purāṇa and the Dharmaśāstras.[34] Yājñavalkya also holds the same view.[35]

---

29. *dhātorgamanārthamarthaviccakāra* । —*Raghu*, III.21
dhātoḥ sthāna iva deṣam
pravṛttirāsīt śabdānāṁ caritārthacatuṣṭayī ॥
30. *phalānyupāyuñkta sa daṇḍanīteḥ.* —*Ibid.*, XVIII.46
31. *adhyāpitasyośanasyāpi nīṯim* । —*Kumāra*, III
32. *sāmadānavidhibhedanigrahaḥ siddhimanta iva tasya bhūpateḥ* । —*Raghu,* XI.55
33. *"vidyāparisamkhyayā me koṭiścatasro daśa cāhareti".* —*Ibid.*, V.21
34. *aṅgāni vedaścatvāro mīmāṁsānyāyavistaraḥ* ।
purāṇam dharmaśāstram ca vidyā hyetā caturdaśa ॥
—*Manu-smṛti*
35. *purāṇanyāyamīmāṁsādharmaśāstrāṅgamiśritāḥ* ।
vedāh sthānāni vidyānām dharmasya ca caturdaśa ॥
Yāj

Kālidāsa has used the term in Śruti and Veda in the *Raghuvaṁśa*.[36] In these stanzas the *dvijas* are entitled to study the Vedas is clear. So the importance of *upanayana saṁskāra* is also revealed here. Here *vedavidām* indicates proficient in all the four Vedas. In the *Vikramorvaśīyam* the Brahmā is described as *vedābhyāsajaḍa*.[37] The *Sāmaveda* is referred in *Kumārasaṁbhava*.[38] Again the *Atharvaveda* is referred to in *Raghuvaṁśa*.[39]

The term *Dhanurveda* is mentioned in the *Vikarmorvaśīyam* and other terms, i.e., *ālīḍha*, *vājinīrājanā* show the existence of other Upavedas.

We find reference to *varṇas* (alphabets) and their *sthāna* or pronunciation[40] which are part of Śikṣā, an *aṅga* of the Veda. The study of etymology is fairly advanced in the Gupta age. The reference are ample in the *kāvyas* of Kālidāsa. The inseparability of a word from its sense or the expression of the sense of a word through etymological analysis — these core ideas of the phonetics have been revealed. The etymologty of the word *kṣatra* is described in the *Raghuvaṁśa*.[41]

The *Rāmāyaṇa* is alluded to as the first in style and model of *kāvya*.[42] *Mahābhārata* and other *kāvyas* are referred to by the

---

36. . . . . *noparodhulpetaratvācchruta niṣkrayasya* —
itthaṁ dvijena dvijarājakāntirāvedito vedavidām vareṇa —
gurvarthamarthī śrutāparadṛ̥śvā raghoḥ . . .
— *Raghu*, V.22-4

37. *vedābhyāsajaḍaḥ* . . . — *Vik*, I. 10, p. 344

38. *sāmabhiḥ sahacarāṇ* . . . *Kumāra*, VIII.41

39. *athātharvarnidhestasya* । — *Raghu*, I.59

40. *vāgarthāviva sampṛ̥ktau vāgartha-pratipattaye*
jagataḥ pitarau vande pārvatīparameśvarau । — *Ibid*., I.1

41. *kṣatāt kila trayata ityudagraḥ kṣatrasaya śabdo bhuvaneṣu rūḍaḥ* ।
— *Ibid*., II.53

42. *kaviprathamapaddhatim*. — *Ibid*., XV.33

expression, *pūrvasūribhiḥ*.[43] *Purāvids*, i.e., the narrators of the Purāṇas[44] are mentioned. It is clear that the study of the Purāṇas was essential. The names of eminent predecessor-authors have been mentioned in the prelude of *Mālavikāgnimitra*. The names of Bhāsa, Saumilla and Kaviputra are mentioned.[45] Poetics was well established and the study of it practised by learned people.

The subject of polity and administration of government reached its excellence. This subject was particularly studied by the king and ministers. In the dramas of Kālidāsa the mention of this subject can be found among discussion.[46]

Guru is referred in the *Raghu* as *brahmayoni* and *brahmavarcasa*. It was believed that the uttering of *mantra* could drive the enemies far away.[47] *Mantra* is referred to in the *Raghu*, XIII.45.[48] The preceptors did not take any fee. The teacher who offered learning in lieu of cash is called *jñānapaṇyabaṇija*.[49] *Guru*, *vidyā* and *trivarga* — all are referred

---

43. *athavā kṛtavāgdvāre vaṁśe'smin pūrvasūribhiḥ* ।
— *Raghu*, I. 4

44. *pūrvavṛttakathitaiḥ purāvidaḥ*
. . . *purāvido yaṁ vyuṣitāśvamāhuḥ*".
— *Ibid*., XI. 10 and XVIII.23

45. *prathitayasasāṁ bhāsa-saumilla-kaviputrādīnāṁ prabandhānatikramya vartamānakaveḥ kālidāsasya kriyāyām kathāṁ bahumānaḥ* । — *Mālavikā*, Prelude

46. *tena hyavitathaṁ tantrakāravacanaṁ*. — *Ibid*.,1. 8

47. *tava mantrakṛto mantrairdūrāt, prasamitāribhiḥ*
. . . . . *hetustvad brahmavarcasam*
tvaivaṁ cintyamānasya guruṇā brahmayoninā ।
— *Raghu*, I.61-4

48. *yo mantrapūtāṁ tanumapyahauṣiṭ* । — *Ibid*., XIII.45

49. *yasyāgamaḥ kevalajīvikāai taṁ jñānapaṇyaṁ baṇijaṁ vadanti* ।
— *Mālavikā*, p. 270

to in the *Raghu*.[50]

The branch of philosophy reached high exaltation. The view of the Buddhist philosophy that the *pratyaya* is the cause is echoed in *Kumārasaṁbhava*[51] and also in the *Raghu*.[52] *Śabdaguṇa* is referred to in the *Raghu*.[53] *Yoga* is also alluded to in the *Raghu*.[54]

Kings learnt along with other branches of learning, diplomacy and various other deceptive items of the statecraft as the part of *daṇḍanīti*. The learning of the Vedas by the would-be kings was considered to be important. In the *Kumārasaṁbhava*, the initiation of king and the study of the Vedas are mentioned. Like all other twice borns, the life of the king is described in the following verse —

śaiśave abhyastavidyānām yauvane viṣayaiṣināṁ |
vārddhakye munivṛttinām yogenānte tanutyājām ||

The thorough study of scriptures would help to achieve success in duty. The knowledge in Scriptures would serve as king's eye and he could hope to attain foresight and unattained end and subtle ends of his endeavours.[55] So the Gupta kings also studied the scriptures and prepared themselves to achieve success in administration. In this matter the reference of Samudragupta is similar in the Allahabad

---

50. *sa purvajanmāntaradṛṣtapārah-smarannivākleśakaro guruṇāṁ tisrastrivargādhigamasya mūlam jagrāha vidyāḥ prakṛtiśca pitṛyaḥ* — *Raghu*, XVIII.50
51. *apekṣate pratyayamuttamaṁ tvam bijāṅkurah prāgudayadivāmbhaḥ* | — *Kumāra*, III.18
52. *atiṣṭhat pratyayāpekṣasantatiḥ sa ciraṁ nṛpaḥ* | — *Raghu*, X.3
53. *athātmanaḥ śabdaguṇam guṇajñaḥ* | — *Ibid.*, XIII.1
54. *vīrasanairdhyānajuṣāmṛṣināmamī samadhyāsitavedima dhyāḥ* | *nivātaniṣkampatayā vibhānti yogādhiruḍā iva śākhino'pi* || — *Ibid.*, XIII.52
55. *cakṣusmatā tu śāstrena sūkṣmakāryārthadarśinā* | — *Ibid.*, IV. 3

Pillar Insciption. There, he is depicted as master of the essence of the *śāstras*.[56]

Besides the religious education, the king studies other *śāstras*, as for example, the *Mānava-dharmaśāstra* and *Arthaśāstra* of Kauṭilya, *parābhisandhāna vidyā*[57] and also other *vidyās* by which one can attain experience or wisdom of an old man without attaining old age.[58]

Other arts which was learnt by the king was magic or charm. *Aparājitā*[59] was a kind of magic, otherwise known as *śikhābandhinī vidyā* which made one free from all molestation. It was chanted while the *śikhā* was being tied. Another kind of magic is *tiraskariṇī vidyā* which made one invisible. Another kind of *vidyā* was that which controlled the movements of a snake within a charmed circle.

Music, dancing, acting and the dramaturgy were other important subjects. These subjects were mostly specialized by ladies. Particularly the courtesans practised these fine arts and utilised the knowledge of these fine arts in their trade. In the *Mālavikāgnimitra* Śarmiṣṭhā is depicted as the inventor of a new kind of dance based on a certain order of pacing called *catuṣpada*. The entire dance is known as *chalika* with accompanying music. From the expression *sarmiṣṭhāyāḥ kṛtiḥ* it seems that a treatise was composed by her. In the *Raghuvaṁśa* we find Aja teaching fine arts to his wife Indumatī.[60] The achievement of proficiency

---

56. *śāstratattvārthabhartuḥ*
— Allahabad Pillar Inscription of Samudragupta, V.3

57. *parābhisandhānapari yadpyasya viceṣṭitam* ।
— *Raghu*, XIVV.76

58. *anākṛṣṭasya viṣayairvidyānām pāradṛśvanaḥ* ।
tasya dharmaraterāsīd vṛddhatvam jarasā vinā ॥
— *Ibid.*, I.23

59. *gaṇadāsa — deva! śarmiṣṭhāyāḥ kṛtirlaya madhya catuṣpadāsti* ।
tasyāstu chalikaprayogamekamanaḥ śrotumarhati devaḥ ॥
— *Mālavikā* II Act, p. 274

60. . . . *priyaśiṣya lalite kalāvidhau* — *Raghu*, VIII. 67

in dancing was considered chiefly due to practice. The art of dancing had to be acquired from teachers who were the acknowledged experts. In the classical age, the ladies of the royal household received their education and culture in every possible way. Besides general education they had to learn various arts for which experts were brought from other parts of the country. In the *Mālatīmādhava*, Agnimitra is described as running a school of fine arts.[61] Thus it may be assumed that kings were proficient in fine arts as well as in other branches of learning. The art of painting was practised and cultivated by both men and women. Kings like Duṣyanta are seen to paint a portrait of Śakuntalā.[62]

We find mention of architecture, sculpture and making of terracottas and pots and utensils of clay and metal and of other useful things done by the goldsmiths and blacksmiths. It may be assumed that the students of the above useful arts must have their training from their respective guilds. The technical education was imparted to students who were interested to acquire particular branch of learning. There were different classes of people, namely kings, nobles, state officers, teachers, priests, militarymen, musicians and actors, workers in metals, other craftsmen, artisans, etc. *Vāstuvidyā* was an art which formed a branch of learning. Soldiers, particularly kings and kṣatriyas were trained in the use of arms. A thorough study of these subjects built up a sense of perfect discipline[63] in the mind of a student. A study of the language[64] started with understanding the alphabets. The characters of the alphabets were first picked up by writing them on the ground.[65]

61. *prayogapradhānam hi nāṭyaśāstram* ।
— *Mālatīmādhava*, Act. I, p.2

62. Kālidāsa — *Śākuntalam*, Act VI, 17, p. 95.

63. *samyagārādhitā vidyā prabodhavinayāviva* ।
— *Raghu*, X.71

64. *liperyathāvad grahaṇena vāṅmayam* ।
—*Ibid.*, III.28

65. *nyastākṣaramakṣara bhūmikāyām kārtasnyena gṛhnāti lipiṁ na yāvad* ।
— *Ibid.*, XVIII.46

Initiation of a Student

Ceremony played a vital role in the life of the people in the Gupta age. *Saṁskāras* are number of practices through which human life from the start purified. The wearing of the sacred thread was called the *upanayana*. *Upanayana* was the marking point of initiation of a student to Vedic studies by the preceptor. In the Gupta age also *upanayana* was distinguished for the first beginning of education. In the *Raghuvaṁśa* we find Raghu was initiated.[66] A good teacher must impart his knowledge to his pupils without any discrimination. Teacher was not supposed to impart his knowledge only to the intelligent student. If the student was meritorious and could acquire mastery in the subject, the teacher was credited with but if the pupil seemed to be dull and slow in grasping his study the teacher was not blamed.[67] Still the teacher was highly esteemed and exalted in a venerable position if the teacher had the power of excellence of imparting education to his pupil of little merits and succeed in grasping the sense of a subtle art of science.[68]

Teacher

The teacher was treated with great reverence and high esteem even by the sovereign.[69] In the *Raghuvaṁśa* we find Dilīpa and Sudakṣiṇā showing reverence to Vasiṣṭha and Arundhatī after reaching the

66. *athopanītam vidhivad vipaścito vininyurenaṁ guravo gurupriyam* ।
— *Raghu.*, III.29

67. *pātraviśeṣe nyāstam guṇāntaram vrajati śilpamādhātuḥ* ।
jalamiva samudraśuktau muktāphalatām payodasya ।।
— *Mālavikā*, I.6

68. *upadeśam viduḥ śuddham santastamupadeśinaḥ* ।
śyāmāyate na yuṣmāsu yaḥ kāñcanamivāgniṣu ।।
— *Ibid.*, II.9

69. *tayorjagṛhatuḥ pādān rājā rājñī ca māgadhī* ।
tau gururgurupatnī ca prītyā pratinandatuḥ ।।
— *Raghu*, I.57

āśrama of the preceptor. In fact, the capacity of the pupil to receive and absorb his teacher's training was supposed to grow in proportion to the *saṁskāras* of his earlier birth.

In the *Raghuvaṁśa* Aja showed reverence to Vasiṣṭha.[70] Everybody including the sovereign showed respect to the preceptor. The idea of preceptor so exalted that it was supposed that nothing was unattainable by him, which he desired. He was pure and mighty as the sun. From the *Raghuvaṁśa* it is clear that the status and ability were such that the king, i.e., Aja again and again approached him for advice to face his difficulties.[71] His position was such that the sovereign along with his wife approached him personally.

The common name for the teacher were *guru*[72] and *ācārya*.[73] The *guru* was generally the head of his establishment. In an institution there were several teachers. The diversity of subjects creates the need of multiplicity of teachers. In this context it may be mentioned that

---

70. *gurorbhavān darśitaśiṣyabhaktiḥ* । — *Raghu*, II.46
71. *Ibid.*, *op. cit.*
72. *vininyurenaṁ guravo gurupriyaṁ* — *Ibid.*, II.44, III.29
gurudakṣiṇārthī । — *Ibid.*, V.1
gurvarthamāhartumaham yatiṣye । — *Ibid.*, V.17
gurudakṣināai । — *Ibid.*, V 20.1
gurvarthamarthī । — *Ibid.*, V.29
gurupradeyādhikaniṣpṛho'rthī. — *Ibid.*, V.31
guroranujñāṁ — *Ibid.*,V.38
yāvadupasthitām homavetām gurave nivedayāmi । — *Śākuntalam*, Act IV
73. *kimidaṁ śiṣyopadeśakāle yugapadācāryābhyāmātropa-sthānam?* — *Mālavikā*, I
ubhāvabhinayācāryam paraśparajayaiṣīnāṁ । — *Ibid.*, I.10

Hiuen-Tsang in his visit eye-witnessed a hundred professors lecturing at one time on many diverse subjects in the University of Nālandā.[74]

The religious preceptor was known by the simple term *guru*. Another type of teacher was called *upādhyāya*[75] who most probably worked under the *guru* or *kulapati*.[76] The term *kulapati* is mentioned when referring Kaṇva in *Śākuntalan*. It may be pointed out that in modern time *kulapati* is generally used in the sense of a Vice-Chancellor of an university.

After the completion of the study, the *godāna* ceremony was performed and the student married. The graduate or *snātaka* married immediately after. Those who are professionals, performed the *godāna* ceremony.[77] Even the sovereign used to please the *guru* by saluting in his feet.[78]

Students

The term *śiṣya* is used in the sense of student. Some students were naturally slow[79] as well as some students were brilliant.[80] As for example, Raghu and Mālavikā were brilliant. Mālavikā is quoted as *medhāvinī* (very intelligent) and *paramanipuṇā* (proficient in her subject). The teacher was credited for choicing and initiating an intelligent pupil. It was presumed that the degree of success varied

---

74. Watter's translation of Hiu-en-Tsang, Nalanda, 165.
75. *Vik*, pp. 60, 61.
76. *api nāma kulapateriyamasavarṇakṣetrasaṁbhavā syāt?*
— *Śāk*, Act I
77. *athāsya godānavidheranantaraṁ vivāhadīkṣāṁ niravartayad guruḥ* |
— *Raghu*, III.33
78. *tayorjagṛhatuḥ pādān rājā rājñī ca māgadhī* |
tau gururgurupatnī ca prītyā pratinanandatuḥ ||
—*Ibid.*, I.57
79. *mandamedhāḥ* | — *Mālatī*, Act I
80. *dhiyaḥ samagraiḥ sa guṇairudāradhīḥ* | — *Raghu*, III.30

according to the proportion of intellect of the student. Otherwise the skill of the teacher had chances of being wasted in the manner of an article placed in an utensil of bad metal,[81] and bad teachers will fail even with the best methods. Indeed, the goodness of the method becomes in such a case a cause of failure, as, to continue the simile, the perfection of the tool becomes in indisciplined hands a source of imperfection. Consequently no discredit was attached to those teachers who had by chance initiated slow and dull pupils.[82] It was contended that the method of teaching on the part of a teacher should be so excellent as to turn a dull pupil into an intelligent one and make him able to receive the secret of his lore. The excellence of art of teaching of the teacher must not be affected by the dullness of his pupil just as gold remains unimpaired even while tested in fire. It was believed that the capacity of the pupil to receive and absorb his teacher's training depended on the proportion of *saṁskāra*s of his earlier birth.[83] The period of study was observed by the student with *brahmacarya*. During the stay of the student in the house of preceptor, the students were used to serve the preceptor by doing household duties. It was their holy duty to collect fuel for the oblation. In *Abhijñānaśākuntalam* we find Vaikhānasa, Śārṅgarava, Śāradvata, Hārīta and Gautama were the dwellers in the hermitage of Kaṇva. If necessary the student performed other types of duties also as ordered by the preceptor. We find that Śārṅgarava and Śāradvata accompanied Śakuntalā while she went to her-in-law's house.

After the period of *brahmacarya* and the education was over, the prince had generally finished the period of learning. We find Raghu as

---

81. *pātraviśeṣe nyāstaṁ guṇāntaraṁ vrajati śilpamādhātuiḥ* ।
— *Mālatī*, I.6

avandhyayatanāśca babhuvuratra te ।
kriyā hi vastūpahitā prasīdati ॥ — *Raghu*, III.29

82. *yadā punarmandamedhā śiṣya upadeśaṁ* ।
malinayanti tadā ācāryasya na doṣaḥ ॥ — *Mālatī*, p. 269

83. *sthiropadeśāmupadeśakāle prapedire prāktanajanmavidyāḥ* ।
— *Kumāra*, I.30

thin by living with fruits of forest.[84] He is called now as *varṇī*[85] and *dvija*. The prince was dressed, in skin[86] and finished the education. The skin was the normal clothes of prince during the study. He went through the ceremony of tonsure, i.e., *godāna*, after which he married.[87] The prince became mature in body resplendent in youth.[88] Manu fixed the age of tonsure in case of a kṣatriya as twenty-two, while Kauṭilya enjoins it in the sixteenth year. According to the *Arthaśāstra* the prince should observe celibacy till he became sixteen-year-old. After that he would observe the ceremony of tonsure and marry. Kālidāsa agrees with the view of Kauṭilya in case of marrying after tonsure and marriage after completion of studies. According to Kālidāsa, the ceremony of tonsure would commence twice — once before, then after education. It is significant that by the first tonsure *cūḍākaraṇa* ceremony has been meant and by the second the completion of the study *godāna* was meant. According to Kālidāsa long hair of the male student, after mastery of the Vedas, was cut at the age of sixteen years.[89] From these it may be concluded that the education of boy as a *brahmacārin* started probably at the age of five or six and the student continued to study in the *āśrama* of his preceptor till he was fifteen or sixteen-year-old. All these studies implied the existence of the organized system of education.

Fees

The ancient education policy was significant in charging the fees. It seems that no fee was charged from the pupil. At the end of the student

---

84. *śarīramātrena narendra tiṣthannābhāsi tīrthapratipāditadhiḥ* ।
araṇyakopattaphalaprasutiḥ stambena nībāra ivāvaśiṣṭaḥ ॥
—*Raghu.*, V.15

85. *varṇāśramāṇām gurave sa varṇī* । —*Ibid.*, V.19

86. *tvacaṁ sa medhayaṁ paridhāya rauravīṁ* । —*Ibid.*, III.3

87. *athāsya godānavideranantaram* ।
vivāhādīkṣām niravartayad guruḥ ॥ —*Ibid.*, III.33

88. *raghuḥ kramād yauvanabhinnaśaiśavaḥ*
puposa gāmbhiryamanoharaṁ vapuḥ ॥ —*Ibid.*, III.32

89. *Raghu*, III.28, 33. — *op. cit.*

life[90] the pupil presented to his teacher *gurudakṣiṇā* which can be described as fee for teaching.[91]

But a section of teachers considered too low for them to receive fee or *gurudakṣiṇā* from the student. Even offering fees to them sometimes caused their wrath.[92] As the person who taught for an income, was particularly marked as those who were in trade of learning[93] and considered as condemnable. So there was a marked reluctance on the part of the *guru* to receive anything as fee.

Kālidāsa has shown us that on meeting one another the practice of salutation was observed.[94] A disciple fell at the feet of his preceptor[95] as a son did to his parents.[96] It was the common practice to show

---

90. *upāttavidyām vidhivad gurubhaystm* । —*Raghu*,V. 38
yatastvayā jñānamaśeṣaprāptam । —*Ibid.*, V.4
91. *śrutaniṣkrayasya* । —*Ibid.*,V.22
92. *samāptavidyena mayā maharṣirvijñāpito abhud gurudakṣiṇāai* । —*Ibid.*, V.20
93. *nirbandhasanjātarūṣārthakārśyamacintayitā guruṇā ahamuktaḥ* ।। —*Ibid.*, V.2
94. R.N. Saletore, *Life in the Gupta Age*, p. 125.
95. *tayorjagṛhatuḥ pādān rājā rājñī ca māgadhī* ।
tau gururgurupatnī ca prītya pratinanandatuḥ ।। —*Ibid.*, I.57
96. *tau nideśakaraṇodyatau piturdhanvinau caraṇayornipatatuḥ* ।
bhūpaterapi tayoḥ pravatsyatornamrayorupari vāṣpavindavaḥ ।। —*Ibid.*, XI.4-5
tau piturnayanajena vāriṇā kiñciduksita śikhaṇḍla kāvubhau । —*Ibid.*, XI.5

reverence to the elder and in turn the elders conveyed their blessings.[97]

The student as well as the ordinary man in the Gupta age had a system of calculating time. Kālidāsa in the *Raghuvaṁśa* has stated that when a pupil was asked how much of the night remained, he announced that it was dawn. He might make the observation by looking about in the open. But most probably a more reliable practice was in use. The night was divided into four watches (*yāma*) after sunset. If the sunset used to take place at six or six-thirty in the evening, then after the first watch, people generally went to bed.

Great care and attention was bestowed on the royal child. After the performance of the tonsure (*cūla*) ceremony, the young prince, associated by the sons of his father's courtiers (*amātyaputrāḥ*) of the same age, learnt the alphabets. After learning his alphabet, the thread ceremony (*upanītam*) was performed in accordance with precept.[98] After the ceremony he learnt the art of using missiles, clad in the sacred skin of the Ruru. After the learning of art of missiles the completion of the ceremony of cropping the hair (*godāna*) took place. After the ceremony of *godāna* he was married.

One of the prominent poet of Gupta age was Vīrasena. Vīrasena was also known as Sāba. He was not only a composer but also a high military official and minister of the King. He was a *saciva* and *sandhivigrahika* of Candragupta II. His family name was Vīrasena and he is described as "known the meaning of words and logic, and the (ways of) mankind". He was a native of Pāṭaliputra, belonged to the Kautsa *gotra*, being a devotee of god Śambhu and a poet.[99]

---

97. *lakṣmaṇānucarameva rāghuvaṁ netumaicchadṛṣirityasau nṛpaḥ* ।
āśiṣaṁ prayuyuje na vāhinīṁ sā hi rakṣanavidhau tayoḥ kṣamā ॥
— *Raghu*, XI.6

98. *abhucca namraḥ praṇipātāśikṣayā piturmuda tena tatāna sārbhakaḥ* ।
— *Raghu*, III.25

99. *Corpus Inscriptionum Indicarum*, III (6), pp. 35-6.

The author of the *Kaumudī-mahotsava* is described as contemporary of Kālidāsa. The writer was most probably a lady and named Kiśorikā. Mr. Ramakrishna Kavi calls her Vijjikā. K.P. Jayaswal called Kiśorikā a contemporary of Kalyāṇavarman of Pāṭaliputra and consequently ascribed her to the time of Samudragupta. He is of the opinion that *Kaumudī-mahotsava* is nearer to Kālidāsa's time than that of Bhāsa's.[100] The language, metre and idea of *Kaumudī-mahotsava* bear similarity with the works of Kālidāsa. The idea that Kālidāsa has borrowed the ideas, etc. from an anonymous and unknown poetess is a far-fetched idea. On the other hand the contrary is certainly possible. Though K.P. Jayaswal[101] is of opinion that the drama was written about AD 340, there are reasons laid by D.C. Sircar and R. Kavi propounding *Kaumudī-mahotsava* a post-Kālidāsa work.[102]

Kumāradāsa of Ceylon was a contemporary of Kālidāsa. Kumāradāsa has been known in India by the name of Nāthakumāra and Kumāradatta. A verse of Nāthakumāra quoted in the *Sūktimuktāvalī* of Jalhana is the same as that in the *Jānakīharaṇa* (I.2). The *Subhāṣitāvalī* cited stanzas under the name of Kumāradatta, which are traceable in *Jānakīharaṇa* of Kumāradāsa. Kumāradatta may be an erroneous reading for Kumāradāsa caused by similarity of orthography.

Bhoja in his *Śṛṅgāraprakāśa*[103] mentions the *Jānakīharaṇa* and Soḍḍhala speaks of Kumāradāsa in his *Udayasundarīkathā*.[104] Two grammatical works, i.e., *Bhāṣāvṛtti* of Puruṣottamadeva, and the

---

100. K.P. Jayaswal, *Annals of the Bhandarker Oriental Research Institute*, XII, pp. 54, 51; *Kaumudi-mahotsava* (Dakshinabhart Sanskrit Series, No. 4), p. 1.

101. K.P. Jayaswal, *History of India*, p. 51.

102. D.C. Sircar, *Journal of the Andhra Historical Research Society*, XI, pp. 63-7; M.R. Kavi, *Journal of Andhra Historical Research Society*, III, pt. II, Intr., p. iv.

103. Bhoja, *Śṛṅgāraprakāśa*, IX.

104. *Udayasundarīkathā*, Gaekwad's Oriental Series, 1920, p. 154.

Uṇādisūtravṛtti of Ujjvaladatta cited stanzas from *Jānakīharaṇa*. Stanzas from the poems have been traced in the following anthologies: *Sūktimuktāvalī*, *Subhāṣitāvalī*, *Subhāṣitaratnabhāṇḍāgara*, and *Subhāṣitaratnakoṣa*. *Jānakīharaṇa* is cited by name in the *Kāvyamīmāṁsā*, and the *Ṭīkāsarvasva* of Sarvānanda.

In the *Jānakīharaṇa* scattered references of education can be found while describing the son of Aja, it is stated that Aja's son whose speed of horses in the form of organs of sense was obstructed by wisdom, originated from his study of all *śāstras*.[105]

While describing slender waist of Kauśalyā, wife of Daśaratha it is described that the waist was fastened by a band or string in order to prevent their further growth. While describing this expression *guṇa*, *vṛddhi* and *niṣedha* — terms of grammar were used. So it is clear that the study of Sanskrit grammar was common to all.[106]

After initiation the student wore triple-string, girdle of *muñja* grass and a dress made of the barks of trees.[107]

The knowledge of Sāṁkhya philosophy was known to the poet. So it is stated that life was regulated by *sattva*, *rajas* and *tamas* quality.[108]

Ascetics were conversant with the Vedas and Vedāṅgas.[109]

The knowledge of politics was in an advanced stage. It is found that Rāma sent Aṅgada to the fort of *rākṣasa* to collect information about the affairs of that state. This information helps us to ascertain which

---

105. *jigīṣurabhyastasamastaśāstrajñānoparūddhendriya vājivegāḥ* ।
— *Jānakīharaṇa*, 1.14

106. *rasanāguṇena śroṇī punarvṛddhiniṣedhahetoḥ* ।
— *Ibid.*, I.30

107. *mauñjī taruvalkalaśca* । — *Ibid.*, I.8

108. *tridhā te samabhūdyogaḥ spṛṣṭasattvarajastamāḥ* ।
— *Ibid.*, II.17

109. *svavedavedāṅgavid* । — *Ibid.*, V.4

of the four means, i.e., *sāma*, *dāma*, *daṇḍa* or *bheda* was fit to win the enemy.[110]

The *Āyurveda* was also cultivated at that age. If one wished one's good, if it was not pleasing, one must be forgiven as if the medicine was pungent, and the motive of physician was not bad.[111] Suṣeṇa, the physician, found the medicinal herb in the slope of the mountain and being pleased, he applied it to Lakṣmaṇa who within a moment opened his eyes.[112]

The knowledge of grammar was well established. The use of *avyaya* by scholar has been compared with the arrangement of dwellings of *kirātas* with famous *siddhas*.[113]

In the *Jānakīharaṇa Kumāradāsa* refers to the painter's brush. The details about the wall-painting show the popularity of it in this age.

The line of new hair of Kauśalyā has been compared with the crops of fallen black colour from the unstable brush of the creators (I.33).

Indragopa (an insect) is compared with the drops of colour fallen from the brush of the creator (XI.80).

---

110. *veditum caturupāyavidhīnāṁ kasya gamya iti kauśikaśatrum* |
— *Jānakīharaṇa*, XV.1

111. *auṣadhāni virasāni tathāpi dveṣyabhāvamupayāti na vaidyaḥ* |
— *Ibid.*, XV.43

112. *havirbhiṣagbhudharasānuto nuto mahauṣadhiṁ prāpya mudā tatastataḥ* |
cakāra rāmāvarajaṁ hṛtaklamamahī punaḥ samunmīlita vīkṣaṇam kṣaṇāt |
— *Ibid.*, XIX.2

113. *nānu vidadhāti pādapuraṇāni prathitayatāvācak kirātadeśāḥ* |
viṣadamatibhikhyayāḥ prabandhe racita ivārthavatīva viprahīnāḥ ||
— *Ibid.*, XX.52

Thus it can be proved that study of painting was well-known at that time.[114]

The *Kundamālā* of Diṅnāga had been a long forgotten name of the domain of Sanskrit dramatic literature. First H.H. Wilson mentioned the name only in the 'list of Hindu plays'.[115] Burnell mentioned the name of this book in Classified Index.[116] From this Index Aufrecht collected his information.[117] The *Kundamālā* is a play of six acts and is based on the conclusion of the *Rāmāyaṇa* story, beginning with the incident where Lakṣmaṇa took Sītā in banishment, and ending with the consecration of Kuśa and Lava as Rāma's heirs. From the different readings of manuscripts four different names of the author have been suggested by the scholars. These are Diṅnāga, Dhīranāga, Vīranāga and Nāgayya. M. Ramakrishna Kavi and Rāmanātha Śāstrī, in their edition of the *Kundamālā* ascribe the authorship of the drama to Diṅnāga, the great Buddhist scholar. Perhaps they might have been influenced by Mallinātha who remarked in the commentary on *Meghadūta*[118] that Diṅnāga was the rival of Kālidāsa. Dakṣiṇāvarta-nātha an ancient commentator, who was earlier than Mallinātha, has also the same reference.[119] It is clear from this discussion that both

114. Ratna Chanda, *Kumāradāsa: A Study,* Calcutta: Sanskrit Pustak Bhandar, 1990.

115. H.H. Wilson, *The Theatre of the Hindus,* 2nd edn., London, 1835, p. lxx.

116. Burnell, *A Classified Index to the Sanskrit Manuscript in the Palace of Tanjore,* London, 1880, p. 168.

117. Aufrecht, *Catalogus Catalogorum*, Vol. I, p. 283.

118. *dinnāgācāryasya kālidāsapratipakṣasya* ।
— Mallinātha on verse 14, *Pūrva Megha*, *Megadūta*

119. *diṅnāgānām anena diṅnāgācāryo vivakṣitaḥ* । *sthūlahastā-valepananena prabandhadūṣana-samaye sthūlahastābhina-yaśca vivakṣitāḥ* । *ayaṁ abhiprāyaḥ-dinnāga iti ko'pyācāryaḥ kālidāsaprabandhān anyatrokto'yamārtha iti sthūlāhastā-bhinayair dūṣyati* । *tam ācāryaṁ svaprabandhasyāpūrvār-thābhidhāyitvam āśritya meghopadeśavyājena kavir upālabhata iti* ।

these commentators cited Diṅnāga as a learned *ācārya* and rival of Kālidāsa, but do not specifically mention him as the Buddhist logician. Veda Vyāsa and Śarandās Bhanoṭ, the other joint editors of the drama, is of opinion, that Diṅnāga was a Hindu poet and not a Buddhist logician.[120] Jayacandra Śātrī refers to the Tanjore manuscript where the author's name is given as Dhīranāga[121] but he is of the opinion that it is a scribal mistake and the author's real name should be Diṅnāga. Krishna Kumar Dhavan Śāstrī also is of opinion that the name Dhīranāga is erroneously scribed and the author is Diṅnāga.[122] V. Varadacārī[123] and F.W. Thomas[124] have also ascribed the authorship of the drama to Diṅnāga.

M. Krishnamachariar opines that the mention of Diṅnāga as the author of *Kundamālā* is an error and the name of the author is Dhīranāga, a Bhadanta, who lived at Āralapura, sometime earlier than the fifth century AD.[125]

In spite of difference of opinions, the name Diṅnāga is very familiar and seems to be the real one. As the drama deals with such theme which is against Buddhistic beliefs and ideas, Diṅnāga's identity with the Buddhist logician cannot be tolerated.

Though the definite date of Diṅnāga is uncertain, the influence of Bhāsa and Kālidāsa can be distinctly perceived in his drama. As the theme and treatment of the *Kundamālā* are closely identical with the *Uttararāmacarita* of Bhavabhūti, the author of the *Kundamālā* might have flourished near about the time of Bhavabhūti, i.e., around AD 700.

120. *Kundamālā*, edited by Veda Vyāsa and Śarandās Bhanoṭ, Lahore, 1932, Introduction, pp. iv ff.
121. *Kundamāla*, edited by Jayacandra Sūri, Lahore, 1929, p. 2.
122. *Kundamālā*, Jallandhar, 1995, Introduction, pp. 2 ff.
123. V. Varadacārī, *A History of Sanskrit Literature,* Allhabad, 1960, p. 150.
124. F.W. Thomas, "The Kundamālā of Diṅnāga Ācārya", in *JRAS*, 1924, p. 61.
125. M. Krishnamachriar, *History of Classical Sanskrit Literature,* p. 604.

Scholars like Krishnamachariar and Varadacārī are of the opinion that Bhavabhūti was inspired by the *Kundamālā*, while Dr. S.K. De is in favour of detecting the influence of Bhavabhūti on the *Kundamālā*.

It is depicted that in the hermitage of Vālmīki the chanting of *Sāmaveda* can be heard. The recitation of the Vedas was practised in the hermitage[126] — it was a common scene of India at the Gupta age. The dwellers of the hermitage though inarticulate were being familiar with and charmed by the song of *Sāmaveda*.[127]

Vālmīki composed the *Rāmāyaṇa* and he was zealous in making the *Rāmāyaṇa* to Lava and Kuśa with great care. He wanted to evaluate his work among the common people. Parhaps he had the same feeling of Kālidāsa that unless the audience appreciate the work the author cannot be satisfied (*ā paritoṣād vidūṣām na sādhu manye prayoga-vijñānam*). So the hermitage of Vālmīki was full of song of the *Rāmāyaṇa*.[128]

It is stated that the preceptor was adept in imparting knowledge and good counsel as is evidenced is the comparison made by Sītā with couple of swans.[129]

Kulapati was the term used as synonym of Vice-Chancellor of an university. The sages who managed to teach many students in their hermitages are called *kulapati*, viz., Vālmīki and Kaṇva. In the *Kundamālā*, Vālmikī is called *kulapati*.

---

126. *śrotreṣu saṁmurcchati sāmanādaḥ* |
— *Kundamālā,* Act III, Śl. 9, p. 38

127. *sāmadhvaniśravaṇadattamanovadhāna* |
niṣpanda-manda-mada-vāraṇa-karaṇa-tālāḥ || 8 ||

munīnāṁ sāmagītāni puṇyāni madhurāṇi ca |
pravāsināmapi mano haranti kimu dantīnām || 9 ||
— *Ibid.*, Act III, Śl. 9, p. 38

128. *rāmāyaṇasaṁgīda-aṇimittaṁ vammīli-tapovanam* |
— *Ibid.*, Act IV, p. 48

129. *upadeśaniyuṇo upajjhāyo* — *Ibid.*, Act IV, p. 53

Vālmīki planned the performance of the *Rāmāyaṇa-gīta* to the public by the disciples, Lava and Kuśa. They were proficient in the art and lyre (*vīṇā*) and vocal music. The students always obeyed the order of their preceptor. Obeying the teacher was the first and foremost duty of the student. Vālmīki ordered Lava and Kuśa to perform the song which was taught to them, according to *Gāndharvaveda*.[130]

The relation with the preceptor is established through the initiation ceremony. After the initiation the preceptor started to teach the Vedas and other subjects to the student. In the *Kundamālā*, Lava stated that his preceptor was Vālmīki the realtionship with whom was established by the initiation.[131]

Lava and Kuśa were always obedient to their preceptor. While they were talking with Rāma, the messenger came to call them. They immediately obeyed the order of the preceptor and bade farewell to Rāma.

Three Vedas were taught in the curricula of the study at that age.[132]

The *Mudrārākṣasa* of Viśākhadatta is a historical play. Sten Konow thinks it more likely that Viśākhadatta was one of the court-poets of Candragupta II.[133] The theme of the drama is Candragupta's

---

130. *jadā ahme mandamaddassudigahīraṁ tālalayadukkara-viṇṇāsaṁ mahākayisaṁgadhita mahāpuruṣa caritta bandhaṁ mahātthagaṃbhīram kena bi assudapuvvaṁ āmaṁ gandhabba-vedasamvādi sarasaṁ joavirayivaṇna ramaṇīyayaṁ vīṇātanti-rasidāṇuviddhaṁ gīdaṁ gāyahma tadā viṇṇāṇa-visesa-pasaṇna-hiyayo rāyā jaṁ buttantaṁ aṇuciṭthissadi eso jāṇidavvoti ahmāṇaṁ bhayavado vaṁmīyimahesino ādesotti* । — *Kundamālā*, p. 57
131. *upanayanopadeśena* । — *Ibid.*, p. 85
132. *tribhivedaiḥ* । — *Ibid.*, Act VI
133. *JBORS*, Vol. XXIII, pt. IV, 1937, p. 451.

elevation to the throne of Magadha after the fall of the Nanda dynasty, and the adoption of measure to strengthen his rule by Cāṇakya, the famous politician. In seven Acts the drama depicts the political intrigue of Cāṇakya to win over *rākṣasa*, former minister of the Nandas, to his side.

The passages (i.e., I.2, I.3) of the *Mudrārākṣasa* give some information about the author.[134] He was the grandson of Vaṭeśvara, who was petty chief and son of Pṛthu, raised to the status of a *mahārāja*. His patron was king Candragupta, if the reading *pārthivaścandragupta* is correct. K.T. Telang accepts this reading. There is another reading Avantīvarmā instead of Candragupta. There were two kings named Avantīvarmā. One is the king of Kashmir. As the style of the play is Gauḍī most probably he belonged to the Gauḍa country. The other king was belonged to Maukhari of Kanauj. His eldest son was Grahavarman. Harṣavardhana, whose date was AD 606 sat on the throne after the death of Grahavarman. So king Avantīvarmā cannot be placed later than the close of the sixth century. Prof. Dhruva concludes that he belonged to the sixth century. Jacobi is of opinion to place him under king of Kashmir. The tolerance shown to the Jaina mendicant, Jīvasiddhi confirms the earlier date. The high esteem to Buddha in the seventh Act of the drama (*buddhānāmapi ceṣṭitaṁ sucariteḥ kliṣṭaṁ vaśuddhātmanā*) also supports the earlier date because 'Śaṅkarācārya (*circa* AD 800) dealt a death blow to Buddhism'.

As the theme of the play is political, reference to the education is scattered here and there but has not been discussed properly.

The knowledge of the astronomy with sixty-four divisions was

---

134. *ājñāpito'smi yathādya tvayā sāmanta-vateśvaradatta pautrasya mahārāja-bhāskaradattasunoḥ kaver-viśākhadattasya kṛtirabhinavaṁ mudrārākṣasam nāma nāṭakam nāṭayitavyamiti* । — *Mudrā*, I.2, I.3

known to the *sūtradhāra*. The eclipse of the moon is referred to in a dialogue.[135]

The relation between *upādhyāya* and *śiṣya* is depicted in Cāṇakya and his disciple Śārṅgarava. Śārṅgarava was always eager to attend the preceptor, Cāṇakya. He is seen in the drama supplying the seal and obeying commands of Cāṇakya. It is also clear that Śārṅgarava was residing in the house of the brāhmaṇa preceptor. He had reverence and high esteem for his preceptor. When the spy was asking about his preceptor, he remarked—"Blockhead, do you wish to rob our preceptor of his omniscience?[136] Do you pretend to be better conversant with *dharma* than our preceptor?[137] Sometimes the preceptors were harsh towards the pupil—this is referred to in a dialogue of Cāṇakya. He said that "not the roughness of temper towards pupils naturally is to be found in preceptors".[138] Cāṇakya is compared with Vṛhaspati, the preceptor of gods.

Cāṇakya appointed emissaries conversant with various places, dresses, languages, manners and modes of dealing with strangers. This fact threw a light on subjects of study.[139] Induśarmā is described as proficient in the science of politics, of Uśanas and astronomy in all its sixtyfour divisions. There is no doubt that the study of astronomy and politics was well practised at that age.

---

135. *ārye kṛtaśramo'smi catuḥṣaṣṭyange jyotiḥśāstre . . . candroparāgam prati tu kenāpi vipralabdhāsi*
— *Mudrārākṣasa,* Act 1, ed. by M.R. Kale, p. 16

136. *mūrkha, sarvajñatāmupādhyāyasy corayitumicchāmi* ।
—*Ibid.*, p. 27

137. *dhiṅg mūrkha kiṁ bhavānasmadupādhyāyādapi dharmavittarah* ।
— *Ibid.*, p. 27

138. *na punarupādhyāyasamabhūḥ śiṣyajane duḥśīlatā* ।
— *Ibid.*, p. 20

139. *bahuvidhadeśaveṣabhāṣācārsañcāravedino nānāvyāñjanāḥ praṇidhayaḥ* ।। — *Ibid.*, p. 25

Cāṇakya referred to Induśarmā as his fellow-student (*sahādhyāyī*). So, the relation between the co-students, which is still strong even in matured age is referred.

The relation of teacher and pupil is reflected nicely in some *śloka*s of *Mudrārākṣasa*.

> In this world a pupil, acting in the right way, experiences no check (from his preceptor) when, however, he strays from the proper path through infatuation, the preceptor becomes a good to him, hence a good man who delight in acting according to instruction are ever free from restraint, we for our part are averse to any idependence beyond this.[140]

The ideal preceptor is depicted in Cāṇakya in the *Mudrārākṣasa*. He was honest and free from desire; he could treat even a king as an object of disregard like a grass. So he could call Candragupta, the king, by the name of simply Vṛṣala. He led a very simple life, devoid of any thing of luxury. His house is described like that —

> Here is a piece of stone for breaking cowdung-cakes; here is a stack of the holy grass brought by his young disciples, and the house with its dilapidated walls appears to have the skirts of its roof bent down by the holy sticks exposed for drying.[141]

The study and knowledge of the political science was highly advanced. This fact can be shown through the contents of the play. Three forms of administration is described by Cāṇakya. This shows that the minute details of the political science were cultivated.

Cāṇakya advised Candragupta to pick a sham quarrel with him and manage matters independently for sometime. This pretention also made the obeying disciple unhappy. He expressed his feeling thus:

> My mind has as it were begun to enter the very cavity of the earth though I overstepped the limits of respectfulness by the

140. *Mudrā*, ed. by M.R. Kale, Act III. 6.
141. *Ibid.*, Act III, Śl. 15.

> command of His Honour himself. How indeed, does not shame rend the heart of those who really (wantonly) slight their preceptor?[142]

The study of *Āyurveda* and astronomy was highly advanced and widely practised. So, we find allusion to healing the disease of delusion by the physician.[143] The auspicious day was fixed for marching of kings by calculating the position of constellations.[144]

The preceptor was the guardian of the pupil and was always eager for the welfare of the pupil.[145] In turn, the pupil was eager to obey and respect the preceptor. Thus the highest ideal picture of teacher-pupil relation is depicted in the drama *Mudrārākṣasa*.

The tenth introductory stanza[146] of Subandhu's *Vāsavadattā* states that Vikramāditya, like a lake hath passed away on earth. Taking this line into consideration, Hall is of opinion that Subandhu lived long posterior to the great Vikramāditya of Ujjayinī. But according to Macdonell[147] this view can scarcely be supported and there is good reason to believe him to be identical with Candragupta II who reigned from about AD 374 to 413.[148] While the known basis for assigning a latest date to the composition of Subandhu's romance, the allusion to

142. *Mudrā* ed. by M.R. Kale, Act III, Śl. 33, p. 97.
143. *Ibid.*, Act V, Śl. 18, p. 111.
144. *Ibid.*, Act V, Śl. 20, p. 112.
145. *Ibid.*, Act VII, Śl. 11, p. 93.
146. *sā rasavattā vihatā navakā vilasanti careti no kaṁ kaḥ sarsī'va kīrtiśeṣam gatavati bhūvi vikramāditya*

     Subandhu, *Vasavadattā* edited by Śaṅkaradeva Śastrī, Varanasi, 1954, p. 5.
147. Subandhu — *Vasavadatta: A Romance;* edited by Fitzerald, Hall, Calcutta, 1859; Bibliotheca Indica Series, Introduction, p. 6.
148. A.A. Macdonell, *History of Sanskrit Literature,* London, 1900, pp. 323-4.

Uddyotakara,[149] who probably flourished in the later half of the sixth century. So it cannot be placed prior to the late sixth century AD. The most important allusion is contained in the eleventh stanza of Bāṇa's introduction to *Harṣacarita*.[150]

The morning was described as when the huts of the ascetics awoke intent on studying,[151] the streets were resounded with poetic tales chanted by mendicants in the *vibhāṣā* mode.

The advanced study of philosophy can be proved from the reference to the Mīmāṁsā and Nyāya philosopohies which is reported to have concealed the views of the Digambara Jains.[152]

The popular study of the *Mahābhārata* and the *Harivaṁśa* can be proved from the line — As the *Harivaṁśa* is delightful on account of the appearance of Puṣkara.[153]

The study of astronomy can be traced from the passage which refers to the pairs of fishes and crabs as the zodiac has Pisches, Gemini

---

149. V.A. Smith, *Early History of India From 600 BC to the Muhammadan Conquest,* 2nd edn., Oxford, 1908, pp. 275-83.
nyāyasthitim ivo'ddyotakārasvarūpaṁ ।
— *Vāsavadattā*, edited by Hall, *op. cit.*, p. 235

150. *kavīnāṁ agalad darpo nūnaṁ vāsvadattayā* ।
— Bāṇa, *Harṣacarita,* Introduction, 11th stanza.

151. *prabuddhādhyanakarmaṭheṣu maṭheṣu* ।
— Subandhu, *Vāsavadattā*, edited by Louis H. Gray, 1924, p. 140

152. *mīmaṁsānyāya iva pihita digambara darśana* ।
— *Ibid.*, p. 157

mīmāṁsādarśanena iva tiraskṛtadigambara darśanena ।
— *Ibid.*, p. 257

153. *yaś ca harivaṁśair iva puṣkaraprādurbha varamaṇiyaiḥ.*
— *Ibid.*, p. 157

and cancer.[154] There is thought of *śūla* and *vyāghāta* in *yogas*.[155] Ginzel has discussed this fact.[156]

The advancement of study of Prosody can be proved from the reference to *kusumavicitras*, *vaṁsapatrapatitas*, *sukumāralalitās*, *puṣpitāgrās*, *śikhariṇīs*, *praharṣiṇīs* and *latās*.[157]

The study of *Kāmasūtra* has also been referred to.[158] The advance study of art of writing is stated in a passage.[159] Grammar was cultivated to a great extent.[160] Music is referred to in 'there is interruption of Gāndhāra mode in the musical scele'.[161] Sixtyfour arts have been alluded.[162] The study of philosophy has also been mentioned. The

---

154. *rāśibhir iva mīnamakarakutila mithunāsāṁ gataiḥ* I
Vāsavadattā, p. 157

155. *śūlavyāghātacintā* I —*Ibid.*, p. 162

The *yoga's śūla* (106° 0'-120° 0') and *vyāghāta* (160° 0'- 173° 20') correspond to the ninth and thirteenth lunar mansions respectively.

156. Ginzel, *Handbuch der mathematischen und technischen chronologie*, I., Leipzig, 1906, pp. 359-61.

157. *Vāsavadattā*, p. 157.

158. *Ibid.*, p. 156.

159. *śṛṁkhalabandho varṇagrathanāsu utprekṣā kāvyālaṁkāreṣu* I
—*Ibid.*, p. 163

160. *kvipāṁ sarvavināśaḥ* I —*Ibid.*, p. 163

cf. Pāṇini, 3.2.61, 76; 87, 177.

vyākaraṇameva vitata-strīnadīkṛtyabahulam I
—*Ibid.*, p. 237

161. *gāndhārnavicchedo rāgeṣu* I —*Ibid.*, p. 163

162. *catuḥṣaṣṭikalākalāpavidagdha*
—*Subandhu*, *Vāsavadattā*, edited by Śaṅkardeva Śāstri, Varanasi, 1959, p. 122.

followers of Mīmāṁsā philosophy vanquished the theory of Buddha.[163] The theory of Nyāya philosophy with the knowledge of *samavāyī* cause has been described.[164]

The theory of negation of the Buddhist philosophy regarding perception is also used.[165] The denial of Śruti by Jaina philosophy has been described.[166]

The allusions referred to the subjects of study are many. Vāsavadattā was brilliant with a pair of legs with reddened feet as a grammar had rubricated *pāda*s: with goodly joints as the Bhārata has a hundred books: charming with beautiful ankles as the *Rāmāyaṇa* is charming with its *Sundarakāṇḍa*; with a glorious slender waist as the *chandoviciti* has the glorious *tanumadhya* metres; with hands and ears that must be reckoned with as astronomy has *hasta* and *śravaṇa*; revealing her beauty as the permanence of the Nyāya system has its from Uddyotakara; decked with ornaments as an assembly of Buddhists is decked with the *alaṁkāra*; showing the essence of delight as an Upanisad shows him

---

163. *kecijjaiminimatānusārina iva tathāgatamatadhvaṁsinaḥ* ।
— *Vāsavadatta* p. 127

164. *māneye svasyava naipunyatyaikatre darśanotsukamanasā vedhasā jadattraya-samavāyirūpa-ramāṇūnādāya viracito'yamiti* ।
—*Ibid.*, p. 137

165. *bauddhadarśanamiva pratyakṣadravyamapahnuvānaṁ* ।
—*Ibid.*, p. 164

166. *śrutivacanamiva kṣapitadigambaradarśanam*
—*Ibid.*, p. 164

kaścid baudahasiddhānta iva kṣapitaśrutivacana-darśano'bhavat ।
—*Ibid.*, p. 257

whose being is bliss;[167] beautified as Tārā being the wife of the teacher (Vṛhaspati). Legs of the grammar means the colophons of the *pādas*, or quarter-divisions, of each book of Pāṇini's grammar. The scheme of the *tanumadhya* is — — ∪ / ∪ — —.[168] Two *nakṣatras* or lunar mansions corresponding to Carvi and Aguilae are referred to. The reference to Uddyotakara helps to assign the date. The book of astronomy written by Śūrapāla is referred to in the text.[169]

Bhāravi was a writer probably nearer to this age under consideration, but his date is not yet free from speculation. He himself did not think it necessary to state anything about his family, his native place, his predecessors or contemporaries or even his *guru*. He is remembered in the Aihole Inscription along with Kālidāsa.[170] It is evident from this inscription that Bhāravi was acknowledged as a great poet placed in same row of Kālidāsa in the middle of the seventh century. The Gummareddipur Plate Inscription[171] says that king Durvinīta wrote a commentary on the Canto XV of the *Kirātārjunīyam*. This inscription is assigned to the early part of the sixth century. It

---

167. *vyākaraṇene'va saraktapādena (mahā) bhāratena'va suparvaṇā rāmāyaṇene'va sundarakāṇḍacāruṇā jaṅghāyugalene virājamānām chandovicitim iva bhrājamānatanumadhyāṁ nakṣatravidyām iva gaṇanīyahastaśravaṇām nyāya (vidyām) ivo'- ddyotakārasvarūpam (satkavikāvya-racanām) ivā'- laṁkāra (prasādhitam) upaniṣadam iva (sānandam raviprabham iva lokam)* — *Vāsavadattā*, pp. 207-8

168. Weber, *Über die Metrik der Inder,* Berlin, 1863, pp. 365-6.

169. *śūlapālacittavṛttimiva phalitaganikārikām* ।
— *Ibid*., pp. 216-17

170. *yenāyoji na veśma sthiramarthavidhau vivekinā jinaveśma* ।
sa vijayatāṁ ravikīrtiḥ kavitāśrita kālidāsa bhāravi-kīrtiḥ ।
— *Epigraphia Indica*, VI, No. I, p.7

171. *Indian Antiquary*, Vol. XLII, p. 204.

rarely happens that the merits of an author are recognised in a few years. So it can be assumed that Bhāravi most probably wrote his work one century before the date of writing commentary on his work by royal commentator. Thus it may be assumed that Bhāravi lived by or before the end of the fourth century AD. Bhāravi was certainly not the contemporary of Kālidāsa. Bhāravi lived in an age of artificial poetry quite contrary to the style of Kālidāsa. R.C. Dutt's remark on the merit of Bhāravi may be quoted. "In the richness of a creative fancy, in true tenderness and pathos, and even in the sweetness and melody of verse, Kālidāsa is incomparably a greater poet. But nevertheless Bhāravi boasts of a vigour of thought and of language, a spirited and lofty eloquence in expression, which Kālidāsa seldom equals."[172]

That the study of politics was well advanced and practised — can be proved by the study of the *Kirātārjunīyam*. In the second canto of the work it is stated that the science of politics, though intricate, can be divided into (well grasped) when a passage to it is made (by close study), just as a body of water (a lake, etc.) can be entered into when a descent to it is made, but, in such a case it is exceeding difficult to find that person who can well set forth the path of action to be pursued.[173] Policy of statecraft has been delineated as five constituents.[174]

Efficacy of speech is compared with medicine. The speech should be short (as compared with the vastness of the subject), of high significance, beneficial in the end though painful to those who have lost their spirit, as is observed in a highly potent medicine, though very small in quantity, which is repugnant to the weak, put productive of good in the end.[175] This shows the study of oratory as well as the science of medicine in this age.

---

172. R.C. Dutt, *Civilization in Ancient India.*

173. Bhāravi — *Kirātārjunīyam,* ed. by M.R. Kale, 4th reprint edn., Varanasi, 1988, Canto II, 3, p. 90.

174. *prabhavaḥ khalu kośadaṇḍayoḥ kṛtapañāṅgavinirṇayo nayaḥ* ।
— *Ibid.*, II.12, pp. 102-3

175. *Ibid.*, Canto II, 4, pp. 91-2.

The subjects of study have been described. The four branches of learning are referred to.[176] They are *ānvikṣikī*, *trayī*, *vārtā* and *daṇḍanīti*.

Bhāravi is famous for his *arthagauravam*. So, the excellence and requisite of a good speech or composition has been mentioned in the second canto of the *Kirātārjunīyam*.[177]

The knowledge is the only means of obtaining the object like a well placed lamp. Regular incessant study is the means of acquiring knowledge. Correct knowledge of the *śāstras* adorns a person. In the matter of execution of duties, correct and definite knowledge of the *śāstras* acquired by keen study helps one to discriminate the right path.[178]

The essential quality of a student is humility. Arjuna's approaching to Vyāsa is compared with the nature of a disciple.[179]

The power of *yoga* is described. *Yoga* is the training of proper contemplation or concentration of the mind on one object, drawn away from others and suspension of its functions. It is assumed that when perfection is reached in contemplation, one gets superhuman power.[180] It shows the training of mind, propagated by the ancient India, was essential as the preparation for acquiring knowledge which is difficult to be attained otherwise. By the word *tattva*, the knowledge of Sāṁkhya is referred to. In the third canto of the *Kirātārjunīyam*, Vyāsa advised Arjuna to prepare himself by practising *yoga* and following the code of moral conduct for acquiring *vidyā*. This shows that the importance of psychological training was thoroughly understood and followed by the eminent educators at that age.

---

176. *catasṛṣvapi te vivekinī nṛpa vidyāsu nirūdimāgatā* |
— *Kirātārjunīyam,* Canto II, 6, pp. 94-5

177. *Ibid.*, Canto II.27, p. 122.

178. *Ibid.*, Canto II. 32, 33, pp. 128-31.

179. *vasannivānte vinayena jiṣṇuḥ* ||
— *Ibid.*, Canto III.24, p. 192

180. *Ibid.*, Canto III. 26f., pp. 194f.

Bhartṛhari as a poet is a very popular name. Almost nothing of his life, even to his actual period, can be stated with any certainty. But popular belief place him in the Gupta age.

In *Nītiśataka* while describing *vidvatpaddhati* section it is stated that *śāstra* is to be handed over to disciples.[181] Knowledge is such a treasure which cannot be stolen; it enhances when it is given in charity and never diminishes.[182] The science of speech is the only ornament of men.[183] Knowledge is the greatest wealth. Knowledge embellishes a man. It is hidden treasure, preceptor among preceptors, friends in distant land, and cause of reverence even among kings. A person deviod of knowledge is devoid of everything.[184]

Bāṇabhaṭṭa is another source of information and indispensable authority. He is the author of the early seventh century. But his reference must be cited in the discussion on the education as the educational theory and policy did not change in short interval. In his works, *Kādambarī* and *Harṣacarita*, he narrated the social as well as cultural picture of that day. That Kālidāsa must have invariably recorded contemporary usage concerning the details of teachers and the student life can be proved by internal evidence pertaining to the days of Bāṇa, though there was gap of a century between two writers.

---

181. *śāstropaskṛtaśabdasundaragiraḥ śiṣya pradeyāgama* |
Bhartṛhari — *Śatakatrayam*, ed. by Dāmodara Dharmānanda Kosāmbī, Bombay, 1946, Śl. 11, p. 7

182. *haturyātī na gocaram kimapi śaṁpuṣpāni yat sarvadā* |
pārthibhyaḥ pratipādyamānamaniśaṁ prāpnoti vṛddhiṁ parām ||
— *Ibid*., Śl. 12, p. 7

183. *satataṁ vāgbhūṣaṇaṁ bhūṣaṇam* || — *Ibid*., Śl. 15, p. 9

184. *vidyā nāma narasya rūpamadhikaṁ pracchannaguṇaṁ dhanaṁ* |
vidyā bhogakarī yaśaḥsukhakarī vidyā gurunāṁ guruḥ |
vidyā bandhujano videśāgamane vidyā parā devatā |
vidyā rājasu pūjyate na hi dhanaṁ vidyāvihīnaḥ ||
— *Ibid*., Śl. 16, pp. 9-10

Bāṇa was himself a great scholar. He thoroughly studied the Veda with its six *aṅgas* and heard lectures of *śāstras* as far as possible.

Bāṇa in his *Harṣacarita*, has given his family history. As he was born in Vātsyāyana clan and his father was reputed brāhmaṇa as well as a teacher the atmosphere of his house was filled with advanced culture and study. Young lads recited the hymns of the *Yajur* and *Sāma-veda*. Even the parrots and *sārikā* birds could recite verses. As his father daily expounded all the extensive lores, the ever-growing crowds of pupils used to come there, intent on listening to those in the morning.

According to Bāṇa, the students had to study not only the Vedas but in addition had to attend to the daily mastery of the Vedas, they had to follow classes in the exposition of grammar, without idly spending their time in a series of emulous discussions. They had to participate in 'Logic Society' where they discussed the problems of science of logic (*Tarkaśāstra*). They exhibited excessive delight in the Mīmāṁsā.[185]

A boy at the age of five or six years was sent to a teacher's house and lived under the preceptor's roof till the age of fourteen years and returned from his teacher's house as a *snātaka*;[186] when a boy was such a student he wore long tawny braids of hair and forehead was marked with white sectarian marks.[187] It is evident that the tutorial system and repetition of instruction of oral system of imparting knowledge was prevalent; while describing Bāṇa's brothers, who were preceptors, Bāṇa describes them as "man of culture, holding the status of preceptors, expounders of Nyāya, deep in the study of able works, receiving only good words, both in the world and in grammar versed in the acts of all monarchs and sages of old, inspired in mind by the *Mahābhārata*, acquainted with all legends, great in wisdom and poetry, full of eagerness to know stories of heroes, thirsting not for elixir, but that of listening to

---

185. Bāṇa, *Harṣacarita*, p. 71.
186. *Ibid.*, p. 32.
187. *Ibid.*, pp. 73-4.

well-turned phrases, foremost in years, speech, distinction, asceticism, the conference, the festival, in person and in sacrifice". Teachers were expected to attain a high standard of knowledge, specially in the fields of Veda, Nyāya, Purāṇa, Nītiśāstra, Vyākaraṇa and general knowledge.

The study of medicine was in practice. Bāṇa gives an elaborate account of the treatment administered by the court physicians to king Prabhākaravardhana. Harṣa saw in the palace where his father lay ill; he "detected an ardour of boiling oil, butter and decoctions emitting a steam scented with various draughts".[188]

Dancing and visual performance were common in this age. An eloquent picture of a dance in action has been given by Bāṇa when he describes the festivities of the dancing girls on the birth of prince Harṣa.[189]

According to a tradition there were nine contemporaries of Kālidāsa.[190] Bhartṛ Maṇṭha, the author of *Hayagrīva-vadha* has been ascribed to *circa* AD 430.[191] As his work is lost, nothing can be said of him. He does not seem to have one of the nine. Varāhamihira, the astronomer is believed to be one of these jewels. As he selected Śaka 427 or AD 505 as the initial of his astronomical calculation, it is very likely that he lived about this age.

Ancient India could be boast of a few persons devoted to the advancement of mathematics and astronomical calculation. Generally astronomical works includes some chapters on mathematics.

---

188. Bāṇa, Harṣacarita, p.138.

189. *Ibid.*, pp. 113-4.

190. *dhanvantariḥ kṣapaṇako amarasimhaḥ śankur* ।
vetālabhaṭṭa ghaṭakarparo kālidāsaḥ ।
khyāto varāhamihiro nṛpateḥ sabhāyāṁ
ratnāni vai vararucir nave vikramasya ॥
— cited from *Jyotirvidābharaṇa* by Vidyābhūṣaṇa, *History of Medieval School of Indian Logic,* p. 15

191. Krishnamacariar, *History of Classical Sanskrit Literature,* p. 129.

Colebrooke is of opinion that as Varāhamihira is mentioned by name in the first book of the *Pañcatantra* he must be anterior to or contemporary with Khusrau Nushirwan, king of Persia, in whose reign (AD 531-79) it was rendered into Pahlavī.[192] Varāhamihira perhaps flourished towards the close of the fifth century AD.[193] L.D. Swamikannu Pillai arrives at AD 523 as the year of zero *ayanāṁśa* and therefore the epoch of *Pañcasiddhāntikā*.[194] Varāhamihira shows acquaintance with *Arthaśāstra* of Kauṭilya and *Kāmasūtra* of Vātsyāyana.[195]

Varāhamihira wrote works in three branches of astronomy, viz. (1) *tantra* or mathematical astronomy, (2) *horā* including nativity, horoscopy etc., (3) *saṁhitā* or mundane astrology.[196] He wrote *Pañcasiddhānitkā*, *Vṛhatsaṁhitā*, *Vṛhajjātaka*, *Vṛhadvivāhapaṭala* and *Vṛhadyātrā* along with the abridged versions, the *Laghujātaka*, the *Svalpavivāhapaṭala* and the *Svalpayātrā*.

Varāhamihira has cited four traditional *vidyās*.[197] Varāhamihira referred to grammarians,[198] *mīmāṁsakas*,[199] poets,[200] *kāvyajña*[201] and gatherings of poets and scholars.[202] It is stated that one well-versed in grammar alone, is laughed at in a poets' gathering. A student who change teachers frequently is alluded to with pointed scorn. He directs that *yogayātrā* should not be taught to a pupil who has stayed only for

---

192. Colebrooke, *Miscellaneous Essays*, II, pp. 167, 173; cf. Kern, *Introduction to Bṛhatsaṁhitā*, pp. 19-20.
193. Colebrooke, *Miscellaneous Essays*, II, pp. 481-2.
194. *Indian Ephimeries,* Vol. I, pt. I, Appendix II, pp. 457-8.
195. A.B. Keith, *A History of Sanskrit Literature,* pp. 461, 469.
196. Varāhamihira, *Bṛhatsaṁhtā,* I.9.
197. *Ibid.*, XIX.11.
198. *vyākaraṇābhiyukta — Yogayātrā,* V.6.
199. *Ibid.,* IV.24.
200. *"Kavi", Ibid.,* V.3, 17, XVI.18, XIX.12, XXXII.11.
201. *Ibid.*, V.6.
202. *viduṣām samavāya — Ibid.*, V.7.

a short time with his teacher.[203] A student revering his teacher has been complimented.[204] A tree, palm-leaf, cloth, lotus-leaf, reeds leather and silk are named as writing materials.[205]

In the works of Varāhamihira references to the *Arthaśāstra*, *Kāmasūtra*, philosophy, palmistry, study of metrics amply prove the vast literature on various subjects flourished at that age.

In the history of science in India, Āryabhaṭa I (born in AD 476), who made notable contribution to the development of astronomy and mathematics, has a distinct place. The year of birth of Āryabhaṭa is stated with precision in his work. He has stated that "when sixty times sixty years and three quarter-*yuga*s has elapsed (of the current *yuga*), twenty-three years had been passed since my birth".[206] Since the *kali* year 3600 corresponds to AD 499 it follows that Āryabhaṭa I was born in the year AD 476. Buddhagupta reigned at Pāṭaliputra from AD 476-96. So he was born in the year when Buddhagupta ascended the throne.

Āryabhaṭa is hailed as the originator of the Epicyclitic astronomy in India.[207] He remodelled the prevalent system of Indian astronomy on a scientific basis, provided it with modified parameters, new tools and techniques, also more accurate methods of calculation.

Āryabhaṭa I worte at least two works on astronomy, viz. (1) *Āryabhaṭīya* and (2) *Āryabhaṭa-siddhānta*. The latter work is known only through references to it in later works. The *Āryabhaṭīya* deals with both mathematics and astronomy with superb mastery over the subjects. The subject-matter is divided into four *pāda*s or chapters, viz., (1)

---

203. *Bṛhatsaṁhitā*, IV.3.

204. *Ibid.*, IV.40.

205. *Bṛhatsaṁhitā*, LXXXV.76.

206. *ṣaṣṭyabdānām ṣaṣṭiryadā vyātītāstrayaśca-yugapādāḥ* |
tryedhikā viṁśatirabdāstadeha mama janmano'tītāḥ ||
—*Āryabhaṭīya,* edited by S.K. Sukla and K.V. Sarma, Delhi, 1976, III.10, p. 95.

207. P.C. Sengupta, "Āryabhaṭa, the Father of Epicyclitic Astronomy", *Journal. Department of Letters*, Vol. XVIII, 1929, pp. 1ff.

Gītikā-pāda which sets forth the basic difinitions of important astronomical parametres and tables, (2) *Gaṇita-pāda* dealing with mathematics, (3) *Kālakriyā-pāda* dealing with various units of time, (4) *Gola-pāda* dealing with the motion of the sun, moon and the planets on the celestial sphere. Āryabhaṭa held the view that the Earth rotates about the axis and the stars are fixed in space. The period of one sidereal rotation of the earth, according to Āryabhaṭa I, is $23^n 56^m 4^8 91$.[208] The corresponding modern value is $23^n 26^m 9^8$. 091.[209]

The famous university of Nālandā was in a flourishing state at that time. There was astronomical observatory which was the special feature of this university.[210] Āryabhaṭa I has been designated as *kulapa* = *kulapati* or head of a university.[211] It is quite likely that he was a *kulapati* of the University of Nalanda. Bhāskara I mentions the names of Pāṇḍuraṅgasvāmī, Lāṭadeva and Niśaṅku among his pupils.

Lāṭadeva was one of the great scholar and teacher of astronomy of that age. Bhāskara I has called him *ācārya* and *sarva-siddhānta-guru* (teacher of all systems of astronomy). Lāṭadeva was the author of at least two works. *Śiṣyadhīvṛddhida* is one of them. The verse are in *āryā* metre and their language and style are similar to those of the *Āryabhaṭīya*.

Thus the *Āryabhaṭīya* schools of astronomy and mathematics show the advanced stage of culture of these two sciences.

In the field of science of grammar, Bhartṛhari is a well-known name. As he is a pupil of Vasurāta, a contemporary of the great

---

208. *Āryabhaṭīya, op.cit., Gītikā-pāda, verse* 3.

209. W.M. Smart, *Text-book on Spherical Astronomy,* Cambridge, 1923, p. 492.

210. D.G. Apte, *Universities in Ancient India,* p. 31.

211. *siddhāntapañcakevidhāvapi dṛgviruddha-*
mauḍhyoparāgamukhakhecarcārakḷptau ।
sūryaḥ svayaṁ kusumapuryabhavat kalau tu
bhūgolavit kulapa āryabhaṭābhidhānaḥ ॥

Buddhist philosopher Vasubandhu, he belonged to the period not much later than AD 500. He is the author of *Vākyapadīya* and *Mahābhāṣyapradīpikā*. He propounded the theory of *sphoṭa*.

Some other treatises are occasionally ascribed to the Gupta age. According to some, Amarasiṁha, author of the *Nāmaliṅgānuśāsana* or *Amarakośa*, was one of the nine jewels of Vikramāditya's court. Kālidāsa has been popularly stated to be the author of some minor works. But, in fact these cannot be the works of Kālidāsa, because of their weak representation. The *Śrutabodha*, a treatise on metre, *Nānārthaśabdaratna*, and *Maṅgalāṣṭaka* are among those works.

From the works discussed above it can be shown that some aspects of the educational system that was current in the Gupta age have been reflected in the poems, dramas and some other minor works of that time. An impression may be created by these works that the Gupta age had encouraged and strengthened to form an atmosphere suitable for propagating a systematised pattern of education.

4

Education in Buddhist and Jaina Literature

Chinese Travellers' Account

WITH the advancement of Hinduism, Buddhism occupied the next most important creed of Gupta age. The majority of historians agree that the Buddha, the founder of Buddhism was born towards the end of the sixth century BC.[1] After the death of the Buddha three Council settled the texts of the teachings of the Buddha. These texts, i.e., the sacred scriptures are known by the name of *Tipiṭaka* in Pāli or *Tripiṭaka* in Sanskrit, signifying the "Three Baskets", i.e., collections. The Kuṣāṇa king Kaniṣka (Scythian) assembled the Fourth Council perhaps at Jalandhara in Kashmir towards AD 100, which demarked the schism between the Buddhist, i.e., the followers of the great vehicle (Mahāyāna) and the followers of the little vehicle (Hīnayāna).

With the advent of the imperial Guptas, the Buddhist religion continued to survive along with other faiths. It is stated that during the

1. The exact date of Buddha is not known but the date of his *nirvāṇa* has been discussed by scholars.

   According to Fleet, Buddha's death occurred between 470-480 BC, cf. Fleet, *JRAS*, 1904.

   The *Mahāvaṁśa* places Buddha's death in 432 BC cf. Vidyābhūṣaṇa, *History of the Mediaeval School of Indian Logic*, p. 57

reign of Samudragupta, king Meghavarṇa of Ceylon sent an embassy to the Gupta court for obtaining permission to build a monastery at Bodh Gayā.

Hīnayāna Buddhism was subdivided into several sects. Three or four of these sects survived and carried on with vigour and energy their activities in different parts of India. The sects, such as, Sarvāstivādins, the Sammitīyas or the Vatsīputrīyas and Thera or Sthaviravādins tried their utmost for setting up of monasteries into magnificent academic centres. In this mission the patronage of rulers as well as of rich devotees was obtained. These academic centres were the footsteps for propagation of learning. They taught not only the Buddhist doctrines but the other views also. The method of ancient philosophical tracts was to set up the concerned doctrines after refutation of views against it. In this way the students of Philosophy was bound to learn other different views in order to proof their own view. The followers of each sect were busy to elucidate their particular doctrines. So the spirit of literary activities sprang from propagation of individual doctrines. The philosophy of this age was exalted and occupied a seat of subtle fineness. During the Gupta period a good number of distinguished writers flourished. Their contributions to philosophy opened a new era. The Buddhist monasteries of Gupta age served as the educational institute of high esteem.

The advent of Mahāyāna with its ultra-altruistic principles, by the scope if afforded to worship and devotion, occupied and conquered the mind of the people. Though the writings of distinguished Hīnayāna writers and Hīnayānic monasteries were in this age but it was losing its hold gradually. The Mahāyāna movement embraced anyone, even a householders to commence the career of Bodhisattvahood.

The beginnings of the history of Buddhism during the imperial Guptas is shrouded in mystery although some light of information can be gathered from the accounts of Chinese travellers.

The traveller Yuan Chwang names the ruler of India as Mahā Śrī Rāja, who has been identified with Samudragupta who had the title of *mahārājādhirāja*.[2] According to Wang Hiuen Tse, two monks came to India but according to Yuan Chwang only one monk came to India with a view to visit Buddhist religious places and complained about the scant hospitality during their visit to king Meghavarṇa. Thereafter the king of Ceylon sent an embassy to the Indian court with a request for permission to build a monastery at Bodh Gayā where Ceylonese monks could stay in peace during their visit to India.

There is no account about the position of the Buddhist faith during the reign of Rāmagupta.

But during the reign of Candragupta II the existence of Buddhism can be proved by contemporary epigraphs and a reputed traveller's account. The Sāñcī Stone Inscription dated AD 412-13 shows that at that time there was a great *vihāra*.[3] Fa-Hien depicts a detailed account of Buddhist faith in northern India between AD 399-414.[4]

Starting from the reign of Kumāragupta I some other traces of Buddhism can be noticed. The Mankuwar Stone Image Inscription of Kumāragupta I records that the *bhikṣu* Buddhamitra installed an image of the Buddha.[5]

The Mathurā Stone Inscription, issued during the reign of Skandagupta dated AD 454-5, records the gift of a statue by Vihārasvāminī *devatā*.[6] There are ample proof of existence of Buddhist faith during the reign of Gupta kings scattered in the inscriptions found in different places of India.

---

2. Yuan Chwang, II, pp. 137-8; John Fleet, *Corpus Inscriptionum Indicarum*, Vol. III Varanasi: Indological Book House, 1970.
3. *siddhaṁ kā [kanā] daboṭa-śrī-mahāvihāre*, pp. 29f.
4. Fa Hien, pp. 31-2.
5. *bhagavato samyak-sambuddhasya sva-mataviruddhasya iyaṁ pratimā pratiṣṭhāpitā bhikṣu-buddhamitrena* ।
   — Fleet *CII*, Vol. III, p. 47
6. *deya-dharmyaṁ vihārasvāminyā devatāyāḥ* ॥
   — *Ibid.*, p. 263

The early Pāli texts mention the first three Vedas. It includes *Atharva* as the fourth Veda by implication and *itihāsa* is the fifth Veda. Vedāṅgas are enumerated in a different way. They comprised works on *nighaṇṭu* (vocabulary), *ketubha* (*kappa* or ritual), *akkharappabheda* (*sikkhā* and *nirutti*, or, *pada* and *padārtha*); *veyyākaraṇa* (*vyākaraṇa*, or grammar) and *lokāyatam*. The term may include the works on metre. The term *lokāyatam* is explained as the stories of creation, etc. But it may be inferred from the reading of *Vinaya Cullavagga*[7] that it was employed to mean all the popular sciences and arts including astronomy, astrology, demonology, quackery. The fuller list is supplied in the *Milinda*.[8] It comprises of *Irubbeda* (*R̥gveda*), *Yajubbeda* (*Yajurveda*), *Sāmabeda* (*Sāmaveda*), *Atharbbanaveda* (*Atharvaveda*), *Lakkhanam* (science of signs), *Itihāsa*, *Purāṇa*, *Nighandu*, *Ketubham*, *Akkharappabhedam*, *Padam*, *Veyyākaraṇam*, *Bhāsāmaggam* (prosody, modes of chanting), *Uppadam* (science of portents), *Supinam* (dream-portents), *nimittam* (science of omens), *Chalangam* (six Vedāṅgas), *Jotisam* dealing with the eclipses of the sun and the moon due to the action of Rāhu and Ketu, fall of metres, forecast of earthquakes, thunderclaps, conflagrations, etc. and the interpretation of omens drawn from the barking of dogs and cries of beasts and birds.

In later Pāli literature the three terms *vijja*, *sippa* and *kalā* comprehend together three Vedas and the whole fields of learning, theoretical and practical. In earlier nomenclature the two terms, *vijja* and *sippa* were considered sufficient for the purpose.

In some of the *Jātakas*, the eighteen *sippas* are *vijjatthānas* or subjects of study apart from the three Vedas.

---

7. *Vinaya Cullavagga*, V.33.2.

8. *ekeneva uddesena tayo vedā hr̥dyaṁgatā vācuggatā sūpadhāritā . . . sakimeva cakkhuṁ udapādi tīsu vedesu sanighaṇṭuketuhesu sākkharappabhedesu itihāsapañcamesu padako veyyākaraṇo lokāyatamahāpuriṣa-lakkhaṇesu anavayo ahosi.* — *Milindapañho*, (8), p. 7

In the *Milindapañho*, the nineteen subjects of study are enumerated. These are *satthas* (*śāstras*), which includes the four Vedas and described as *Suti* (*Śruti*), *Samuti* (*Smṛti*) *Sānkhya* (*Sāṁkhya*), *Yoga* (*yoga*), *Nīti* (*Nyāya*), *Viśeṣika* (*Vaiśeṣika*), *Gaṇikā* (arithmetic), *Gandharbba* (music), *Tikicchā* (medicine), *Catubbeda* (four Vedas), *Purāṇa*, *Itihāṣa*, *Jotisa*, *Māyā* (magic), *Hetu* (causistry), *Mantanā* (polity), *Yuddha* (military science), *Chandasa* (prosody) and *Muddā* (conveyancing). The number nineteen may be reduced to eighteen by taking the *suti* to mean four Vedas. This enumeration is not available in the *Jātakas*. They do not also explain why the first three Vedas were excluded from the list. But it may be assumed that eighteen number of *sippas* or subjects of study is fixed, as also for the alphabets and the dialects other than the Indo-Āryan (*deśībhāṣā*, *milakkhabhāsā*).

There are other enumerations of *sippas* (science and arts), *sippathhānas* or *sippāyatanas* (crafts or professional arts) where their total number is not mentioned.

The *Jātaka* and other Pāli canonical texts show that the science of royal polity was developing under the name *Rājadhamma* or principles of royal polity. In one of the oldest Pāli literature a list of topics which were included in a work on royal polity were enumerated. The list includes the topics concerning the kings, thieves, robbers, bandits, the *mahāmattas*, or, ministers and high officials, the army, wars, food stuffs, drinks, clothes, beds, articles of luxury, friends and relatives, conveyances, villages, towns, cities, countries, men, women, warriors, etc.

The *Mahābodhi Jātaka* mentions Pāli *khattavijja* which is the same term as *kṣatravidyā* in the *Chāndogya Upaniṣad*. This enumerates the *Dhanurvidyā*, the science of archery or military science. Those persons whose intention was attaining the position of *senāpatis* and other military ranks were required to study the branch of this learning. The art of warfare, the forming of battle arrays, the mobilisation of forces, the training of the four divisions of the army, the principles of war and peace, the knowledge of handling of weapons of war comes under the scope of this subject.

The canonical Pāli text throw abundant light on the study of *Tekicchā sattha* or *Āyurveda*. The *Tekicchā sattha* developed into *Tekicchā* in general and *Agadatantra* and *Śalyatantra* or surgery.

The veterinary science was a side development of the *Āyurveda*. The study of *Āyurveda* includes the knowledge of medicinal plants, minerals and other organic and inorganic substances and their properties. For treatment of diseased person the anatomical knowledge, the physiological function, the selection and preparation of drugs and their application was necessary. The *Satipatthana Sutta* under *Majjhimanikāya* shows clearly that dissection was not necessary for the anatomical knowledge. The *sutta* itself throws light about the development of the knowledge of anatomy.

The early Buddhist texts as well as Jaina texts show the development of *Gandhabbabeda* or musicology, etc. The musicology was concerned with four main divisions. These are dancing (*nacca*), singing (*gīta*), playing on instrument (*vādita*) and dramatic performance (*visūkadassana*). A classified list of musical instruments is supplied. Ballad-recitation was also practised. The canon of Ājīvikas included two treatises namely *gīta-mārga* and *nṛtya-mārga*.

We see the development of *vatthuvijjā* (*vāstuvidyā*) or architecture. The architects were known as *thapatis* (*sthapatis*) or *vaḍḍikis*. Carpentry, wood carving, stone masonry, etc. were all connected with the art of building.

The early Jaina and Buddhist texts bear ample testimony to the progress of *Jyotiṣa* known as *Nakkhatavijjā*. People were acquainted with solar and lunar eclipses, planets, comets. The person proficient in astronomy was able to forecast all coming events, celestial or terrestrial.

The term *nirutti* in Pāli has been used in the sense of 'explanation, etymological interpretation, pronunciation, dialects, expression'. In a *Dhammapada* verse it is stated that a saint is conversant with the sequence of letters in words as well as in the modes of expression.[9]

9. *niruttipadakavido — Dhammapada.*

Buddhists compiled two treatises called *Nettipakaraṇa* and *Peṭakopadeśa* which are exegetical in the model of *Nirukta*. The *Cullaniddesa* and *Mahāniddesa* which are canonical, explain the words of *pārāyaṇavagga* and *atthakavagga* consisting of sixteen archaic poems. The *niryuktis* of the Jaina Āgama contain the characteristics of *Nirukta*.

The Jaina *Kalpasūtra* presented the *vinaya* or discipline followed by the followers of Jainism. The *Ācārāṅga-sūtra* may be considered as *Vinaya* work of Nirgantha sect of śramaṇas The *Caluḥsarana*, *Ācārādarśa* are of the same class. The *Upāsakadasāṅga* is the oldest known text of the Jaina *gṛhivinaya*.

The *Pātimokkha* is prescribed as a code of discipline for the *bhikkhus* and *bhikkhunīs*. The *Suttavibhaṅga* is an annotation of Pātimokkhas. It may be considered as a masterpiece of criminal jurisprudence. *Vinya Mahāvagga* and *Cullavagga* enumerate with details the rules regarding the initiation, ordination, residence, dress, food, personal hygiene, internal concord of the order and their amendments. The *Parivārapāṭha* is a canonical digest of the whole of the *Vinaya* discipline.

The example of Buddhist *gṛhivinaya* is *Siṅgālovāda Sutta* in the *Dīghanikāya*. The *Maṅgala Sutta* is the versified summary of *Siṅgālovāda Sutta*. This *Maṅgala Sutta* was promulgated by Aśoka through his edicts.

Buddhist, have referred to 9 *aṅgas* (classes or types of literature). These are — (1) *Sutta*, (2) *Geyya*, (3) *Veyyākaraṇa*, (4) *Gāthā*, (5) *Udāna*, (6) *Itivuttaka*, (7) *Jātaka*, (8) *Abbhutadamma*, (9) *Vedalla*.

Vaṁsa and *Apadāna* were developed in connection with the *Jātaka*.

The *suttas* are prose discourses of Buddha, particularly embodied in *Dīghanikāya* and *Majjhimanikāya*.

Geyyas are *suttas* in which the prose portions set up the framework for the verses, as for example, the *Sagāthavagga* in the *Saṁyutta Nikāya*.

The *Veyyākaraṇas* are typified by the *Abhidhamma* books in which the *dhamma* is analysed and expounded in a most prosaic or scientific form.

Gāthās are those poems or groups of stanzas which are not the part of any prose framework, i.e., *gāthās* in the *Dhammapada*, *Thera-Therīgāthā* and some stanzas in the *Suttanipāta*.

The *Udānas* are examples of this type. These are not outcome of any direct religious experience.

The *Itivuttaka* class is a book of quotations.

The *Jātakas* are birth stories of Bodhisattva.

The *Abbhutadhamma* are particular *suttas* through which Buddha describes wonderful things.

There are only 2 *suttas* under *Majjhimanikāya* which are designated as *Vedalla*.

The Jaina Āgama showed much interest in secular and scientific subjects as the study of organic and inorganic matter, different forms of life, astronomy, arithmetic, geography, drama, music and the similar subjects. *Gaṇitavijjā* is a textbook of arithmetic; *Caṁdapaṇṇatti* and *Sūrapaṇṇatti* are works on astronomy and the *Jambudīvapaṇṇatti* is a work on geography. The *Anuyogadvāra* is a treatise on Jaina system of education.

The Ardha-Māgadhī language is used in various stages of its development in the texts of the Jaina *Āgama* of Śvetāmbara canon.

Lalitavistara as well as Jaina *Nandisūtra* mention Brāhmī, Kharoṣṭhī and Puṣkarasārī as the three parent scripts of India.

Side by side there were schools of Bhānakas that bore the responsibility of preserving Buddhist texts by repetition of orally transmitting the texts.

Kāṭhaka Jātaka recorded the story of a son of a rich merchant of Benares who went to learn alphabets and a son of a female slave accompanied him with his wooden board and other things. He learnt art of writing alphabets, also other arts. *Lalitavistara* records that a qualified teacher taught Siddhārtha the knowledge of numerals and various forms of writing (*lipis*).

Milindapañho recorded a story of Nāgasena, whose father appointed a teacher on payment of an honorarium of 1,000 pieces of money to teach him three Vedas with auxiliary branches of learning. After learning these subjects, he joined the Buddhist order to quench his thirst of learning and followed a different course of learning.

According to the *Jātakas* the sixteenth year is the normal age of brāhmaṇa and kṣatriya youths for completion of study. According to the Buddhist order, a boy or girl under twenty, even under ten, was allowed to be initiated into religious life as a novice (*sāmaṇera*) but the age limit was twenty to be ordained as a *bhikkhu*. The *Vinaya Mahāvagga* throws some light on primary education.

In some of the *Jātakas*, the parents offered to their sons two options of either worshipping the fire in the wood or studying. The option was between going to an *āśrama* or hermitage of a *ṛṣi* for religious training or going to some seat of learning for vocational education. Jotipāla, son of the *purohita* of the king of Benares, returned from Takṣaśilā with great proficiency in archery or military science. Jīvaka went to Takṣaśilā to learn the science of medicine.

Citta-Sambhūta Jātaka records that the maintenance of a school depends on its head at Takṣaśilā. He had to depend for the maintenance of himself and his residence-pupils on occasional invitations and contributions from the local people as partly received from some of his pupils.

Benares was an important centre of learning. There were in Kośala and Aṅga-Magadha several *mahāśālās* or *snātaka*-institutions.

Buddhist *ārāmas* or *vihāras* enforced the rules of conduct and discipline which were formed according to their own idea of morality and religious ideal. The discussions on the causes of truth and knowledge in all branches of learning (by open discussion) were the remarkable feature of their educational and cultural activities. The *ārāma*-

institutions depended wholly on public charities. The Śāmanas freely admitted into their orders men and women from all social status. Their attitude towards the existing social and religious institutions was the attitude of disapproval. Their aim of learning was democratisation of learning, the social and moral uplift of men and women, the development of living languages.

The Buddhists practised among themselves an institution of *Dhammakathikās* or popular preachers who preached mainly three topics, namely *dāna, śīla* and *sagga* (heavenly reward for meritorious deeds) to spread popular education. Their preaching was rich in similes mostly drawn from everyday life. Mahāmoggallāna and Kumāra Kassapa were prominent among popular preachers.

The Jainas compiled for same purpose a text known as *Nāyadhammakahā*.

The technical schools were grown up side by side. There was a school of archery for teaching military science. The *Suppa-nipāta* commentary mentions an ancient institution of carpenters and wood-carvers at Benares. Private craftsmen and professionals had *antevāsīs* or resident pupils under them.

Anuyogadvāra Sūtra states about the Jaina system of education that it meant the equipment for acquiring proficiency in the *laukika* or general knowledge as well as proficiency in the *lokottara* or special knowledge of the Jaina doctrines. The Jaina system included in their syllabi the study of grammar, arithmetic, astronomy, geography, science of music, *Rāmāyaṇa*, *Mahābhārata*, drama and allied subjects. It also included *adhyānas* or lectures, *praśna-vyākaraṇas* or typical question and answers expositions, manuals and digests. *Upādhyāya* initiated the learners into the order and *ācārya* one or more to teach the texts.

The Buddhist doctrines also prescribe an *upādhyāya* to initiate him into the order and *ācārya*, the number of which may exceed one, to teach the texts. The intention was to make the learner proficient in *lokīya* and *lokottara* matter. These constituted the motto of *samma-dassana* or *samma-diṭṭhi*, i.e., right direction of mind, *samma-caritta*, i.e. right conduct and *sammaṇāṇa*, i.e., right knowledge. The Buddhist education system prescribed the study of *Jātakas* and cognate subjects to cope with the matters that are *lokīya*. It prescribed the numerical groupings of the doctrines, catechisms (*panhapucchakam*), manuals and digests to be equipped with matters that are *lokottara*.

Elaborate rules were laid down to specify the duties of the *upajjhāya* and *saddhivihārika* towards each other. Rules were also formulated for specifying the mutual duties of the *ācārīya* and the *antevāsika*. The *ācārīya* ought to consider the *antevāsika* as a son; on the other hand, the *antevāsika* ought to consider the *ācārīya* as father. Thus *ācārīya* and *antevāsika* united themselves by mutual reverences, confidence and union of life; thus they advanced and could reach higher stage in Buddhist doctrine and discipline. This point was elaborated in the *Milindapañho* which enumerated twenty-five qualities of a teacher.[10]

The *Buddhāpadāna* depicts the picture of the Buddhakhetta as an ideally situated place of learning in the midst of peaceful natural surroundings of an eternal school. There the Buddhas and their disciples are all teachers and everyone is a pupil, all engaged either in asking questions or answering them and helping each other in annotating the points of the doctrine.

The Jaina and Buddhist texts do not fix any rule about the period of education.[11]

Several *Jātaka* stories[12] depict a boy leaving his home for receiving instruction at the age of sixteen years. But according to Fick[13] it does not mean that before the age of sixteen, a child did not receive any education. Up to this age a boy received instructions in elementary

---

10. *pañcaviśati ācarīyaguṇa* — *Milinda*, p. 94
11. Singh, *Ksatriyas in Ancient India*, pp. 93-102.
12. Cowell (ed.), *Jātaka*, I, No. 51, p. 126; I, No. 51, p. 128; II, No. 128, p. 60; II, No. 287, p. 287; IV, No. 456, p. 67.
13. Fick, *Social Organisations in North-East India in Buddha's Time*, p. 94.

sciences and physical education at home, most probably by his father. At the age of sixteen he was ready to start the study of higher spiritual and religious subjects. Man had to be twenty-year-old for full ordination, *upasampadā* to be permissible.[14]

In the *Milindapañho*, nineteen subjects of study including the four Vedas have been enumerated. In some of the *Jātaka*s eighteen subjects are mentioned apart from three Vedas.

Lalitavistara[15] narrates the proficiency in all worldly occupations, — in writing, arithmetic and numeration, in mechanical arts, in the practice of the sword, bow and arrow, and in all sorts of gymnastics.

King Milinda mastered many arts, as for examples, the revealed tradition, secular lore, the Sāṁkhya, Yoga, Nyāya (here called *nīti*), Vaiśeṣika system, accountancy, music, medicine, the four Vedas, the Purāṇas, the oral traditions, astronomy, conjuring, logic, spells, fighting, poetry, reckoning on the fingers; in a word, the nineteen arts.[16]

In the *Milindapañho* Nāgasena learnt Brāhmaṇical subjects of study, i.e., the three Vedas with their vocabularies and rituals, with the phonology and exegesis and the oral tradition as the fifth; he learnt the lines (of the Vedas), the expositions, and popular philosophy of the marks of a great man.[17]

After acquiring mastery in the Brāhmaṇical subjects, he learnt and mastered the whole of the *Abhidhammapiṭaka*. It consists of *Dhammasangani*, adorned with triads and dyads, the *Vibhaṅga* composition adorned with eighteen analysis beginning with that on the *khandhā*, the *Dhātukathā* composition, its fourteenfold division beginning with inclusion, non-inclusion; the *Puggalapaṇṇati* with its sixfold divisions beginning with the *khandhā* and the exposition of the *āyatana*, the *Kathāvattu* composition, divided by combining a thousand

14. *Vinaya*, IV.130 (Pāṇ 65).
15. *Lalitavistara*, ed. by R.L. Mitra, Calcutta, *RASB*, 1881, p. 4.
16. *Milinda*, p. 5.
17. *Milinda*, V.l, tr. by I.B. Horner, London, Luzac, 1963, p. 17.

discourses — five hundred from own and five hundred from dissenting speakers; the *yamaka* with its two-fold division beginning with the pair on roots (*mūla*), and the pair on *khandhā*, the *paṭhana*-composition with its twenty-four division.

The *Mahābodhi Jātaka*[18] mentions the term Pāli *Khattavijjā* as the same as kṣatriya in the *Chāndogya Upaniṣad*.[19] *Pāṇinisūtra*[20] explains the term *Dhanurveda* in the sense of science of archery and military science. According to B.C. Law[21] the *Dhanurveda* was studied by those willing and aspiring for the position of *senāpati* and other military ranks. *Kṣatravidyā* constitutes the art of warfare, the forming of battle arrays, the mobilisation of forces, the methods of offence and defence, the training of the four divisions of army, the strategy of war, the principles and rules of war and peace, the knowledge of handling of weapons of war, the maintenance of military discipline and control over the rank and file, etc.

According to Pāli canonical text, i.e., *Dīgha Nikāya*[22] *Khattavijjā* comes under a group of low arts and wrongful occupations by which false ascetics and the brāhmaṇas used to earn their livelihood.

According to U.N. Ghosal[23] the topic *Khattavijjā* is kṣatriya science. The reference can be traced in the *Jātaka* story No. 528 and No. 546.[24] *Khattavijjā* conceived to be a systematized body of knowledge, which may be identified with the *Arthaśāstra*. *Mahābodhi Jātaka*[25] describes that it teaches selfishness and cruelty even to the extent of killing one's

---

18. *Jātaka*, V, No. 528, p. 117, tr. by E.B.Cowell.
19. *Chāndogya Upaniṣad*, VII.I.2.
20. *Pāṇini*, XXXII.12.
21. B.C. Law, *India as Described by the early texts of Jainism and Buddhism*, p. 258.
22. *Dīgha Nikāya*, I, p. 9.
23. U.N. Ghosal, *Indian Political Ideas*, pp. 65-6.
24. *Jātaka*, Story No. 528, 546.
25. *Jātaka*, No. 528, Vol. V, p. 117.

own parents. As the ethical tendencies is predominant in the Buddhist order this type of teaching is not supported.

The *Jātaka* stories delineate that the princes were generally sent to the brāhmaṇa teachers for study.[26]

There are fixed rules regarding behaviour of teacher with the pupil.[27] A monk who is angry and displeased must not strike another. If novices were disrespectful towards monks, the monks were able to prohibit them, within limits, from entering the monastery.

From *Milindapañho*,[28] we come to know of a brāhmaṇa teacher accepting fee. It is described that the brāhmaṇa Sonuttara gave a teacher's fee of thousand (probably *kahāpaṇas*) to a brāhmaṇa for study of Nāgasena.

As in the case of the Brāhmaṇical education, the Buddhist *bhikkhu* also has to make a formal application to *Upājjhāya* uttering the application three times. The *Upājjhāya* will accept by nodding or uttering his acceptance of the applicant as his pupil.[29]

The duty of the pupil was to rise early from bed and arrange for his teacher's teeth-cleanser and water and, after preparing a seat, serve him rice milk. Washing the vessel of his preceptor and sweeping the place was his duty. He had to help the preceptor to be ready for begging. If he was to follow the preceptor in begging he must had not walk too far from or near him. After the begging, he had to offer food to his teacher and to help him in bath by serving him cold or hot water as desired by the teacher, to provide him with kneaded powder, moistened clay and a chair.[30]

After bath an interval of teaching occurred. The teaching would be

---

26. *Musika Jātaka*, No. 373, V.III, p. 142.
27. *Vinaya*, IV, p. 146; I, p. 84.
28. *Milinda*, p. 14.
29. *Mahā*, V, i.25.7.
30. *Mahāvagga*, I.48.

in the form of answering questions or delivering a discourse.[31]

To sweep clean in every means the *vihāra* where his teacher dwell was the duty of the pupil. It was his duty to clean out other apartments of the *vihāra*, as for example, storeroom, refractory, fire-room, etc.[32] There is a detailed description in *Cullavagga*[33] about the duty of cleaning of *vihāra* by the junior *bhikkhu*.

He was not allowed to give or receive anything without his teacher's permission.[34] If his teacher felt sick his duty was to nurse him as long as his life lasted and wait until he had recovered.

On the other hand the teacher must give the *bhikkhu*, under his charge, all possible intellectual and spiritual help and guidances. He would train the pupils not only by teaching but by instructing the doctrine of the Buddha. If the pupil lacked his necessary articles, such as, robe, etc. the teacher was expected to supply them from his own belongings. If the pupil felt ill, the teacher must had nursed him as long as his life lasted and wait until he had recovered. It is noteworthy that in the period of illness of the pupil, the teachers was to serve him in the same way as he served him in his health.[35]

The relation between the pupil and the teacher was so intimate that the pupil tried to reconcile his teacher's mental trouble. The relation of the pupil towards his teacher and *vis-a-vis* did not transcend those towards the order as a whole to which they both owed a common responsibility as members. Where the teacher made offence towards the order the pupil's duty was to get him puished by the order. Similar was the case with the pupil.[36]

The duties of the teacher demanded the qualification of the teacher.

---

31. *Mahāvagga*, 14.
32. *Ibid.*, 15, 16.
33. *Cullavagga*, VIII. I.3.
34. *Ibid.*, I.25.24.
35. *Mahāvagga*, I.26.
36. *Ibid.*, I.36.

"He must be equipped with moral practices, self-concentration, wisdom, emancipation, knowledge as well as insight. He must be able to help others and to train a pupil in good conduct. He must be proficient in educating in the elements of morality, *dhamma*, *vinaya* and to convince others who are believer of false doctrine and to instruct him in true knowledge."[37] Apart from that he must be modest, fearful of sinning, of ready memory, not guilty of transgressions in morality or conduct, not uneducated or foolish. If a monk bore these qualities he was entitled 'to give a *niraya*' or ordain a novice.

A learned competent *bhikkhu* could ordain two novices or to ordain as many novices whom he was able to instruct in the instruction of the order.[38]

Thus the Buddhist education like Brāhmaṇical one was centred around one teacher or *upājjhāya* or *ācārīya*. He was the guradian of his pupils and was responsible for their health and studies, morals, their spiritual progress. But unlike Brāhmaṇical schools these group of schools were not isolated. They were under the large unit called the *vihāra* or monastery. So the Buddhist culture was the product of confederations of such individual schools in larger monastic institution. The rules and regulations of larger institutions controlled the individual life which was merged in large group.

There were three objects of the *vihāra*: (1) the indpendence of each constituent group of pupils, (2) the adjustment of relations between the different groups, (3) the framing of laws governing the establishment as a whole.

There were ten serious offences, namely (1) destroying life, (2) stealing, (3) committing impurity, (4) lying, (5) drinking intoxicating liquors, (6-8) defaming the Buddha, the *dhamma* and *saṁgha*, (9) holding false doctrines, (10) misconduct with *bhikkhunīs*. If one committed such serious offences he would be punished by immediate expulsion from the order. If a *bhikkhu* forced other *bhikkhus* not to

37. *Mahāvagga*, I. 50.

38. *Ibid*., I. 55.

receive alms, meeting with misfortunes and if he caused division between *bhikkhus*, he was punishable. The punishment was forbidding his entrance in the monastery.[39]

There were some fixed common laws and regulations prescribed for all groups in a *vihāra*. The life of an ascetic and householder was marked by gulf of difference which must not be surpassed. It is noteworthy that Buddhist asceticism developed its own system of rules and regulations according to its particular view and definition of the ascetic life. Buddha expounded the middle path. So Buddhist order followed the middle path, avoiding the one extreme of self-indulgence and other of self-mortification. Buddhism did not approve any positive and artificial additions to the sum of life's sufferings by the infliction or disease on one's own self or on others. This type of life's suffering is classified by the Buddhist Canon into — (1) self-tormentors or self-burners (*attantapo*): those who practise penance, (2) tormentors of others, such as butchers, fowlers, hunters, fishermen, thieves, all perpetrators of cruelties, (3) tormentors of both self and others, as for example, when holding sacrificial ceremonies one performs rites which causes some personal discomfort and also causes herds of animal to be slaughtered. Thus they cause pain to self and others, (4) tormentors neither of self nor or others. Those who have left the home and the world for life of recluse, renouncing the worldly life in which exist the courses and connections that torment the world, owning no property and filled with charity and compassion for all living beings. There are cool (*śītabhūta*) and not in a state of burning.[40] Buddha believed the path of the middle way. He condemned the bitter course of painful hardship. So he propounded the middle path between the extremes of self-indulgence and self-suppression. So Buddhist monastic life and discipline have considered three primary human requisites, viz. food, clothing and shelter. Unlike Hindu asceticism Buddhist asceticism has considerably dealt with these human requisites.

The structure of worldly life has its basis in marriage and property.

39. *Majjhima*, I.57.1.

40. *Ibid.*, I.341, 411; II.158.

When a man is involved in his worldly life he tries to attain property and generally one longs for property when he has children to inherit his property. Children are the result of marriage. So if one is not tied in bond of marriage or sexual life he can attain detachment easily than a person who has accepted the bond of marriage and lead a worldly life. So the first and foremost rule of ascetic life is self-restraint from any sexual relationship. So a *bhikkhu* who practised sexual intercourse was no Samana.[41] *Mahāvagga*[42] suggests a monk to address his abandoned wife as sister. Monkhood deserves cutting off all blood relationship.[43] Buddha was addressed by his son Rāhula not as a father but as a Samana.[44] But in the Buddhist faith it was not necessary to disown him. The relationship continued and it was open to the monk for resumption whenever he wanted it. A man was also allowed to visit his sick relatives if they desired to do it.[45] Even he was allowed to give robes to his father and mother if he so desired.[46] But the vow of chastity must be maintained by a monk.

Poverty was the another important thing to be maintained for monastic life. So he was called *bhikṣu*, *bhikkhu* or beggar. To embrace homelessness, abondoning the home meant the surrender of all property and wishfully accept poverty. An intending *bhikkhu* must declare that as it was difficult to live the higher intellectual life in its fulness, purity and bright perfection in dwelling at home he would go forth from the household life into the houseless state. He would renounce all the worldly objects in the former house.[47] While at the time of ordination, the instruction to the monk was not to take gold and silver as presents. This instruction must be obeyed seriously. If one violated this instruction, it was regarded as serious offence. It was a *Pacittiya* offence involving

41. *Mahāvagga,* I. 78. 2.
42. *Ibid.*, I.78.1.
43. *Oldenberg's Buddha,* p. 335.
44. *Mahāvagga,* I. 54. 1. 2.
45. *Ibid.*, III. 7.
46. *Ibid.*, VIII, 22.
47. *Ibid.*, I, 13.

forfeiture.[48] The offending *bhikkhu* had to surrender the treasure to the *saṁgha*. *Saṁgha* also did not keep the treasure. *Saṁgha* would then transfer it to some *āramika* or *upāsaka* for getting in exchange honey, ghee or oil which would be treated as common property of the *saṁgha*. "If the guilty monk did not agree with this proposal he would be asked to throw it away. If he did not agree to do both the proposals, a morally strong *bhikkhu* was to be appointed by the *saṁgha*. He would cast it away in such a way that he would leave no sign where it might be. *Saṁgha* accepted gifts in kind alone but not their money values.[49] If in his way one *bhikkhu* got gold, silver or jewel he must had layed aside them. He must assume that the man to whom it may belonged, might take it away.[50] He must be devoid of worldly greed which might contaminate his moral character. The property which were not prescribed for an individual *bhikkhu* was not prescribed for *saṁgha* even in its corporate capacity. The ploughing of field was not allowed by the *bhikkhus*. The propensity of accumulating money grew from the agriculture.

Some articles and property were not allowed to possess by individual monk but treated as indivisible common property of the entire *saṁgha*. The list including following things — (1) park (*ārāma*) or the site for a park, (2) a monastery (*vihāra*) or the site for it, (3) a bed or a chair or a pillow, (4) a brass vessel, jar, pot or vase, (5) creepers, bamboos, *muñja* or common grass or clay, (6) things made of wood or crockery.[51] The vow of poverty which was so rigorously enjoined upon the individual monk, was not at all meant for the *saṁgha*. Some of things might form part of the possession of an individual monk on whose death they would be considered as the common property of the *saṁgha*. The *saṁgha* also received property by bequest of the dead.[52] Buddha prescribed the dedication of all such gifts to the *saṁgha* and encouraged it by

48. *S.B.E.*, XIII, p. 26.
49. *Mahāvagga*, VI. 34.21.
50. *Pātimokkhasutta*, p. 53.
51. *Cullavagga*, VI.15.2.
52. *Ibid.*, X. 2.

declaring it very meritorious. It was a duty of the Buddhist to offer all facilities to the *saṁgha*. The vow of the poverty for a monk was so rigid that he could possess not more than eight articles. These were three robes, a girdle for the loin, an alms bowl, a razor, a needle and a water-strainer. This self-imposed poverty of the monk was shown by his begging rounds.

Begging for food was common to both Brāhmaṇical and Buddhist systems of training. The rule of Buddhist system was to beg in silence. The mode of the daily begging was to be clad in proper robe, be must had begged with down cast eye specially while taking alms from a lady. He should not stand too far off, nor too near, nor too long, and should not turn back easily. After accepting the food, he should cover up the bowl with his robe and turn back slowly.[53] The begging bowl was made only of iron or clay and not of other materials. It was usually put in a bag (*thavika*) carried by a shoulder strap.[54] The *bhikkhu* carried needles, scissors, drugs, a strainer for filtering water, he also might use sandles if the path was rough.

Two kinds of food are distinguished, hard, such as cakes, meat, fruits; and soft, such as boiled rice and curries.[55] Buddha accepted *pāyasam* or milk-rice from Sujātā at Uruvela.[56] Aśvaghoṣa mentioned three sweet substances — sugar, honey (and *ghī*) and milk.[57] *Bhikkhus* on journey were permitted to provide themselves with rice, salt, *ghī*, beans, oil and molasses.[58] Fermented liquors and strong drinks were forbidden.[59] He who came first from the round for alms would make the arrangements for the dining of the whole fraternity. He would prepare the seats, water for washing and drinking and towels, etc. He who came

53. *Cullavagga*, VIII. 5. 2.
54. *Ibid.*, V. 9.1.
55. *Ibid.*, V. 13.1.
56. *Pātimokkhasutta,* pp. 37-42.
57. *Buddhacarita*, XV.61.
58. *Mahāvagga,* VI. 16.2.
59. *Pātimokkhasutta,* pp. 37-42.

last, took his meal and clean out the dining room.[60]

Seeking food without invitation from a household was forbidden. Not more than three *bhikkhus* were permitted to seek alms at a common place together.[61] The monks were not allowed to choice the invitations but he had to accept them as they come. When invited the *bhikkhus* must take food and water patiently, everyone must be served with same quantity of food. Their manner of taking food must be accomplished. The senior monk would sit apart from the juniors. He would accept water for washing while all the monks finished their meal. Before parting, the senior monk would thank to the host. Monks were entertained as guests by both individuals and collective bodies.

The monks used to take rest in public rest-house (*āvasatha*) for meal, but they did not take more than one meal.[62] These rest-houses were most distinguishing features of the Gupta period as is shown by Fa-hien's first hand observations regarding the public charities in middle kingdom and central India.

The daily meal of the *bhikkhu* would start with slight fruit and cakes with milk or water in the early morning. Sometimes rice-milk was used to be served for the early morning meal or breakfast. After that the *bhikkhus* must start on their begging round. The principal meal of a day was usually made up of rice and curry; the schedule time of this meal was between eleven and twelve, because the regulation regarding meal time was not to be prolonged beyond the time when the sun cast a shadow.[63] After the principal meal no more solid and heavy food was permitted. Only some fruits, etc. were allowed in the afternoon after sun-turn.

Medicine was prescribed for the sick *bhikkhu*. Many articles were prescribed as medicine. Extra allowances of food was prescribed for the

---

60. *Cullavagga*, VIII. 5.3.
61. *Ibid.*, VII.3.13.
62. *Pātimokkhasutta*, p. 56.
63. *Cullavagga*, XII. 2-8

sick *bhikkhu*. The best diet for health is stated to be rice-milk. Surgical treatment for *bhikkhus* was also prescribed.

The duty of nursing of the sick was a must for the *bhikkhus*. The duty of nursing the sick *bhikkhu* fell upon his immediate associates. They were his *upājjhāya*, *ācārīya*, *suddhivihārika*, *antevāsika*, a fellow *suddhivihārika* or a fellow *antevāsika*. The duty of nursing a teacher and a student was reciprocal. A *bhikkhu* who was neither a teacher nor a student should be nursed by the *saṁgha*.[64] The nurse must knew the medicine and should nurse the patient out of love and should not bear bad feeling. He might make delightment of the patient with religious discourse.[65] Nursing was encouraged by a special reward.

There was a minimum prescription regarding clothing, like food, of the *bhikkus*. But the dress of the *bhikkhu* was designed with correct conception of decency and decorum. *Bhikkhu*'s dress comprised three parts and was called *ticivara*. The three parts were called *antaravāsaka*, *uttarasaṁga* and *saṁghati*.[66] The robes must be dyed.

When the *bhikkhu* had to walk in rough paths, use of shoes was permitted.

The need of a shelter was imperative in the rainy season when the monks were enjoined to take to a retreat. The retreat was chosen on the principle that it must not be liable to interruption. Monks were permitted to change their retreat when they were troubled by beasts of prey or by snakes, etc.[67]

Different kinds of dwellings were provided for a *bhikkhu*, for example, hut, cave which may be an artificial structure made of brick, of wood, or an excavation out of a rock. The storyed house, the *vihāra* and the *ārāma* were the examples of dwelling place. The *vihāra* was the

---

64. *Pātimokkhasutta,* 40.
65. *Mahāvagga,* VIII.26.
66. *Ibid.*, I. 76; VIII.13.
67. *Cullavagga,* X.17.

single apartment of a single *bhikkhu* and situated near one another.[68] Later it denoted a large building.

It is noteworthy that this growth of collective life and organisation in education was a main feature which distinguished the Buddhist and Brāhmaṇical education. The social atmosphere of the *saṁgha* with a large number of monks in the neighbourhood of locality, where they used to go for hunting, set up the education of the *bhikkhus* in a quite different way. Some of the larger *vihāras* were set in the midst of a large compound with extensive grounds technically called the *ārāma* or Park.

While taking their bath, the *bhikkhus* were not allowed to sport in water.[69] The ordinary mode of shampooing was allowed.

The *saṁgha* was well managed with staff including following officers[70] — (1) distributor of lodging places, (2) the regulators of rations, (3) overseer of stores, (4) receiver of robes, (5) distributor of robes, fruits, etc., (6) distributor of dry foods, (7) disposer of trifles (needle, pairs of scissors, girdle, stainer, etc.), (8) receiver of under-garments, (9) receiver of bowls, (10) *ārāmikas*, (11) superintendents of *ārāmikas* to look after their works, (12) superintendent of Samanera to keep them to their duties.[71]

Monks were engaged in various types of practical jobs to manage to live properly. So apart from religious training, they were educated in the practical arts and crafts. So it is found that *bhikkhus* were deputed as the building overseers. Such *bhikkhu* overseer was called *navakammika*. They were superintendents of repair work of the building also. They were also expected to prepare their own robes and keep them in fit condition with the help of weaving appliance.

The training of a monk in the faith of order was the main objective

---

68. *Cullavagga*, II.I.2.
69. *Pātimokkhasutta,* p. 44.
70. *Cullavagga*, V.I.5.
71. *Ibid.*, VI.21.

of the *saṁgha* life. The *Vinaya* texts prescribe four principal kinds of probation for the *bhikkhus*. When the follower of another reforming sect was received into the Buddhist order, the first type of probation started. A probation time (*parivāsa*) of four months was imposed upon him to examine him. He had to pass through strict discipline. He was also expected to be pleased when the Buddha was praised and not be displeased when the sect he had abandoned was criticised.[72]

A probationary *bhikkhu* was not entitled to the full privileges generally enjoyed by a regular *bhikkhu*. There were many practices forbidden by the monks under training. Injuring plants or vegetables, storing up property, witnessing public spectacles, ornamenting bodies, indulging in mean talk were forbidden.[73]

Though there were disciplines and restrictions on monastic life, there were provision for games and sports.

The ordinary instructions imparted to pupil-monks comprised of reciting, examination, making exhortation and explaining *dhamma*.[74] In the *Mahāvagga*, we find some *bhikkhus* specializing in reciting the *dhammas*, some in *suttantas*, some in the *Vinaya* and some preachers of *dhamma*.[75] It was in vogue that the *bhikkhus* were assigned to different classes according to their progress in studies. In the lowest class the pupil had to learn by heart the *suttantas*. The students used to learn *Vinaya* by discussing it with one another. Those *bhikkhus* who trained themselves up as teachers of the *dhamma* belonged to the next higher class. They discussed with one another academic issues as part of their training so that they could be able to preach them to others. The *bhikkhus* belonging to the highest classes were dedicated in practice of the four *thanas* or meditations. There were some *bhikkhus* who were distinguised as wise in worldly lore and abounding in bodily vigour. So

---

72. *Mahāvagga,* I.38.
73. *Cullavagga*, I.13.
74. *Ibid.*, VIII. 7.4.
75. *Mahāvagga*, IV.15.4.

the *bhikkhus* were divided into different grades of talent, maturity and progress in studies.

The curricula of study for the monks included *suttanta*, *dhamma*, *vinaya*, together with *suttas* and *suttavibhaṅgas*. In the oldest tradition the discourses or conversations now called *suttas* were not termed by that name, but were referred to as *suttantas*.[76] There were some *bhikkhus* and *bhikkhunīs* who were well versed in the art of reciting some well-known *suttantas*. In *Cullavagga*[77] we find the *bhikkhus* reciting the *dhamma*, those versed in the *suttantas* explaining some *suttantas* and who were well versed in *vinaya* discussing the *vinaya*, the preachers of the *dhamma* made discourse in the *Dhamma*. *Suttavibhaṅga* means some parts of the *vinaya* literature as distinct from the *suttas* of *Pātimokkha*.

According to the Buddha, spiritual upliftment could be attained only by those who embraced the life of a recluse. Buddha did not prescribe one particular course of training for all of his disciples. First he studied the mental inclination of a *bhikkhu* and then prescribed a certain course of training for him. It is narrated that one of his disciple suggested that the teachings of the Buddha must be expressed in Sanskrit language to avoid mutilation by the *bhikkhus* expressing in local speech. But Buddha was against this view and according to him the teachings of religion must be expressed in living language which was common to all and easily approachable by common people. Sanskrit would repel the ordinary people or masses who were to be reached through their own vernaculars. The religions of Buddha meant specially for masses.

There were some general rules which could be profitably followed by most of his disciples. Buddha's view expressed in conversations with *Ganaka-Moggatana-Brāhmaṇa* is that all kinds of training needed a graduate course, as for example, in constructing a building, in study, and in mathematical calculations. Buddha also described the gradual

---

76. *S.B.E.*, V.13, pp. xxvii, xxx.
77. *Cullavagga*, IV. 4.

courses of training. These are as follow:

(1) A monk was first to observe the moral precepts,[78] to abide by all the 227 disciplinary rules codified in the *Pātimokkha* and to be discreet in his conduct; he would beg round so carefully as that slightest wrong might not be committed.

(2) He was then enjoined to exercise control over his sense-organs so that by seeing an object his mind might not be attracted to the characteristics of the objects, because such attractions led to the rise of mental impurities such as greed, despair, etc. This was the case with hearing, smelling, tasting, touching and thinking.[79]

(3) He was next instructed to take food without causing injury to any living being, for the bare maintenance of his body, to keep it just fit for leading a pure and holy life and not for embellishing or beautifying his body. He should at the same time bear in his mind that he was going to destroy his old inclinations and to watch that he was not developing new inclinations and he was living in a pure and good manner.

(4) The *bhikkhu* was then advised to sit at a place after the circumambulating walk and try to rid his mind of the impurities which caused hinderance to spiritual advancement. He must continue the same attempt in the first watch and the third watch of the night. In the second watch, though he was permitted to sleep, he should be lying on his right side with one leg on another and the sleep should be so light that he must keep himself alert to get up whenever required.

(5) He was then instructed to practise the first *saṭipaṭṭhāna* (*smṛtyupasthāna*), i.e., being aware of what was connected with physical matters, never to be absent-minded in any action, be it in extending or contracting his hands, in seeing

78. *Chabbiśodhanasutta* (*Majjhima*, III, p. 33).

79. *Saṁyutta*, IV, p. 104.

any object, in eating or drinking, or in passing urine or excrements, or in putting on robes and taking up the bowl, or in standing, sleeping or remaining awake or silent.

There are four *saṭipaṭṭhānas* — (1) *Kāya-saṭipaṭṭhāna*, (2) *Vedanā-saṭipaṭṭhāna*, (3) *Citta-saṭipaṭṭhāna*, (4) *Dhamma-saṭipaṭṭhāna*.

(6) He was then sent to a lonely place, a forest or a forest-path or the base of a tree, or a hill or a cave, or a cemetery or an open space. After his midday meal, he was to sit cross-legged, keeping his body erect and mind alert. He must try to purify his mind of greed, hatred, idleness, arrogance, doubts about the true *dhammas*.

(7) When his mental impurities had been almost eliminated by knowledge, he had to practise meditation of which there are four stages:

(a) Disassociating mind from evils and desires. Thus making the mind free from fault one should try to concentrate one's mind on a certain object. At first one's mind roamed (*savitakka-savicāra* means reflection and judgement) around the object of meditation, but the meditator derived the satisfaction that he had almost get rid of evils and desires, was seated in a solitary place.

(b) In the second stage, the meditator's mind did not roam about (*avitakka-avicāra*) and concentrated on the objects of meditation (*cetaso ekodībhāvam*); it became internally serene, and derived pleasure on account of full concentration.

(c) In the third stage, the meditator's mind rose above pleasure, caused by acquisition of certain virtues and displeasure caused by the thought in impermanence, death and so forth and to attain mental equilibrium. He felt happy and remained alert, being watchful on what was passing in his body and mind, and his body felt at east like that of a person after a deep sleep.

(d) In the fourth stage, the meditator's mind remained undisturbed by any kind of feeling, whether happy or unhappy and as a result of being freed from all mental impurities, his mind attained perfect equanimity and remained alert to the subtlest movement of his mind and body.

(e) After advancing in the meditations, he should try to comprehend the four Truths [*Ārya-satya*],viz., suffering its origin, its removal and the path leading to its removal, as well as he should apply his mind to the four impurities (*āsavas*), their origin, removal and the path to their removal.

Buddha personally trained his disciples and kept a watchful eye on the new entrants into the order. According to him they should be nurtured as young plants which needed looking after by a gardener.[80] He attempted to correct many monks who were arrogant, quarrelsome, distracted and negligent.[81]

According to Buddha his disciples should be remained unconcerned about their food and clothing and be satisfied with whatever they got by begging without expressing their intention to have any particular food or thing needed by them. He laid down elaborate rules codified in the book, called, *Pātimokkhasutta*. According to Buddhaśīla comprised of *Sammagvāca* (means, right speech), *Sammākammānto* (means, right deeds), and *Sammā-ājīva* (means, right means of livelihood). *Citta* comprises of *Sammā-vāyāma* (means, right exertion), *Sammā-sati* (means, right mindfulness), *Sammā samādhi* (means, right meditation). *Paññā* comprises of *Sammā-saṅkappa* (means, right

80. *Saṁyutta*, III, p. 91.

81. *Ibid*., V, p. 269.

resolution), *Sammā-diṭṭhi* (means, right view). The eight items are classified under three heads, moral precepts (*śīla*) mental development (*citta*) and knowledge (*paññā*).[82]

Lokāyata system together with the 'low arts', such as, spells, omens, astrology, sacrifice to gods, witchcraft and quackery was forbidden as the subjects of study by the *bhikkhus*.[83]

Education was transmitted orally in the age of earlier texts. Though art of writing was developed, the teaching was not yet fully depended upon written literature. In the *Mahāvagga* it is described that writing was a source of livelihood or an occupation.[84] The *Vibhaṅga* recommends to the *bhikkhunīs* the art of writing. But the evidence available does not point to the use of writing for the purpose of preserving and transmitting an extensive sacred literature. In the *Vinaya* texts, the exhaustive list of personal property has been enumerated. But there is neither the least trace of any reference to manuscripts, nor mention of accessories of writing as ink, pen, style, or other materials. If the manuscripts played an important part in education of monks there should have been reference of copying manuscripts by monks. Though writing was not prevalent largely but there is positive evidence showing the very limited use of writing in those days for education. The *bhikkhus* of a certain place not knowing the *Pātimokkha*, was sent to learn it from a neighbouring fraternity and import the knowledge[85] to his own fraternity. In *Mahāvagga* there is a reference to an *upāsaka* inviting a fraternity of *bhikkhus* to hear him recite an important *suttanta* so that they might learn it and preserve it from oblivion.[86] So these citations prove that the oral

---

82. *śīle patitthāya naro sapañño cittaṁ paññan ca bhāvayaṁ*
ātāpi nipako bhikkhu so imaṁ vijataye jaṭam ।
— *Saṁyutta Nikaya*, I, p. 165

83. *Cullavagga*, V. 33.1.

84. *Mahāvagga*, I. 49.1.

85. *Ibid.*, II.17.5, 6.

86. *Ibid.*, III. 5, 9.

transmittance of teaching was in vogue. It is probable that the convenient practical material for writing was not sufficient and caused absence of writing.

The method of debate and discussion was the main feature of Buddhist education like Brāhmaṇical education. It may be said that Buddhists layed more stress on debate than brāhmaṇas as by debate only it could spread and win converts from other religions. Buddha spent whole of his religious life in debates and discussions either with the exponents of other schools of opponent thought or answering of questions put to him at the assemblies of his own disciples. The canonical Buddhist texts are full of conversation of Buddha during the discourse. There were constant meeting at assemblies for discussions of different doctrines by the believer of different philosophical faith in the period. The *Sutta Nipāta*[87] describes these brāhmaṇa ascetics, Parivrājakas as Vedaśīla, disputatious, Vitaṇḍas, Lokāyatas, sophists, casuists and materialists. These Brāhmaṇical ascetics met at different discussions with Buddha. The Jainas also took part in the religious disputes of the day. The followers of Pārśva led by Keśī had discussion with the followers of Mahāvīra under Gautama in the Park called Tinduka at Śrāvastī. As a result Jainism divided into two sects. There were similar controversies between the followers of Mahāvīra and Gosāla.

Buddhist literature throws considerable light on the rules of conduct of such discussion and proceedings of the *saṁgha*. The earliest work discussing on the methods of disputation is the *Kathāvatthu*.[88] The *Cullavagga* describes the working of *saṁgha*s as democratic parliamentary assemblies.[89] *Saptadaśabhūmi-śāstra-yogācarya* of Maitreya was a special treatise on the subject of debate. This work deals with the art of debate. The first chapter defines the subject of debate.

---

87. *Sutta Nipāta*, p. 382.
88. *Kathāvatthu*, I. 1-69.
89. *Cullavagga*, pp. 209-16.

It bars the useless subjects. The second chapter deals with the place of debate which should be an assembly of scholars, the palace of a king, or the office of a minister, or the *pariṣad*. The third chapter points out the means of a debate. There are eight kinds of proof, viz., (1) *Siddhānta*, conclusion, (2) *Hetu*, reason, (3) *Udāharaṇa*, example, (4) *Sādharmya*, affirmative example; (5) *Vaidharmya*, negative example, (6) *Pratyakṣa*, perception, (7) *Anumāna*, inference, (8) *Āgama*, scripture. The fourth chapter lays down the qualifications of the debaters. They must be well versed in each other's scriptures and must be conversant to speak continuously without break and intelligibly and should speak in harmony, sometimes soft, and sometimes loud, to convince their audience. The fifth chapter mentions the point of defeat (*nigraha sthāna*) viz. (1) opposing a proposition and then speaking in agreement, (2) leaving the subject started and introducing another, (3) talking irrelevantly (*atīta-vākya*). The next chapter discusses the fitness of debate by its subject, place or audience. The seventh chapter recommends self-confidence in the meeting. Thus Buddhist education trained a student in debating skill to its highest elevation and helped to be equipped with essential qualities for leadership.

There was an arrangement of periodical gatherings of the monk from different monasteries in religious gathering for purpose of confession of sins twice in the month, at full moon and at new moon. The meeting was conducted by senior monks. It was prescribed that the complete fraternity must be present at the meeting. The place of the gathering had to be fixed and announced well in hand. The *saṁgha* as a corporate body must fix the place of the meeting by a resolution. First the *Theras* must assemble and they would guide the young resident *bhikkhus* of that place to prepare seats, light and make arrangements for food and drink. If a member of the fraternity was sick, he would send a declaration of his innocence through another *bhikkhu*. Otherwise he must be carried on to the assembly, or, if he was unable to come, the assembly must go to him and hold their meeting to secure his attendance. Only a mad member of the fraternity was exempted from attendance. The confession was individual.

There was yearly recurring ceremony of *pavaraṇa* or invitation that was to be initiated.[90]

Apart from regular teachers, known as *upādhyāyas* and *ācāryas*, imparting of education by distinguished teachers who were specialists and authorities in their subjects was also current. In the *Cullavagga*[91] we find that Upāli taught *vinaya* classes which were very popular and largely attended. Upāli delivered his discourses standing, out of respect for the senior monks. And the seniors heard him standing out of respect for the subject of his discourse. Delivering religious discourses and listening to them was a means of instruction. One of the ideal *saṁghas* situated at the Eastern Bamboo Park (*Venuvana*) made it a rule that every five days they should spend a whole night, sitting together, in religious discourse.[92]

The *Vinaya* mentions five kinds of false teachers, who falsely announced that their conduct, mode of livelihood, preaching of the *dhamma*, system of exposition and insight arising from knowledge were above all reproach.[93]

Some monks sought the solitude of the forest for a life of meditation. The elderly and maturer *bhikkhus* were eligible for the forester's life.

But Buddhists, as in other matters, followed the middle path regarding solitary life. They had to attend the confessional meetings and had to live not far from a village so as to be able to reach it on their daily begging rounds.[94] He had to expect and entertain visitors.

Buddha, after the double pressure of his foster-mother Mahāprajāpati and his favourite disciple Ānanda, consented to admit women as his disciples on their renouncing the world and householder's state.[95] They

---

90. *Mahāvagga*, IV.2.1.
91. *Cullavagga*, VI.13.I.
92. *Mahāvagga*, X.4.5.
93. *Cullavagga*, VII.2.3.
94. *Ibid.*, VIII.6.
95. *Ibid.*, X.1.

kept the nuns in a condition of complete subordination to the monks. The probationary period of the nun was fixed as long as two years, after which the ordination must be sanctioned by both the *saṁghas* of nuns and monks. Other rules prescribed strict separation between monks and nun. A monk selected by the brotherhood had to impart instruction to the nuns twice in a month in the presence of another monk. The discipline and duties of daily life were the same for nuns as for monks. But the solitary life was not prescribed for nuns.

But it is noteworthy that with all these restrictions the order of nuns opened up avenue of culture and social service to the women of Buddhist India. It was able to draw sympathy and generosity of lady lay devotees. The order of nuns was the training ground of numerous remarkable women. Some of nuns trained and qualified themselves in the sacred texts and were able to teach other junior nuns. Some distinguished nuns took a prominent part in the work of the early Buddhist Reformation and Church. There were several nuns who were known as *Therīs*. In the *Therī-Gāthā* information regarding these women leaders are given. Mahāprajāpati, sister of Buddha's mother entered the order with 500 other Śākya ladies. This nucleus of the order was formed of members representing different classes and ranks of society. Some of these *Therīs* took an honourable share in social service and missionary work for their faith. Buddhist faith opened to women opportunities for education, self-culture and varied spheres of social service.

In the *Majjhima*,[96] during a conversation, Buddha said that one could derive serene pleasure internally by being truthful, by *tapasyā*, by leading a pure and holy life, by study and by making gifts. Buddha described certain duties and practices prescribed by him for lay-devotees. Buddha did not chalk out a clear-cut course of training for the laymen but there are a few stray instructions for their guidance. Buddha defined *upāsaka* as whoever, without any reference to his caste or creed, complied with the conditions described below would be regarded as a *upāsaka*.

96. *Majjhima*, II. p. 206.

(1) *Triśaraṇa*, i.e., an *upāsaka* must take refuge in Buddha, *dhamma* and *saṁgha*.

(2) *Pañcaśīla* — He must abstain from killing living beings, from stealing, from leading an unchaste life, from speaking falsehood and from indulging in drinks.

(3) *Saddhā* (*śraddhā*) — He must have faith in Buddha as the enlightened one.

(4) *Cāga* (*tyāga*) — He should give up miserliness, be open-minded in making charities.

(5) *Paññā* (*prajñā*) — He should be wise and try to comprehend the origin and decay of objects and the path leading to the cessation of misery. He should get rid of misery, hatred, slothfulness, arrogance and doubt about *triratna*.[97]

(6) *Suta* (*śruta*) — He should listen to the religious discourses and ponder over the teachings.

In the *Dhammakasutta* it has been propounded by Buddha that lay devotee must observe the first five of the ten moral precepts (*śīlas*) and who wanted to be more earnest should observe three more —

(1) to refrain from meals at night;

(2) to refrain from using scent and garlands;

(3) to sleep on low bed spread on the floor.

A lay devotee usually took the vow of observing the eight precepts on the *uposatha* days and for doing so he often resided in the monastery.

According to Buddha a lay devotee should not only himself comply with the six conditions but persuade others to do so. There were also occasions when Buddha asked his spiritual advanced *upāsakas* to take recourse to more arduous practices. Once while inquired by Nakulapitā Gahapati, an advanced *upāsaka* Buddha advised him to be *anātura* (in

---

97. *Saṁyutta*, V. p. 395.

good health). Sāriputta explained *anātura* as that one should not establish and relation of himself with one of the five constituents of the body, i.e., he must know that his self was not *rūpa* (matter), nor *vedanā* (feeling), nor his self was endowed with *rūpa*, *vedanā*, etc., nor his self was in *rūpa*, etc., nor *rūpa*, etc., were in his self. In another occasion Buddha advised Dhammadinna Upāsaka to study the *suttanta*s (discourses) and particularly those dealing with transcendental (*lokottara*) topics and with non-existence of worldy objects (*sunnatā-patisaṁyutam*).

The system of education, the condition of learning as described in the *Jātaka*s may throw light in the social background of the age. These stories throw reflection of the contemporary conditions of life.

The *Jātaka* stories bear the picture of atmosphere of learning and culture. These also bear glimpses of educational system prevailing in this age.

The subjects of study under the sciences and arts are not mentioned separately. But their number is frequently mentioned. *Milindapañho* mentions the then current *sippa*s. *Jātaka*s, however, make individual mention of some subjects which may come under the *sippa*s. There are scattered references from which it may be assumed that the following arts were taught in some of the colleges of Takṣaśilā:

(1) Elephant lore (*Hatthi Sutta*)[98]

(2) Magic charms[99]

(3) Spell for bringing back the dead to life[100]

(4) Hunting[101]

---

98. *Majjhima*, II. 47.
99. *Ibid.*, II. 100.
100. *Ibid.*, I. 510.
101. *Ibid.*, II. 200.

(5) Spell for understanding all animal's cries[102]

(6) Archery (*Issatthasippa*)[103]

(7) The art of prognostication[104]

(8) Charm for commanding all things of sense[105]

(9) Divining from signs of the body[106]

(10) Medicine.[107]

It is noteworthy that students selected only one of these subjects in which they wanted to specialize and make themselves expert.

The education before attainment of the age of 16 is not described properly anywhere. Regarding education of princes, description is available of the education after attainment of the 16th year (*viññutaṁpatvāsoḷasavassapadese*).[108] They became discreet enough and were considered fit for going abroad with a view to educate themselves at the feet of world renowned teachers. They generally went to Takṣaśilā which was noted as the prominent centre of learning and culture in this age. Instances, however, are rare where princes at the age of 16 are mentioned as having already completed their education and holding important posts at home.[109] Though there might be a famous teacher living in their own city the custom of sending princes to foreign countries to complete their education was in vogue. It may be assumed that by this means they might learn to throw away their pride

---

102. *Majjhima*, III. 415.
103. *Ibid.*, V. 127.
104. *Ibid.*, III. 122.
105. *Ibid.*, IV. 456.
106. *Majjhima*, II. 200.
107. *Ibid.*, IV. 171.
108. *Jātaka*, No. 55.
109. *Dummedha Jātaka*, No. 50.

and high-mindedness, and enduce heat and cold from happy luxurious life of palace. Thus the princes might be acquainted with the ways of the world. Kings were particularly solicitous for promoting, to the fullest extent possible, the development of the manly faculties of their children. By going abroad for the purpose of education they would acquire valuable practical experiences about men and affairs. Lessons were gathered as to how to make their physique strong and sound, urging them frequently to bring their spirit of adventure into play, and such other beneficial matters.[110] Thus the objects which the system of education was desired to aim at were most practical in their nature, and its effects on individual as well as social life, industries, trade and commerce and the result must be beneficial and progressive.

In many *Jātaka*s a conventional list of the subjects of study at Takṣaśilā is found comprising the 'three Vedas' and the eighteen or all the liberal arts.[111] These also formed the course of study on the part of a brāhmaṇa student. The usual fee (*bhāga*) which a prince had to offer to his teacher amounted to a thousand pieces of money.[112] There were two classes of students: those who paid fees to their masters, *ācārīyabhāga-dāyaka*, and those who did not bring any fee but offered their services known as *Dhammantevāsika*. The former were privileged groups, while the *Dhammantevāsika*s had to attend on their teachers at daytime and in return were taught by them at night.

It was perhaps the general custom to hand over the fee to the teacher at the commencement of the course.

It is noteworthy that the system of education in vogue did not favour anybody, whether rich or poor. It is found that the prince from

---

110. *porāṇakarājāno ca attano putte evaṁ ete nihatamānadappā sītuṇhakkhamā lokacarittaññū ca bhavissantīti* ।
— *Tilamuṭṭhi Jātaka* No. 252

111. *tayovede sabbasippāni* — *Jātaka* No. 338.
aṭṭhārasannaṁ vijjaṭṭhānānām — *Jātaka* No. 50.

112. *Saharsam* — *Pañcavudha Jātaka* No. 55.

Benares walking alone in the streets of Takṣaśilā. He had to come in the robe of an humble student, leaving aside the equipments of a prince, conscious of the fact that he was now placed in a situation which did not recognise any earthly distinctions. If a young prince committed any offence or was unusually boisterous, defying all rules and regulations, then it was believed to be the clear duty of the teacher to offer him advice, chastise him, or even beat him according as the mischief committed. But reference has been made to the fact that the proud kṣatriya lad considered all this as an insult, planned to take revenge by murdering his teacher after his return to his country.[113] Instances of student's misbehaviour are also to be found in some other *Jātaka*s also.

One teacher advises his pupil, a prince, to win the cruelty and violence of his nature, as power, attained by viloence, does not last long and when it is lost, one's condition becomes like that of a ship wrecked at sea.[114] Some teachers in the distant city of Takṣaśilā certainly took a good deal of interest in procuring information about the internal affairs of the different kingdoms from their representatives, viz., the princes who came to study in Gāndhāra. They were so serious about the welfare of their pupils that on the basis of such reports they tried to form some idea regarding the prospects of their pupils in their own countries and the dangers they were likely to face in the near future. Besides this, by their experience and wisdom they had a general notion about the motives that inspired struggles and rivalries in the field of politics and how these could be cleverly countered without any bloodshed.

We can find in the *Jātaka*s certain pieces of advice, which are highly practical and often cited in verses, which were imparted by teachers to their pupils on the eve of their departure for home; this

---

113. *tata takkaśīlam gantvā sippam ugganahanti*
itinām maraṇena sanjajjento evam āha ।
— *Jātaka* No. 252

114. *pharusena nāma laddham issariyam aciraṭhitikaṁ hoti, so issariye vigate bhinnanavo viyo samudde patiṭṭhaṁ na labhate* ।
— *Jātaka* 353 — *Dhonaśāka*

proved really practical and useful in averting calamities, immediate or remote.[115] A king succeeded in stupefying a plotting son with the help of some verses which were imparted to him by his teacher.[116] A teacher at Takṣaśilā presents five weapons to a prince when he starts for his home after the completion of his study, with the help of which he defeats a very powerful enemy on the way.[117] Though different from usual practice of sending princes abroad for education, there is an instance of a king who makes arrangements for the education of his hundred sons under the supervision of a separate courtier.[118] The courtier who takes charge of the youngest prince imparts to him some advices along with the mere academic education. The advice that he offers him at the completion of his study is considerably thoughtful and secures for the prince the throne of his father.

In a *Jātaka* story it is found that in a school 500 brāhmaṇa pupils gathered firewood from the forests for their master.[119] Sometimes, a student wanted to spend his whole time to study without spending any time for menial work, while he was very poor so as to unable to pay the teacher's fee in cash in advance. In such a case the pupil promised to pay his fee after completion of his study.

In case of poor student, unable to pay the fee, a charitable community

---

115. *vidilam thusam undurānam, vidilam pane taṇḍulaṁ thusan thusam vivajjetvā taṇḍulaṁ pane* ।
— *Jātaka* No. 338

116. *Jātaka* No. 462.

117. *so tattha gantvā sippaṁ sikkhitvā ācāriyena dinnaṁ pañcāvudhaṁ gahetvā ācariyam vanditvā takkasīlānagarato nikkhamitvā sannaddhapañcāvudho bārānasīmaggaṁ patipajji* । — *Jātaka* No. 55 — *Pañcaruddhā*

118. *rājā puttasatassa ekkekam puttaṁ sikkhitabbayuttakaṁ sikkhāpethā ti ekekassa emaccassa adāsi* ।
— *Jātaka*, Vol. IV, No. 462, p. 131

119. *atīte . . . bodhisatto ācāriyo hutvā pañca mānavakasatāni mante vācesi* ।
— *Jātaka* No. 97 — *Nāmasiddhijātaka*, Vol. I, p. 402

often extended hand to provide for him free education. It is found that 'Benares folk' bore the responsibility of maintaining 500 students of a 'worldwide fame' teacher.[120] Philanthropic householders often extended their help by inviting to dinner. It is found that 'a country family' at Takṣaśilā invited 500 students of a school. These invitations came by turns to make permanent provisions of meals for the teacher and students to remove the burden.

There was again another class of students who paid the teacher's fee from the state scholarship. Generally such students were sent as companions of the princes. Apart from that, students were sent to Takṣaśilā, by a king of Benares for the purpose of specializing in the science of archery.[121] Fees paid by the students were not adequate to the cost of his education. The fee was required to cover the cost of the maintenance also.

Day scholars were also admitted to institution.[122] The admission of day scholars as students implied the householders or married students.

The maximum or standard number of pupils which an individual teacher admitted to his school was 500.[123] The students were drawn

---

120. *tadā bārānasīvāsino duggatānam paribbayaṁ datvā sippaṁ sikkhāpenti* ।
— *Jātaka*, Vol. I, p. 239 — *Losakajātaka*

121. *so tato paṭṭhāya devasikaṁ sahassaṁ labhitvā rājānam upaṭṭhahi* ।
— *Sarabhaṅgajātaka*, Vol. V, p. 127

122. *tadā bodhisatto bārānasīyam disāpāmokkho ācariyo hutvā pañca mānavakaśatāni sippaṁ vācesi* ।
— *Jātaka*, Vol. I, p. 239, 317, 402; *Losakajātaka*, (41)

123. *takkaśīlāyāṁ todhisatto disāpāmokkho ācariyo hutvā pañcamānavakaśatāni sippam uggaṇhāpeti* ।
— *Varanajātaka*, No. 71

→

from all ranks and classes of society and represented diverse social conditions. Youths of brāhmaṇa and kṣatriyas, princes, sons of magnetes, sons of merchants and tailors, and even fishermen were in the folk of students. Generally Buddhistic view was to preach the moral law to anyone except Cāṇḍalas.

There was freedom of choice of studies and did not always confine themselves to their traditional subject of study. So it can be found that a brāhmaṇa boy was specialised in archery,[124] another specialised in magic charms,[125] another brāhmaṇa boy studies 'science'. Sometimes the students are referred to as selecting the study of the Vedas alone.[126] We find even the direct mention of a *Vinaya* scholar and a *sūtra* scholar.[127]

So it can be inferred that youths of all classes and castes merged in the eqality of learning. Certain standards of simplicity and discipline in life maintained by the school were on level with all distinctions. Thus

---

→ *atīte takkasilāyāṁ bodhisattva disāpāmokkho ācariyo hutvā pañca mānavakaśatāni mante vācesi* ǀ
— *Nāmasiddhijātaka,* No. 97

124. *tadā eko barānasībrāhmaṇo mānavo takkaśilāyā dhanukamme nipphattiṁ . . . . pandito nāma ahosi* ǀ
— *Jātaka,* Vol. III, 219
— *Jātaka* — *Culladhanuggahajātaka*

125. *bodhisattvo hatthācariyakule nibbattitvā vayappatto hatthācariyasippe nipphattim . . . upaṭṭhasi* ǀ
— *Jātaka,* V, II.94

126. *kittim hi pappoti adhicca vede santim pun'eti caraṇena danto ti.*
— *Jātaka* I. 402, III, 235; *Setaketujātaka* (377)

127. *tadā kira due bhikkhū ekasmin āvase vasimsu vinayadharo ca suttantiko ca.*
— *Jātaka*, III. 486; *Kosambijātaka* (426)

the prince entered his school as a poor man leaving all riches. In the story of Prince Junha we see that the prince accidentally broke the alms-bowl of a brāhmaṇa and was asked to pay the price of meal which he could not pay, but promised to pay when he would come to his kingdom. It proves that there was no money with the prince when he was a student.

The food of the students was the simplest kind. Rice-gruel was prepared as breakfast by a maid of the teacher's house.[128] At invitation they were given sugar-cane, molasses, curd and milk.

Side by side with these colleges there were also references to colleges of particular communities only.

The most advanced of senior pupils were appointed as assistant masters (*piṭṭhiācārīya*) who helped to manage the school.[129] These senior pupils, by practising teaching, soon became fit to be teachers.

Instruction was imparted at times, convenient to the students. The teacher taught by shifts both in the day and the night for the poor as well as for the pupil who could pay for their study.[130]

Students seem to have commenced their studies very early in the morning with the crowing of the cock. Probably a cock was domesticated in every school to serve as a clock. It seems that there was time for the private study of the students at which time they spent on repeating new lessons and revising old ones.

The students of those days had to travel long journey after their graduation. It helped to acquire mature and practical turn to their theoretical studies at the college and qualify themselves for the life for broadening the range of their experience. It helped to grow insight into

---

128. *te pāto va yāgupācanatthāya dāsiṁ uṭṭhāpetvā, "khippaṁ no yaguṁ pacāhīti" ahamsu* ।
— *Jātaka*, Vol. I, p. 318; *Silavanāgajātaka* (72)

129. .... *ekapade pi nikkaṁkho piṭṭhiācariyo hutvā mante vācesi* ।
— *Jātaka*, II, 100; *Anabhiratijātaka* (185)

130. *Mahāsutasamajātaka* (537), *Jātaka*, Vol. V, p. 457.

human affairs by close study of the diverse manners and customs prevailing in the different parts of the country. It also helped to build up the physique of the student and to cope with the hardships of travelling to bear all types of weathers and climate. Because of the necessary travelling and living under new conditions in school, they had the chance of being more humanized, with their native pride of position and aristocracy crushed out of them under the spirit of thoroughgoing democracy and fraternity.

Buddhist in all probability carried on an educational practice which they inherited from Hindu ancestry and precedent. Buddhists worthily maintained the legacy of regard for learning and zeal in its pursuit; moreover they seem to have extended its scope. From the practice of later centuries it is evident they spread it beyond the confines of the purely religious or philosophical to subjects of a more general and popular interest.

Takṣaśilā was famous for its special schools. Medical school which produced physician like Jīvaka may be mentioned. It was also noted for its school of law, which attracted students from Ujjeni (Ujjayinī).[131] Among its military schools, one such school could boast of counting all the then princes throughout Indian numbering 103 as its students.[132] People of this age was keen for training offered by its schools of archery. So the teachers were as famous as the knowledge of the arts of peace as for that of war. The Veda of the bow (*Dhanurveda*) attracted as many students as the sacred triple Vedas in those days. Thus the demand for the knowledge of the *sippas* (*śilpas*) or for teachincal and scientific education was not less keen than that for general education or religious studies.

Bhikkhus (*bhikṣus*) got the facilites in their own monasteries for training and practice in the handicrafts, such as, spinning, weaving,

---

131. *tadā so ācariyo diṭṭhadiṭṭhānām kevattadinam.*
— *Jātaka*, Vol. IV, p. 392; Vol. III, 171; *Kāraṇdiyajātaka* (356)

132. *Jātaka*, Vol. II, p. 457.

tailoring, etc. The *Vinaya* texts refer to some occupations such as writing or the occupation of the clerk or scribe (*lekham*), accountancy (*gaṇana*) and drawing (*rūpam*). The *Vinaya* texts bears testimony of drugs, surgical operations and treatment that was in vogue at that time. It seems that the course of medical study is extended to seven years, after which a practical examination was held. The student had to prove his skill in medical botany, or medicinal plants and their properties. Considerable progress in surgery was achieved in this age. So the physicians must have known the antiseptic medicine which was necessary for surgical operation. In the *Milindapañho* when the course of medical training is described, it is said that a medical student must be an apprentice to a teacher. Then the training was imparted to him either relating to the subjects under surgery or subjects under medicine.

A treatment of a boil is described.[133] In the *Jātaka*s it is found that a family of physicians in Benares were specialists in the cure of snake-bite.[134]

While studying medicine the practical course had to be learnt under the direction of expert teachers. The practical course of study of medicine at Takṣaśilā was based on a first hand study of the plants. In case of other subjects after completion of the study the student had to complete the practical course with their own effort. So it is found that a prince of Magadha mastered all the arts of Takṣaśilā and travelled over vast land to acquire all practical usages and to understand country observances.[135] There is an instance of prince of Kośala, who, after studying the three Vedas and eighteen liberal arts, went to study

133. *Milindapañho*, IV.2.13.

134. *tayā daṭṭhatthānato tvaṁ yeva mukhena visaṁ ākaḍḍhāhīti* |
—*Jātaka*, I. 311; *Visavantajātaka* (69)

135. *darīmukha... sabbasippāni ugganhitvā sabba-samayasippāni ca sikkhissāma descārittañ ca jānissāma ti gāmanigamādisu caranta ....*
— *Jātaka*, Vol. III, p. 238; *Darīmukhajātaka*

the practical uses of the sciences.[136]

Benares ranks next to Takṣaśilā as a seat of learning. Mostly ex-students of Takṣaśilā set up as teachers of Benares. There were schools for the teaching of spells and magic cherms.[137] There were of course many established schools for the study of ordinary subjects. Benares seems to have specialized in teaching certain subjects. A school of music was managed by an expert of that age.[138]

Education, as revealed in the earlier Buddhist texts was mainly based on oral teachings and not on written literature. But it seems that art of writing was known at that time. In *Mahāvagga* it is regarded as a source of livelihood. *Vibhaṅga* prescribed art of writing to the *bhikkhunīs*. *Suttavibhaṅga* refers to the possibility of causing the death of a person by misleading representations in writing. But it is not proved that writing was used for preserving extensive sacred literature. There is no reference to manuscripts, manuscript-writing and accessories of writing. In the *Jātaka*s there is reference to drowsiness preventing the students from understanding the subject already learnt; it may be indicate the use of books for their studies. The *Jātaka*s use the expression *sippaṁ vācheti* means 'getting the science read'. In a certain *Jātaka* there is a reference to Bodhisattva making a book of judgement which is written and instructed for the purpose that suits should be settled by consulting this book. There are references to the writing of epistles,[139] contents of a message given, forging of letters, inscription on

---

136. *kosalarañño pana putto . . . tayo'veda aṭṭhārasañ ca sippāni uggaṇhitvā . . . ekaṁ paccantagāmakaṁ papūhi* ।
— *Jātaka*, Vol. III, p. 115; *Brahāchattajātaka*

137. *rājā tiracchānānām pi nāma āsayam janissatīti.*
— *Jātaka*, Vol. II, p. 99

138. *guttilakumāra . . . gandhabbasippe nipphattiṁ patvā guttilagandhabbo nāma sakala-jambūdīpe ayyagandhabbo ahosi* । — *Jātaka*, p. 243; *Guttilajātaka*

139. *sādhukārasaddapuṇṇo antalikho ahosi* ।

mahāsatto: vinicchaye potthakaṁ likhipetvā imaṁ potthakam olokentā aṭṭaṁ tireyyāthā । — *Jātaka*, Vol. III, p. 292

gold plate, inscription over a hermitage, inscriptions upon garments, to impart a message on an arrow and a leaf. There is clear reference to art of writing being taught to the young pupil in the elementary or primary schools. There is a description of carrying the board and other accessories by a son of a servant for the rich man's son and the young servant learnt to write. The three R's are taught in this elementary school.

It is difficult to present a consecutive history of educational theory of practice among Buddhist in the absence of proper historical records or materials. There is no evidence at how early a date, or under what circumstances, the monasteries of Buddhism became general centres of instruction and training.

The eagerness with which the Chinese pilgrims and students came to the great Indian schools of learning during many centuries for the advantages which they offered, is proof of the real worth of these schools. They were ready to face dangers and endure the trouble of long journey.

Wholly dominated by the religious interest and occupied with matters of doctrine and philosophical speculations, Buddhist literature was even less informative than that of the Hindus; this was mainly with regard to the matters of historical detail of the rules and regulations and condition of the opportunities open to all to obtain the training in knowledge or the art which is needed for daily life. Such educationl opportunities apart from monasteries did not exist. The monks controlled secular as well as religious education and they imparted knowledge. The duty of the senior monks was to teach. Ths subject of their teaching was mostly religious faith and doctrine. Manual toil was honoured by the layman and was an obvious necessity if he was to minister to the support of the numerous inmates of the monasteries.

The writing of the Chinese Buddhist monks and pilgrims who visited India offer abundant proof of the active pursuit of learning and many opportunities for study. The purpose of their travels was to secure copies of Buddhist sacred books. These books were translated into Chinese and were carefully preserved. A close and active intercourse between India and China was prevalent with this purpose. The earliest of these scholars whose narrative has been preserved is Fa-Hien.

Fa-Hien travelled and stayed outside his home in the early part of the fifth century, for a period of fifteen years and visited in India the sacred sites of Buddhism. He stayed for two or three years at a time at monasteries in Pāṭaliputra, and Tāmralipti. In all these places he was busy in study and secured copies of sacred texts.

Many of the monasteries visited by him were large, with 600 or 700 residing monks. He describes the students restoring learning in search of truth. In northern India he travelled in Punjab and adjacent districts. Fa-Hien noted that all the instructions were orally made. But in the eastern part of the country, the monasteries preserved written copies of the *Vinaya*, the *sūtras* of the schools and the *Abhidhamma*. Fa-Hien received freedom and facility for study and copying of manuscripts. After returning to China, he himself translated some of the Buddhist books into Chinese.

The Nala or Nālandā received a single reference. This was the famous site of the Buddhist monastery or university in later age. In Fa-Hien's time the place did not attain the importance. He refers to it as the birthplace of Sāriputta.

Though the age of the Guptas is frequently described as an era of Brāhmaṇic imperial renovation and of Sanskritic renaissance; it is also noteworthy that they also made an important contribution to the progress and prosperity of the Buddhism. Buddhism obtained a firm hold on certain sections of the people. The Gupta age is remarkable in the history of the religion because of the religious toleration of Gupta empire.

I-tsing and Hiuen-Tsang mention Śrīgupta, the first ruler of the Gupta dynasty as at first a prosecutor of Buddhists but, who later on became a follower of Buddhism. It is clear that Buddhism was patronised by Śrīgupta, the first known king of the Gupta dynasty.

Buddhism never existed in a neglected condition in the age of Samudragupta. The religion flourished under his patronage. In his youth he extended his royal favour to Vasubandhu, the celebrated Buddhist scholar.[140] Vasubandhu is the author of several Buddhist philosophical works. It is said that at the request of his father Samudragupta studied Buddhism and doctrinal philosophy under the guidance of the philosopher and teacher in his early age. The Buddhist philosopher occupied a prominent place in the religious world. He was patronised by kings, nobles and intellectual people. Samudragupta appointed Vasubandhu as a minister or an intimate counsellor in his government.[141]

Samudragupta's reign is important in the history of Buddhism for establishment of cultural relation between India and Ceylon. Samudragupta gave permission to the Ceylonese king Meghavarṇa to build a monastery with great splendour at Bodh Gayā for Ceylonese pilgrims. The Chinese traveller Wang Hiuen ts'e gave this account. Hiuen Tsang refers to the same story with little variations. Hiuen Tsang also mentions that about one thousand monks of the Sthavira school of the Mahāyāna lived in this monastery during his visit. Scholars like V.A. Smith, Sylvian Levi and W. Geiger have agreed that the Mahābodhi monastery near the northern wall of the Bodhi tree enclosure was erected by king Meghavarṇa of Ceylon with the permission of the Indian king Samudragupta.

Two inscriptions found at Bodh Gayā may help us to corroborate the statements. There is a clear picture of Buddhism in the reign of Samudragupta. The patronage and contribution to the Buddhist world had caused Buddhism to intensify its activities during this period. He showed a loyal attitude towards Buddhism as a true patron. Samudragupta, no less than Dharmāśoka, made firm the rampart of the true law (*Dharma-prācīrabandhah*).[142]

In the reign of Candragupta II the progress of Buddhism did not retard and did not suffer from any hinderance in its activities. The

140. V.A. Smith, *Early History of India,* pp. 298, 305, 347.

141. *Ibid.*, p. 347.

142. Allahabad Pillar Inscription, *CII*, III, No. 1.

enlightened ruler followed a liberal policy for the development of each and every religion that existed in his kingdom and gave full freedom and protection to the followers of all faiths. Buddhism also attained prominence under his patronage. Candragupta II never hesitated to appoint men to high position irrespective of caste and creed. His military general Amrakarddeva was possibly a Buddist. He played a remarkable role for the progress of Buddhism.

Buddhism continued to flourish and was favoured by the people as one of the important religions in the kingdom of Candragupta II.

From the account of the Chinese pilgrim, Fa-Hien, data about the progress of Buddhism during Candragupta's period can be found. It is curious that he did not mention the name of Candragupta II. But he described vividly the adminstrative system, social condition and the position of Buddhism in the reign of Candragupta II. Buddhism exercised a great influence upon the peoples of all classes. No one killed any living thing or drank wine or ate onions or garlic. Nobody kept pigs, or fowls. There were no butchers' shops or distilleries. Thus the Buddhist way of life was generally accepted by the people at that time. The Buddhist monks and monasteries were patronised by the king as well as by his officials and his subjects. Buddhism made a massive contribution to the social and religious history of the country and it was a popular religion.

Fa-Hien found two monasteries occupied by six or seven hundred Buddhist monks — one belonging to the Hīnayānas, and the other to the Mahāyānas, both at Pāṭaliputra. In the Mahāyāna monastery there lived the famous Buddhist teacher Raivata.

The main object of Fa-Hien's visit was to collect copies of sacred books, legends and to study Buddhism in India. But in various countries of north India, the sacred works were handed down orally from one patriarch to another. "There was no written volume. Most probably at Pāṭaliputra he found a copy of the discipline, a further transcript of the same running in 7,000 stanzas as used by the Sarvāstivāda school which also had been handed down orally from patriarch to patriarch without being committed to writing, extracts from the *Abhidharma* in about 6,000 stanzas, and a complete copy of a *sūtra* in 2, 500 stanzas as well as a role of *Vaipulya Parinirvāṇa Sūtra* in 3,000 stanzas." He studied Sanskrit and Pāli and engaged himself in copying the disciplines for about three years in Pāṭaliputra. He also described the annual procession of the Buddha and Bodhisattva images in the city on the eighth day of the second month.

Fa-Hien, in his journey, visited Punjab where he saw many monasteries with 10,000 monks. He visited Mathurā where he found about twenty monasteries with 3,000 monks. He saw two monasteries in Benares inhabited by monks. He then came to Tāmralipta or Tamluk. In Tāmralipta he visited twenty-four monasteries during his stay of two years. This place was an important centre of Buddhism during his visit.

Kumāragupta I maintained liberal outlook towards all religions. In the reign of Kumāragupta I the valuable services of the common people helped to attain the glorious seat in the religious world. The liberal policy of the king must have played an important factor.

Skandagupta was a tolerant king. During the reign of the successors of Skandagupta, goodwill towards the Buddhists was not barred and Buddhism flourished steadily in their reign. King Purugupta has been mentioned by Hiuen Tsang and the reverence of the king towards the three gems, i.e., the Buddha, *dharma* and *saṁgha* is mentioned. He built a monastery at Nālandā, the great centre of Buddhist learning in those days, as a zealous patron of Buddhism.

In the life of Vasubandhu written by Paramārtha, valuable service rendered by Vasubandhu to popularise Buddhism in the reign of king Vikramāditya of Ayodhyā and his son Bālāditya. Vasubandhu became the tutor of the queen and crown prince Bālāditya. After his accession to the throne Bālāditya invited Vasubandhu to organise Buddhist organisations.

Narasiṁhagupta Bālāditya, the successor of Purugupta, was a great patron of Buddhism. He erected at Nālandā great monastery of more than 300 feet high. Hiuen Tsang includes the description of invitation of Buddhist monks from all quarters as well as laymen to attend the formal opening ceremony of this monastery.

From the historical documents and accounts of Chinese travellers it can be assumed that during the prosperous rule of the Imperial Guptas, Buddhism attained a great prominence indicating their great love, respect and tolerance for other religions. The age of the Gupta monarchs is highly remarkable in Indian history for religious toleration of all religions and noteworthy for direct and indirect services rendered by these rulers.

Kumāragupta II Kramāditya also was a patron of Buddhism.

From the name of the next ruler Buddhagupta (AD 477-95), it can be assumed that this Gupta ruler was a devout follower of Buddhism. Abhayamitra, a prominent figure in the Buddhist world helped to popularise Buddhism in the kingdom of the Gupta rulers in the last quarter of the fifth century AD. Various religions flourished side by side amicably in the Gupta period. Each one played its prominent part peacefully without doing any damage to the progress of the other. Thus the Gupta age was essentially one of religious harmony and toleration.

Vajra, the son of Bālāditya, was another ruler, who occupied a place in Buddhist history for his services to Buddhism. According to Hiuen Tsang he had implicit faith in Buddhism and constructed a monastery at Nālandā. This king ruled for a very short period.

With the great patronage of the Gupta emperors monasteries like Nālandā, Takṣaśilā or Dudda became important centres of Buddhist studies and the Buddhist monks led a peaceful life as well as maintained a very high standard of scholarly activities. Fa-Hien describes that "the kings of the various countries and the head of the vaiśyas built *vihāra*s for the priests and endowed them with fields, houses, gardens and orchards, along with the resident populations and their cattle, the grants being engraved on plates of metal". Hiuen Tsang also refers to such grants of the Gupta emperors to the Nālandā monastery. He states that "soon after the decease of Buddha, Śakrāditya, a former king of this country, esteeming the one vehicle, and reverencing the three precious ones, built a monastery. This king's son and successor

Buddhagupta continuing his father's good work, to the south of this monastery, built another one; to the east, the king Tathāgatagupta built a third monastery and to the north-east of this king Bālāditya added fourth". He also described further that "Vajra, his son and successor built another and a ruler of mid-India afterwards erected a large monastery to the north of this. Thus Gupta rulers patronised the Nālandā monastery. Fa-Hien describes the behaviour of Gupta rulers along with that of the Buddhist monks. He describes that "when they (the kings) make their offerings to a community of monks, they take off their royal caps, and along with their relatives and ministers, supply them with food with their own hands. (The king) has a carpet spread for himself on the ground, and sits down on it in front of the chairman . . . they dare not presume to sit on couches in front of the community.

The attitude of Gupta monarchs towards the Buddhists and Jainas were equally liberal. Buddhism continued to be popular with the masses. The exploration and the discovery of antiquities confirm this belief that the Buddhist community attained its highest prosperity in the Gupta period. Although some of the Buddhist centres life Kapilāvastu and Śrāvastī were in a neglected condition, from the account of Fa-Hien it is clear that Mathurā, Sārnāth, Pāṭaliputra, Bodh Gayā and Nālandā were flourishing centres of Buddhism.

During the Gupta age, patronage to Buddhism offered by the Gupta rulers led to a great intellectual reawakening and a large number of literary works were written in Pāli and Sanskrit. Asaṅga, Vasubandhu, Buddhaghoṣa, Dharmapāla, Āryaśūra, Diṅnāga, Bhāvaviveka wrote on philosophical subjects. Asaṅga was the pupil of Maitreyanātha of the *Yogācāra-Vijñānavāda* school of Mahāyāna philosophy. He wrote the *Mahāyāna Samparigraha*, the *Prakaraṇa-Āryavāna* the *Mahāyāna-Abhidharma-Saṁgīti-Śāstra* and a commentary of the *Vajracchedika*. Vasubandhu was the author of the *Viṁśatikā* and *Triṁśikā* on *Vijñaptimātratā*, the *Vādavidhi*, the *Vādavidhāna* and the *Vādahṛdaya* on logical matters, the *Aparimitāyus-Sūtropadeśa* and several commentaries on the Mahāyāna *sūtras*. Buddhaghoṣa, the renowned Pāli scholar, inspired the whole Buddhist world in India and abroad which resulted in the production of many other Pāli commentaries and other literary works. He is the author of the *Nānodaya*, the *Visuddhimagga*, the *Sāmanta-pāsādikā*, the *Kankhāvitaraṇī*, the *Sumaṅgala-vilāsinī*, the *Papañca-sūdani*, the *Sāratthappakāsinī*, the *Manorathapūraṇī*, the *Dhammapadatthakathā*, the *Jātakatthakathā*, the *Paramatthajotikā*, the *Aṭṭasālinī*, the *Sammohavinodanī* and the *Pañcappa-karaṇatthakathā*. Dharmapāla lived in the monastery of Nālandā and was the teacher of Hiuen Tsang. He wrote a commentary on the *Vijñaptimātraṭāsiddhi*. Āryaśūra wrote *Jātakamālā*.

Diṅnāga is regarded as the father of Indian logic. He is the author of the *Pramāṇa-Samuccaya*, the *Ālambana-parīkṣā*, the *Trikālaparīkṣā* and *Nyāyamukha*. Bhāvaviveka was the founder of the *Sautāntrika* branch of the *Mādhyamika* school. He is the author of the *Prajñāpradīpa* on the *Mādhyamikaśāstra*, the *Mādhyamikahṛdayakārikā* with the *Tarkajvālā*, the *Mahāyāna-karatalaratna* and the *Madhyamārtha Saṁgraha*.

In this period the Tāntric Buddhism was also practised. It consists of the ideas of the Mantrayāna, the Tantrayāna and Vajrayāna. The Buddhist logic also flourished during this period. Buddhist literary world was highly developed and it may be supposed that the ruling families, the nobility and the rich people continued to patronise Buddhism, its *saṁgha* and literature.

The Buddhist art also reached its classic perfection during this period.

The first quarter of sixth century AD witnessed the rise of dynasty known as later Guptas who ruled in Magadha.

In the reign of Jīvitagupta I Buddhism flourished in Magadha. Buddhist monks from foreign countries visited eastern kingdom to study religious texts from local monks in Magadha. First Liang emperor of China, Wu-ti or Hsiao yen, a great devotee of Buddhism, sent a Buddhist mission to Magadha. The object of the mission was to collect original Mahāyānist texts and to make them translated properly.

According to V.A. Smith, this event took place either in the reign of Jīvitagupta I or during the rule of Kumāragupta. Paramārtha, the great scholar, accompanied them to China in AD 546 and translated many works which he brought from India.

The next ruler was Kumāragupta III. Though nothing is known about Buddhism during his reign, it may be assumed that the reputation of the kingdom as the centre of Buddhist centre continued as before.

From the Aphsad Stone Inscription it is known that Śrīmatī, mother of Ādityasena, constructed a religious college which may be belonged to the Buddhist institution, the Nalanda University.

Nālandā attained an important position and reputation in the Buddhist world for the scholastic approach. Many students not only from other parts of India but also from foreign countries used to come to study in Nālandā.

The teaching in Nālandā was both tutorial and professional and there was close touch between the professors and the student. It is evident from the account of Itsing the old idea of serving the teacher was prevalent in these Buddhist establishment. In Hiuen Tsang's time ten thousand students studied the Greater Vehicle and the works of this line covered the eighteen schools of Buddhism. Besides that Vedas and other books, *Hetuvidyā*, *Śabdavidyā*, *Cikitsāvidyā* (the science of healing), the work on Tantra, and Sāṁkhya were studied. The result was that there was one thousand men who could explain the collection of *sūtras* and *śāstras*; five hundred who could explain thirty collections and there were ten men including the master of law (he may be Vice-Chancellor in our modern sense) who could explain fifty collection. The then prominent teachers were Dharmapāla, Candrapāla, Guṇamati, Sthiramati, Prabhāmitra, Jinamitra, author of the *Mūla Sarvāstivāda Nikāya* and *Jñānacandra*. Śīlabhadra was the head of the establishment and an expert in explaining the entire collection of *sūtras* and *śāstras*; under him Hiuen Tsang studied. There were many more of rare ability and talent, whose distinction was great and whose fame spread to distant regions and thereby attracted students to the university.

It is known that Ādityasena patronised Buddhism. A traveller named Hwui Lun or Li who was referred to by I-tsing and a native of Sin-Ko (Korea), and was well versed in the doctrines of Buddhism, visited India as a pilgrim during the latter half of the seventh century AD. He wrote that a king called sun-army (Ādityasena) built by the side of the old temple (Mahābodhi temple near Bodh Gayā) another new temple.

The Korean traveller also mentioned another temple known as Tchina (China) temple and described that according to tradition this temple with the land and revenues of about twenty villages as an endowment was built by Mahārāja Śrīgupta for the use of Chinese priests. The land has now reverted to king Devavarman who was willing to return the temple-land and the endowment in case any priest came from China. According to R.C. Majumdar, king Devavarman was Devakhaḍga of eastern Bengal but, according to R.G. Basak, king Devavarman is identified with Devagupta III, a son of Ādityasena and was ruling in eastern India during Hwui Li's visit.

Though no detailed account is available from the description of the Korean pilgrim and inscriptions, it is clear that Ādityasena and his son Devagupta III wanted to popularise Buddhism by erecting temples and for the spread of Buddhist education, culture and philosophy built a college in Nālandā.

After Ādityasena, Devagupta III, Viṣṇugupta II and Jīvitagupta II ascended the throne. But nothing can be known about their efforts to propagate the Buddhist education.

Nālandā University was the most renowned seat of learning in ancient India. It was then known all over Magadha by the name of Dharmayajña. Nālandā belonging to the age of artistic culture and skill, boasting of a gorgeous and luxurious style of architecture, of a deep philosophical knowledge of profound and learned discussions and of rapid progress along the paths of civilisation and showing a standard of culture and education which may be envied by many modern universities.

It had been in existence for seven centuries. It is said that four kings, Śakrāditya, Buddhagupta, Tathāgatagupta and Bālāditya had devoted much of their efforts to this great monastery. However at the time of Bālāditya, who flourished in the middle of the fifth century AD, its most flourishing period began.

India under the reign of Samudragupta ensured peace, prosperity and orderly government not only in Magadha but throughout the greater part of India. Gupta rulers encouraged and patronised artists, poets and philosophers irrespective of caste and creed. Nālandā is believed to have been founded by king Śakrāditya (Kumāragupta I).[143] Nālandā, before it became an educational centre, was imbued with the holy memories of the Buddha.

The heritage of Nālandā may be divided into two parts — Buddhist and non-Buddhist. According to Hiuen Tsang a student must have studied deeply both old and new (books) before getting admission at Nālandā. By old and new books it included the Vedas, Upaniṣads, works of different systems of Philosophy — Sāṁkhya, Vaiśeṣika, Nyāya and all the works of Mahāyāna and Hīnayāna Buddhism.

Hwui Li, the biographer of Hiuen Tsang recorded that Nālandā was a teaching university because students were instructed here in all the varied subjects. But those students who seek admission into Nalanda University, had to undergo a strict test of their knowledge.[144]

The curriculum of the university was very exhaustive. Nālandā prescribed theology as one of the subjects of study. Theology included all the works on the Mahāyāna besides acquaintance with all the eighteen schools of Buddhism.[145] The Mahāyāna was divided into two schools, from philosophical viewpoints, viz. *śūnyatāvāda* and *vijñānavāda*, i.e., Nihilism and Idealism. Under the general term

---

143. Jayaswal, *History of India*, p. 48.

144. Hiuen Tsang, *Buddhist Records of the Western World,* 1906, II, pp. 170-1.

145. Hwui Li, p. 112.

Mahāyāna, the doctrine of 'sky-flower' was the most popular. This doctrine was explained in *Suraṅgama Sūtra* and probably written by Dharmapāla in Nālandā.

Sthiramati in his *Mahāyānābhidharmasaṁyukta-saṅgitī-śāstra* speaks of Mahāyana elaborately.

Nāgārjuna first preached the philosophy of Mahāyāna doctrine in the *Prajñāpāramitā-śāstra*. The followers of him also carried on this doctrine.

Śīlabhadra made three divisions of the whole Buddhism.

All these doctrines were taught to the students of the Nālandā.

A student of Nālandā had to go through the logic of all systems of thought, viz., Buddhist, Jaina, Sāṁkhya and others. The purpose of the learning of the logic of other systems was the refutation of other systems and defending the Buddhist systems. Diṅnāga, the great *paṇḍit* of Nālandā, established the footstone of Logic. Dharmakīrti made further improvement in Logic after Diṅnāga.

From references in Tibetan works to Nālandā, it is evident that Tantra was very popular among the students as well as the teachers of Nālandā.[146]

Knowledge of Sanskrit was essential for a student of Nālandā. It is based on thorough grasp of Sanskrit grammar technically called *śabdavidyā*. *Śabdavidyā* impresses upon the boy's mind the idea of science, method, order, principle and system of rule.

Six-year-old beginners started to learn *siddha*-composition[147] and finished it within six months.

Usually the student of eight years studied the *sūtras* of Pāṇini and the book on *dhātu*. When he reached the age of ten, he was taught the book on the three *khilas*. It deals with case endings, verbal tenses, *ātmanepada* and *parasmaipada*, formation of words by means of

146. Vidyābhūṣaṇa, *History of Indian Logic,* p. 327.

147. I-tsing, pp. 170-2.

combining a root and a suffix.[148] Boys of fifteen began to study commentaries on various texts. The efforts to train or cultivate the memory of the the students were completed by means of teaching grammar. Now a student learnt the composition in verse and prose. After gaining efficiency in the composition he learnt *hetuvidyā* (logic), and *abhidharmakośa* (metaphysics).

The *Cūrṇi* of Patañjali and *Bhartṛhari-śāstra* and Peina (probably Sanskrit Veda) were studied.

Kṣatriya students would study archery and if anyone was interested in studying medicine or anything else, he could also do so in the University.[149] The old and new books mentioned by Hiuen Tsang includes works, such as, the Vedas, Vedāṅgas, Sāṁkhya, Nyāya, Vaiśeṣika and works on Buddhist *śāstras* with all its subdivisions.[150] Nālandā imparted knowledge in all the heterogeneous arts and sciences, philosophies and religions.

For this reason the Nālandā may be considered as a University of universities.

The method of teaching was based on tutorial system. The discussion was prevalent along with the tutorial method. More attention was paid to the needs of individual students.

A student had to copy manuscripts. For this purpose the slabs of stone were carved out in the Buddhist caves.

The outsider students had to undergo strict examination processes. As the number of unsuccessful students were seven or sometimes eight out of ten, the strictness can be assumed.

The admitted students of Nālandā had to study the Buddhist works and works of other faiths and systems. After finishing certain texts, they were placed in charge of various departments, majority of

---

148. I-tsing, p. 175.
149. Hwui Li, *op. cit.*, p. 113.
150. Hiuen Tsang, *op. cit.*, p. 171.

them being appointed as *ācāryas*.

The students belonging to two ages were admitted in the University. The outsiders entered the University at the minimum age of twenty.

The student dedicated themselves to the teacher for the acquisition of knowledge.

After the completion of education, the student paid whatever he like, and whatever he could pay to his preceptors. The teacher made the students to work in his *āśrama* or *vihāra*. The student had to go for alms.

There was no corporal punishment. The highest punishment was expulsion from the monastery for serious acts of immorality.

Teachers and students were united by mutual reverence, confidence, communion of life. Thus the student succeeded to progress, advance, reach a high stage in doctrine and discipline.[151] The standard of morality of the students was very high.

The dress of the students was prescribed as the same as that of a *bhikkhu*. Sometimes the number of students of a *bhikkhu* must have been about 4000.[152]

The Buddhist *bhikkhu* occupying even the post in the *saṁgha* or University derived no material gain; honour and power were the only emoluments of his services, and of his high office.[153]

Logic, philosophy and theology occupied a prominent place in the curriculum of the study. Thus it results in a class of priests, philosophers and debators. The personal contact with the teacher created a great influence in building up the character and mental outlook of the student. Daily attendance imparted a practical training for life, cultivated the spirit of service, humility and virtues which were essential for all students.

---

151. *Mahāvagga,* I. 25.
152. H.D. Sankalia, *The University of Nalanda*, p. 168.
153. Hwui Li, *op. cit.*, p. 106.

Nālandā was an international University of this age. Streams of pilgrim-students used to come here in search of knowledge from China, Tibet and Korea.[154] Moreover, the princes of Magadha,[155] Kashmir,[156] and those from distant provinces, viz. Kāñcīpura in the south, Puruṣapura[157] in the north and Samataṭa[158] in the east flocked together.

Nalanda University was embellished with *paṇḍits*, like, Vasubandhu, Diṅnāga, Jayadeva, Candrakīrti, Guṇamati, Sthiramati, Prabhāmitra, Jinamitra, Śāntarakṣita, Padamasambhava, Śīlabhadra, Dharmapāla and Candragomin.

Doctorate degree was bestowed on scholars of high degree. I-tsing gave an idea of the standard that was prevalent in the University of Nālandā. "The priests learn besides all the *Vinaya* works, and investigate *sūtra*s and *śāstra*s as well. They oppose the heretics as they would drive beasts (deer) in middle of a plain, and explain away disputations as boiling water melts frost. In this manner they became famous throughout Jambūdvīpa (India), received respect above gods and men, serving under the Buddha and promoting His doctrines . . . of such persons in every generation only one or two appear. . . . These men could compose a work on the spot, whatever . . . subject was required—such men could commit to memory the contents of two volumes, having heard them only once."[159]

---

154. Beal, *JRAS,* XIII, N.S., p. 556.
155. Takakusu, *JRAS,* 1905, p. 44.

    Prince Bālāditya and afterwards king Narasiṁhagupta came from Magadha.
156. Takakusu, *JRAS*, 1905, p. 40
157. Takakusu, *JRAS,* 1905, p. 35.

    Asaṅga and Vasubandhu came from Puruṣapura.
158. Hiuen Tsang, *op. cit.*, II, p. 110.
159. I-tsing, *A Record of Buddhist Religion*, tr. by J. Takakusu, pp. 181-2.

The Jainas were the first and foremost to organise monasteries to preach their religion and culture among the masses and they were followed by the Buddhists. The monasteries of Jaina were scattered over a wide region in India from Magadha kingdom in the east to Gujarat in the west, from the Vijayanagara kingdom in the south to the Kośala kingdom in the north. The Jaina propagators used to make periodical and systematic preaching tours. Jaina education is noteworthy for imparting instructions, both religious and secular, to all ranks of pupils from the prince to the humble folk. The Jainas admitted into their monasteries regardless of caste and creed, and challanged the educational monopoly of the brāhmaṇas.

Teachers were classified by the Jainas into two distinct groups. One group imparted religious instructions to the novices and other imparted knowledge on secular subjects to the young scholars.

It is difficult to ascertain whether it was compulsory for students to reside within the campus of the above types of schools. Majority of students resided with their teachers. In *Kathākośa* a reference to a princess residing with her teacher during her studentship is available.[160]

Among other duties of the monks compulsory duty was the daily studies for at least three hours a day.

The Jaina authorities followed the ideals of the Takshashila University in combining sacred with secular education. In the monastic University of the Jainas there were departments of the Vedic study as well as of the Jaina scripture. In the Vedic school, *ācārya*, *upādhyāya*, *hotṛ*, *udgātṛ*, *adhvaryū*, monitors and tutors were the teachers of various ranks engaged in teaching. The head-teacher of an art school was in charge of the students who used to reside in his house for a specific period.[161]

The curricula in the Jaina monasteries were encyclopaedic, embracing courses of studies of all three sects. The first group includes

160. *Kathākośa*, tr. by C.H. Tawney, p. 195.

161. *Bṛhat Kalpa Sutra,* Vol. I, p. 88.

the Brāhmaṇic education and the art courses. The second gruop included the Buddhist courses and the third group embraced the twelve *aṅgas* of the Jainas. The curricula could satisfy the needs of the scholars of all ranks — the high and the low.

The *Anuyogadvāra Sūtram*[162] records the following courses of studies:

I. The four Vedas, the Vedāṅgas, the Vyākaraṇa, the dramas, and Lokāyata, Sāṁkhya, Vaiśeṣika, *Arthaśāstra,* the *Ṣaṣṭitantra* (a Sāṁkhya treatise), the *Rāmāyaṇa*, treatment of horses, the science of chariots, *Kārpāsika śāstras*, *Nāgasūkṣma*, *Kanakasaptatī śāstra* etc.

II. The *Buddha Śāsana*, i.e., the Doctrine of the Buddha.

III. The seventy-two arts are as follows: (1) *likhitam*,(writing), (2) *gaṇitam*, (arithmetic), (3) *gītam* (singing), (4) *nr̥tyam* (dancing), (5) *paṭhitam* (reading), (6) *vādyam* (music), (7) *vyākaraṇam* (grammar), (8) *chandaḥ* (prosody), (9) *jyotiṣam* (astronomy), (10) *śikṣā* (phonetics), (11) *niruktam* (etymology), (12) *kātyāyanam* (ritual), (13) *nighaṇṭu* (lexicography), (14) *patracchedyam* (cutting of leaves), (15) *nakhacchedyam* (cutting of nails), (16) *ratnaparīkṣā* (testing of jewels), (17) *āyudhābhyāsa* (use of weapons), (18) *gajārohaṇam* (riding elephant), (19) *turagārohaṇam* (riding horses), (20) *tayoḥ śikṣā* (learning the use of arrows), (21) *mantravāda* (science of *mantra*), (22) *yantravāda* (science of surgical instrument), (23) *rasavāda*, (24) *khanyavāda* (mining), (25) *rasāyanam* (chemistry), (26) *vijñānam* (science), (27) *tarkavāda* (logic), (28) *siddhānta*, (29) *viṣavāda* (the science of curing poison), (30) *garūḍham* (the cure of snake bites), (31) *śakunam* (reading omens from the flight and cry of birds), (32) *vaidyakam* (medicine), (33) *ācārya vidyā* (the science of teaching), (34) *āgama* (traditional doctrine), (35) *prāsādalakṣaṇam*

162. *Anuyogadvāra Sūtra*, p. 22.

(architecture), (36) *sāmudrikam* (palmistry), (37) *smṛti* (law), (38) *purāṇam*, (39) *itihāsa* (anecdotes), (40) *veda*, (41) *vidhi* (injunction), (42) *vidyānuvāda* (interpretation of learning), (43) *darśanasamaskāra* (philosophy), (44) *khecarikalā* (yogic practice), (45) *amrikalā* (black arts), (46) *indrajālam* magic, (47) *pātālasiddhi* (an occult practice), (48) *dhūrtasambalam* (cunning art), (49) *gandhavāda* (perfumery), (50) *vṛkṣacikitsā*, (51) *kṛtrimamaṇikarma* (manufacture of artificial gems), (52) *sarvakaraṇī* (sundry art), (53) *vāsyakarma* (enchanting), (54) *paṇakarma* (trade or business), (55) *citrakarma* (painting), (56) *kāṣṭaghātanam* (carpentry), (57) *pāṣāṇakarma* (stone work), (58) *lepakarma* (ointment), (59) *carmakarma* (leather work), (60) *yantrakārasavatī* (manufacture of machines or implements), (61) *kāvyam* (poetry), (62) *alaṁkāra* (rhetoric), (63) *hasitam* (comic), (64) *saṁskṛtam* (sanskrit), (65) *prākṛtam* (prakrit), (66) *paiśācikam* (witchcraft), (67) *apabhraṁśam* (apabhraṁśa, prakrit), (68) *kapaṭam* (art of tricks), (60) *deśabhāṣā* (spoken dialects), (70) *dhātukarma* (metal-work), (71) *prayogopāya* (the mode of recitation), (72) *kevalividhi* (the rule of the *kevalins*).[163]

IV. The twelve *aṅgas* of the Jainas are as follows:

(1) *Ācārаṅga Sūtra*, (2) *Sūtrakṛtāṅga*, (3) *Sthānāṅga*, (4) *Samavāyāṅga*, (5) *Vyākhyāprajñapti*, (6) *Jñātadharmakathā*, (7) *Upāsakadaśāḥ*, (8) *Antakṛddaśāḥ*, (9) *Anuttaraupapātikadaśāḥ*, (10) *Praśna-vyākaraṇam*, (11) *Vipāka-sūtram*, and (12) *Dṛṣṭivāda*.[164]

It is quite probable that all the important Jaina monasteries offered the whole range of encyclopaedic courses of studies with modification to suit the needs of local society and individuals.

It is noteworthy that students of all communities and all religions

163. Rajasekhara Sūri, *Prabhandhakośa*, Vol. I, p. 28.

164. *Anuyogadvāra Sūtra*, p. 32.

could get admittance in the Jaina monasteries. The special feature of the Jaina education was that it was against rot learning. It disapproves the blind memory method and highlighted the importance of reason. The aim of education was to develop the latent faculties of mind.

The method of study in the Jaina monastery was comprehensive and rational. The five steps in the passage of the acquisition of knowledge were followed. The five steps were: (1) rehearsal, (2) repetition, (3) interrogation, (4) concentration, (5) discussion. Study was fivefold: saying or learning one's lessons, questioning the teacher about it, repetition, pondering and religious discourse.[165] Jaina educationists valued the importance of repetition in the method of study.[166]

Jaina monasteries had special provisions for the military and physical education of the princes and perhaps for the children of military classes. While teaching military science, the teachers utilised the mental aptitude of the students.

An ethical code of conduct of a very strict type was applied to the guidance of novices of Jaina monasteries. Special respect must be shown to teachers.[167] The student regularly studied the scriptures with concentrated mind, moral discipline, and faith.

The students of Jaina monasteries availed their education, boarding and lodging free. Begging-tours were prescribed for the students. The teachers were required to follow a prescribed scheme of duties.

The Jaina teachers used to confer degrees on successful students. The title of *paṇḍits* was bestowed on successful students of moderate attainments. In the Nālandā and Vikramaśilā universities, the Buddhists

---

165. *Jaina Sūtras*, Vol. II, tr. by Hermann Jacobi, pp. 179, 4.
166. Yogīndra Ācārya, *Pramātma Prakāśa*, tr. by Rickhab Dass Jain, pp. 59, 34.
167. Kundakundācārya, *Pravacanasāra*, ed. by A.N. Upadhye, p. 32 verse 47.

had *paṇḍits* as the highest degree for the head of the institution.[168] In the Vedic schools also the title of *paṇḍit* was conferred upon a student studying in a Vedic school.

The existence of Master's degree in Buddhist India is evident from *Aṅguttara Nikāya*.[169] It is probable that the Jainas followed the Buddhists in conferring degree on a competent student. Above the Master's degree, there was a title of *Bahuśruta*, in between the degree of the Master and that of the Doctorate.

The Doctorate degree is mentioned in Jaina literature. Eminent Jaina church-fathers like Hemacandra,[170] Śrīdeva,[171] Bappahatti,[172] Abhayasūri,[173] Jayamaṅgala,[174] Jayasena,[175] Śīlaguṇa,[176] Vijayasena,[177] and others were recipients of this degree. It is clear that the requirements for the Doctor's degree in the Jaina monastery were of a comprehensive nature including a thorough knowledge of Jaina, as well as Vedic literature and Arts. Candidates for Doctorate in the Jaina university were well conversant with the technique of research. They used to consult the state records. Originality and research were the most needful thing in a Doctor. The aspiring student had to look for truth in primary sources available in the state library or in the libraries of the

168. *Tāranātha, Geschichte des Buddhismus in Indien,* tr. by Schiefner, 232.

169. "He is a master of logical analysis, master of analysing causal relations, a master of grammatical analysis." *Aṅguttara Nikāya,* Vol. II, tr. by F.L. Woodward, p. 89.

170. Hemacandra Acarya, *Prabandhacintāmani*, tr. by C.H. Tawney, p. 123.

171. *Ibid.*, pp. 98, 102.

172. *Ibid.*, p. 201.

173. *Ibid.*, p. 196.

174. *Ibid.*, p. 93.

175. *Ibid.*, p. 167.

176. *Ibid.*, p. 19.

177. *Ibid.*, p. 157.

monasteries. Kundakunda Ācārya composed his thesis in the state library.

Education in the Jaina monasteries was a systematic, never-ending process. Jaina monks learnt things spiritual and mental by means of meditation, devotion and study.[178]

The Jaina monks used to copy manuscripts of valuable books. Thus they kept the torch of learning always burning.

Debate was an important feature of the Jaina education. Sometimes intra-monastic debates took place when monks from outside monasteries joined the debates. Libraries were also attached to the monasteries. Learned monks wrote books on different subjects—religion, philosophy, astronomy, logic and arithmetic.

Nunneries also sprang up for the spread of Jainism and made valuable contribution. There were two types of female education: (1) The education imparted to future nuns by nuns in nunneries, (2) the education imparted in palace schools by lay teachers with the secular object of training the students in the various duties of life.

The Jaina fathers admitted ladies freely into order of the Jaina. Nuns could rise to the position of a head of the community of nuns under an *arhat*. Brāhmīsundarī,[179] Āryakinī,[180] Puṣpakulā[181] and Candrabālā were heads of the community of Jaina nuns under *arhats* Ṛṣabha, Ariṣṭanemi, Pārśva and Mahāvīra respectively. Nandā, the consort of Bimbisāra embraced Jainism. It was also compulsory for the nuns to study regularly.[182] It can be assumed (1) first, co-education was practised in the Jaina monastery where serman could be attended by the males and females alike, (2) secondly, vehicles played an important role in the

---

178. *The Uvāsagadasāo*, tr. by A.F. Rudolf Hoernle, p. 61, verse 77.
179. *Kalpasūtra,* Vol, I, tr. by Herman Jacobi, p. 278.
180. *Ibid.*
181. *Ibid.*, p. 274.
182. *The Niryāvaliyāo,* ed. by A.S. Gopani, pp. 118-20.

dissemination of Jaina culture and faith among the people.[183] The arrangement for instructions in philosophy and theology, given to female students in Jaina nunneries, was as perfect as possible. Jainism successfully persuaded the ladies to give up a life of luxury and ease in favour of a life of stern asceticism and led a life of hardship.

The nuns of mature age, being well versed both in secular and sacred learning were fit to impart education to female lay students. It is noteworthy there was a sound knowledge of psychology in the background of the steps of education they imparted to their students. in the *Uvāsagadasāo* eight stages of the human life is described. "Eight stages of man (*puriṣabhumīya*) can be designated as the following eight developmental periods of man: the dull stage (*manda-bhūmi*), the playful-stage (*khiḍḍa-bhūmi*), the experimental-stage (*vimaṁsa-bhūmi*), the erect-stage (*ujugata-bhūmi*), the learning stage (*sekhā bhūmi*), the ascetic-stage (*samana-bhūmi*), the Jina-stage (*jina-bhūmi*), and the prostrate-stage (*puṇṇa-bhūmi*).[184]

Jaina fathers prescribed the art of education for the girls in their girlhood instead of the Vedic education. The Vedic education was to be superimposed upon the art of primary and secondary education. The course of studies intended for females were practical with a special eye to the mental aptitude of their students. Specialization was in vogue. Students thoroughly studied a particular branch of knowledge with the study of allied pre-umbral subjects, which was quite in harmony with their bents of mind. Organised games and physical exercises formed a part of training. In the *Prabandhakośa*[185] it is stated that *Madanamañjarī* versed in the higher branches of learning, wrote from behind the screen, five hundred *śloka*s of a book composed by a Digambara saint. It proves that she was competent enough as a scribe.

183. *The Niryāvaliyāo*, ed. by A.S. Gopani, pp. 118-20.

184. *The Uvāsagadasāo*, Vol. II, tr. by A.F. Rudolf Hoernle, p. 23.

185. *digambareṇa granthān kartumārebhe* |
rājaputrī bajraśatīṁ likhati ||
— Rājaśekhara Sūri, *Prabandhakośa,* Vol. I, p. 64

Women were also conversant with varied languages and costumes.[186]

The word *paṇḍita* being prefixed to the names of some of the females proves that diploma of *paṇḍita* used to be conferred upon the competent lady scholars also. Jainas recognized the equality of the two sexes. Only individual interests, aptitudes, temperaments, tastes and needs was the detrimental factor of the type of education meant for any student.

Jaina philosophy must have influenced its educational doctrine. The elaborate psychology and sublime ethical code influenced educational psychology.

The Jaina architecture of marble temples proves the advanced learning of engineering.

The Jaina monasteries had excellent libraries or *bhāṇḍāras* attached to them. Highly educated monks spent their time in studying, copying sacred books and writing books on diverse subjects. These libraries were rich depositories of Indian literature.

186. *nānādeśaveṣa bhāṣāvicakṣaṇān . . . strī*
— *Prabandakośa*, Vol. I, p. 92

5

Education as is known from Sanskrit Inscription

INSCRIPTIONS are the sources of much important and reliable records relating to the Gupta age. They are incised on stones, metals, as well as in the copper-plates. Some inscriptions have recorded religious endowments of secular donations. The donative inscriptions are large in number.

The *praśasti*s or eulogistic *kāvya*s on stone tablets and pillars, copper-plate inscriptions most of which deal with land-grants were composed in great quality and quantity during the time of the Guptas. Inscribed pillars (*stambha*) were of various kinds, viz., (1) *dhvajastambha*, erected in front of a temple, (2) *jaya-stambha*, containing the eulogy of a conqueror, (3) *kīrti-stambha* bearing the praises of a person who made himself famous by performing some pious deeds. Many epigraphic records, including land-grants depicted the donations made in favour of learned brāhmaṇas or deserving individuals. For engraving these grants copper was chosen among other metals and later on it became almost traditional to engrave title-deeds on copper-plates for the purpose of durability.

The Gupta kings and people of that age donated lands for various purposes, specially because of the fact that the Smṛti, *Mahābhārata* and some law-books propagated that the gift of land is most meritorious gift and reliever of any type of sin committed by the donor.

It is an admitted fact that the inscriptions of this period were not written with the aim of recording the educational system current at their time. But some valuable information regarding the status of teacher, nature of students, subjects of study, can be traced in these inscriptions. On the basis of these datas, a picture of the general education prevalent in this age can be discovered.

The Mathurā Pillar Inscription of the time of Candragupta II recorded a custom of offering worship to the teachers, along with the worship of deities. The images and statues of the teachers and founders of religious sects were installed in shrines (*gurvāyatana*).

Education was promoted by public benefactions which usually took the form of gifts made of both cash and kind. The gifts of cash were not usually spent. The Sāñcī Stone Inscription[1] recorded the gifts of cash kept as a permanent fund (*akṣaya-nīvi*), the interest of which only was to be spent on their purpose. Gifts of kind were generally grants of land. The grants of land was in the shape of an *agrahāra* or village to learned brāhmaṇas in the purpose of furtherance of their religious pursuits. The mention of *agrahāra* which was a typically Hindu institution in Gupta times can be traced from many contemporary inscriptions. The rulers of the country donated the land to brāhmaṇas for specified objects. The *agrahāras* were donated to learned brāhmaṇas with the assignment of one particular tax like *uparikaras*. Other privileges were also attached.

Samudragupta donated a village entitled Revatikā of Gayā district, as an *agrahāra* to one Gopadevasvāmī[2] who was a *brahmacārī*. Gopasvāmī came under the Bhāradvāja *gotra* and belonged to Bahvṛccha *śākhā*. This fact is recorded in the Gayā Copper-Plate Grant of Samudragupta. It is noteworthy that the *gotra* and the *śākhā*, i.e., the particular recension of the Veda is mentioned. It may be assumed that the student should study and cultivate the particular branch of the Veda.

1. Fleet, *Corpus Inscription Indicarum*, Vol. III, No.62, p. 260.
2. *Ibid.*, No. 60, p. 257.

The Bihar Stone Pillar Inscription of Skandagupta recorded the grant of a certain *agrahāra*, the name of which is missing. An allusion is recorded to three shares probably granted by one Anantasena in the town of Ajapura.[3] Official *agrahārika* is also mentioned in this connection.[4]

The Khoh Copper Plate Grant of Mahārāja Hastin, dated 482-3, refers to the *agrahāra* of Korpārika. It is granted to Devasvāmin of the Bhāradvāja *gotra*; Gosvāmin of the Kautsa *gotra*; a student of the Vājasaneya *śākhā*; Svātisvāmin, Varuṇaśraman of the Bhārgava *gotra* and a student of Vājasaneya *śākhā*; Bappasvāmin and Maitraśarman, a student of the Vājasaneya *śākhā*, Nāgaśarman. It is probable that Gopasvāmin was the head of the religious institution and the other donees were his disciples. The system of collective possession of the village can be assumed. It is clear that these grants were offered to scholarly brāhmaṇas who specialised in particular *śākhā*s.

This practice was prevalent from the fourth to seventh century AD is evident from the fact that the Aphsad Stone Inscription of Dāmodaragupta, ascribed to the seventh century, related the *agrahāra* grants to virtuous brāhmaṇas.[5] The Shāhapur Stone Image Inscription, dated AD 672-3 during the reign of Ādityasena, recorded that one Sālapakṣa who was a Balādhikṛta, made a *mahāgrahāra* of Nālandā. So, Nālandā appear to have been a great *agrahāra*.[6]

The scholarly Brāhmaṇas enjoyed the privilege of accepting donation of *agrahāras*. Such gifts also helped the rise and spread of Vedic and other studies in this age. The Nirmand Copper Plate Grant of Mahāsāmanta and Mahārāja Samudrasena records the grant to brāhmaṇas who study the *Atharvaveda*.[7]

Mallasore Copper Plate Inscription, though it is undated,

3. Fleet, *Corpus Inscription Indicarum,* No. 12, p. 51.
4. *Ibid.*, No. 23, p. 109.
5. *Ibid.*, No. 42, p. 206.
6. *Ibid.*, No. 43, p. 210.
7. *Ibid.*

palaeographically resembles the Farīdpur Plates of Dharmāditya assigned to the sixth century AD. The inscription records a gift of land measuring 8 *kulyavāpas* to a brāhmaṇa.

The Gunaigaḍh Inscription of Vainyagupta records the gift to a Mahāyāna *saṁgha* of Śākyabhikṣus for provision for their *cīvara* (clothing), *piṇḍapāta* (food), *āsana* and medicine. It was followed by another gift of *agrahāra* to the same *saṁgha*.

The Sāñcī Stone Inscription of Candragupta II records the grant of the village Īśvaravāsaka and twenty-five *dīnāras*. From the interest of the *dīnāras* feeding of five *bhikkhus* was arranged and provision of lamp to be burnt in the jewel house was made.

Educational benefactions of those days were made in the form of grants of lands which could be profitably cultivated to produce to income required to maintain them.

Brāhmaṇas who were versed in all the four Vedas were known as *caturvedins*.[8] Generally they lived together in a village. *Caturvidyāgrahāra*[9] and *cāturvedyagrāmamaryādā*[10] — these type of expressions prove that village had been donated to those brāhmaṇas as *agrahāra*.

Students of the Vedic school followed respective recensions of the Vedas. The students were grouped under *śākhās* and *caraṇas*. Gupta inscriptions recorded some of the recensions, viz., Kāṇva-Vājasaneya[11]

---

8. *caturvidyā-sāmānya-brāhmaṇa* — Indor Copper Plate Inscription of Skandagupta, *CII*, III, No 16, pp. 70, 1. 5.
9. Poona Inscription of Prabhāvatīgupta — *Select Inscriptions*, bearing *Indian History and Civilization,* Vol. I, ed. by D.C. Sircar, Calcutta, 1965, p. 437, 1.16.
10. Rīthāpur Inscription of Prabhāvatīgupta — *Sel. Ins.*, p. 441, 1. 17; Chammak Inscription of Pravarasena II, *CII*, III, No. 55, p. 238, 1.25.
11. Farīdpur Copper Plate Inscription of Dharmāditya and Gopacandra — *Sel. Ins.*, p. 368, 1.10; p. 371, 1.13.

of *Śukla Yajurveda*, *Vājasaneyaṣaḍaṅgādhyāyī*[12] of the *Śukla Yajurveda*, *Chāndoga-rānāyanīya*[13] of the *Sāmaveda*, *Maitrāyanīya*[14] of the *Kṛṣṇa Yajurveda*, *Bahvṛcca*[15] of the *Ṛgveda*, *Atharvaṇikacaraṇa*[16] and *Chāndogakauthuma*[17] of the *Sāmaveda*, *Aupamanyava*,[18] *Kaṭha*,[19] *Nārāyaṇīya*,[20] *Taittirīya*,[21] *Mādhyandina-vājasaneya*[22] of the *Yajurveda*. The branches of Vedāṅga were cultivated with proper attention. Reference is made to one Ṣaṣṭidatta who was the originator of a race of Naigamas, and the chief of the interpreters of the Vedic words.[23]

The esteemed brāhmaṇa teachers were honoured by the title of Bhaṭṭa. Bhaṭṭa Guhilasvāmin in Bihar Stone Pillar Inscription of Skandagupta[24] and Bhaṭṭa Bhavadatta and Bhaṭṭa Haridatta and Bhaṭṭa Gaurīdatta in Rājim Copper Plate Inscription may be mentioned in this context.

---

12. *Sel. Ins.*, p. 366, 1. 19.
13. Indor Copper-Plate Inscription of Skandagupta. — *CII*, III, No. 16, p. 70, 1. 6
14. Eran Stone Pillar Inscription of Buddhagupta, dated AD 484. — *CII*, No. 19, p. 39
15. Mallasurul Copper-Plate Inscription of the Time of Gopacandra — *Sel. Ins.*, p. 374, 1.10
16. Basim Copper-Plate Inscription of Vindhyasakti II. — *Sel. Ins.*, p. 374, 1.10
17. Majhgawam Copper-Plate Inscription of Mahārāja Hastin. — *CII*, III, No. 23, p. 108, 1.80
18. *CII*, No. 41, p. 197.
19. *Ibid.*, No. 22, p. 102.
20. *Ibid.*, No. 16, p. 70.
21. *Ibid.*, No. 16.
22. *Ibid.*, No. 21, 81.
23. *yata uditagarimnas tāvate naigamānām* — Mandasor Stone Inscription of Yaśodharman and Viṣṇuvardhan, dated AD 510. — *Ibid.*, No. 35, p. 153, I.11
24. *Ibid.*, III, No. 12, p. 52, 1. 31.

The term *ācārya* and *upādhyāya* for the teachers and *śisya* for the pupil are referred to in the inscriptions. By the term *ācārya* the Gupta records indicated all those who taught one of the Brāhmaṇical, Buddhist or Jaina learning. *Upādhyāya* connotates a teacher who is conversant with only in a part of the Veda or in grammar and in the other Vedāṅgas.[25] *Brahmacārin* also meant a disciple.[26] The term *brahmacārī* means unmarried student who observed the vow of celibacy.

The three Vedas are collectively called *trayī*[27] The brāhmaṇa who was conversant with four Vedas, is called *caturvedin*. The term *caturvedin* is associated with the *caturvidyāgrahāra*. The Khoh Copper-Plate Inscription[28] has recorded the name of Veda-Vyāsa as the arranger of the Vedas. There were brāhmaṇas who acquired mastery on only one Veda. Mention of the *Atharvaveda* individually has been found in the Gupta inscription.[29]

The inclusion of the four Vedas in the subjects of study is clear from the term *caturvedin*. The fourteen sections of the learning (*caturdaśavidyāsthāna*)[30] comprises four Vedas, six Vedāṅgas, the Purāṇas, Mīmāṁsā, Nyāya and Dharmaśātra or Law. Nyāyaśāstra or Science of Logic was also considered as special branch of study. Reference has been made of one Cakrapālita as well versed in Nyāya, i.e., *Nyāyaśāstravettā* in the Junāgaḍh Inscription of Skandagupta.[31] Six Vedāṅgas along with Dharmaśāstra were mentioned.[32] The Gunaigaḍh inscription of Vainyagupta dated AD 507 recorded Śruti, Smṛti and

25. *CII*, III, No. 81, p. 255, 1. 23.
26. *Ibid.*, Nos. 56, 61, 71; 21, 23, 39, 60.
27. *Ibid.*, No. 39, p. 173.
28. *Ibid.*, No. 21, p. 95.
29. *Ibid.*, No. 80.
30. Khoh Copper-Plate Inscription of Mahārāja Samkṣobha. — *CII*, III, 25, p. 114. 1. 3
31. *Sel. Ins.*, p. 313, 1.19.
32. Farīdpur Inscription of Dharmāditya and Gopacandra. — *Sel. Ins.*, p. 369, Lines 19-24

itihāsa.[33] *Itihāsa* includes also the two great epics, i.e., the *Rāmāyaṇa* and the *Mahābhārata* and probably along with Purāṇas. The large number of land-grants prove the importance and authenticity of the Dharmaśāstras. The influence of Dharmaśāstra mainly provoked the donor to offer these gifts as Dharmaśāstras recommended such type of grant as a sacred act and generator of *puṇya* for the donor or even for his parents. References can be found to the grammar of Pāṇini, which is called *Śālāturīya*[34] after the name of the place where Pāṇini lived; to son of Parāśara.[35] The name of *Mahābhārata*[36] as *Śatasahasrī-saṁhitā* can be found in the different inscriptions.

The fact that the *Mahābhārata* and the Purāṇas were discussed among the people, can be proved from ample references to the characters of these books. Yudhiṣṭhira,[37] Vidura,[38] Uddhava,'[39] etc.

Svādhyāya suggests the study of the particular recension of the Veda.[40] Karamdāṇḍa (situated in Faizabad district, U.P.) Stone Liṅga Inscription of the time of Kumāragupta I, dated AD 436 ,[41] states that a Vedic scholar was used to be well acquainted in the interpretations and significance of Vedic *svādhyāya*, *mantra*, *sūkta*, *bhāṣya* and *pravacana*. *Pravacana* means sacred writings, specially *Brāhmaṇas* and Vedāṅgas.[42] The study of the *Ṛgveda* hymns was specially emphasised. Samudragupta was advised to follow the path of the

---

33. *Sel. Ins.*, p. 342, 1. 8.
34. *CII*, No. 39.
35. *Ibid.*, No. 31.
36. *Ibid.*, Nos. 26, 27, 28 and 31.
37. *Ibid.*, No. 38.
38. *Ibid.*, No. 35.
39. *Ibid.*, No. 35.
40. Mandasor Inscription of Kumaragupta and Bandhuvarman. — *CII*, II, 18, p. 82. 1.8
41. *Sel. Ins.*, p. 313, 1.19.
42. Monier-Williams, *Sanskrit-English Dictionary,* p. 690.

sacred hymns (*adhyaḥ sūktamārgaḥ*).[43] Indraviṣṇu is described as a *viprarṣi*[44] who had read fully the recension of the Veda (*adītarvādhyāyasya*).[45]

Royal officers are sometimes well-acquainted with various subjects. Sāba Vīrasena, a minister of Candragupta II was a poet. He was also proficient in etymology (*śabdārthaḥ*), logic (Nyāya) and statecraft (*lokajña*).[45] Some acquired proficiency in *Jyotiṣa*.[46]

The science of archery (*Dhanurveda*) and wonderful *kathā* literaure, i.e., *vicitra-kathā-vidaḥ* were referred to in the inscription.[47] Some persons were engaged in practising vocal music and some were busy in painting pictures. The great king Samudragupta was also a patron of fine arts and also he himself was accomplished in instrumental music. It is stated allegorically that he had made ashamed Tumburu and Nārada, two celestial musicians, by his musical skill and accomplishments (*gāndharvalalitaiḥ*).[48] The lyrist type of coins of Samudragupta shows the king playing or lyre of *vīṇā* and the image of the goddess on the reverse may be taken as that of Sarasvatī who being the goddess of music, is associated with *vīṇā*.[49] Skandagupta disciplined himself in the different tunes (*tāna*) of music, which is clear from his Bhitarī Stone Pillar Inscription.[50]

Samudragupta was described in the Allahabad Stone Pillar Inscription as a man of letters and as a poet. Samudragupta ruled over a kingdom of poetry as well as a realm of earth — with equal ability. He

---

43. *CII*, III, No. 1, p. 6, 1.16.
44. *Ibid.*, No. 19, p. 89.1.5.
45. *Sel. Ins.*, p. 280, 1.4.
46. Mandasor Inscription of Kumāragupta and Bandhuvarman. — *CII*, III, 18, p. 82,1.10
47. *CII*, p. 82, 1.9.
48. *Ibid.*, p. 81, 1.7.
49. Allan, *Catalogue of Coins.*
50. *Sel. Ins.*, p. 322, 1.9.

was well competent to find out the real truth of the scriptures. (*śāstratattvārthabharttā*). It is stated that he was entitled *kavirāja*. It proves that he was a genius. The study of the hymns of the *R̥gveda* was one of his daily duties (*adhyeyaḥ sūktamārgaḥ* — verse 8).

He made another contribution to learning by upholding its standard. He used to convene conferences of literary critics to judge the true poetry and weed out that literature which would violate its dignity.[51] He was accustomed to associate himself regularly with learned assemblies (*prajñanuṣaṅgocita*). This epithets prove the royal patronage to education.

Learned chiefs were also referred to in the inscriptions. Mātr̥-viṣṇu was a local chief. He was described as brāhmaṇa *r̥ṣi*. He completed his Vedic study. The local chief Viśvavarman is also described as the equal of Śakra and Vr̥haspati.

It is noteworthy that this inscription also recorded the fact that even members of an industrial guild, a guild of silk-weavers (*paṭṭavāya śreṇī*) though proficient in technical topic showed proficiency in cultural subjects. Some of them were proficient in military science (*Dhanurvidyā*), some in stories (*kathāvidhaḥ*) and in astrology (*jyotiṣa*). So this inscription, speaks itself about the advancement of the general education of the masses.

In the Gupta age, the general people were familiar with Sanskrit language and learning. This fact can be supported by the fact that all the Gupta inscriptions were written in Sanskrit, replacing Prākr̥t or Pāli which was the medium of the earlier inscription. So it may be assumed that Sanskrit displaced Prākr̥t as the popular language. Reference to the arrangement of sentences, i.e., compositions of poems both in Sanskrit and Prākr̥t can be found.

vacanaracanābandhe saṁskr̥taprākr̥te yaḥ ।
kavibhir uditarāgam gīyate gīrabhijñāḥ ॥ [52]

---

51. *vidvajjanopajīvyāneka-kāvya-kriyābhiḥ* ।
pratiṣṭhita-kavirāja śabdasya ॥ — I. 27

52. *CII*, p. 153, 1.14.

Inscription-writing was considered as a cultivated art. It was not a mere statement of facts but the authors declared them to be considered as a piece of literature. These were purposely shaped in the forms of excellent poems. In the Allahabad Pillar Inscription, it is declared by Hariṣena that it is nothing but a *kāvya* in nature (*etacca kāvyam* — I. 31). The writer of the inscription was highly esteemed and favoured by the king. This fact can be supported by the fact that Hariṣena held posts as *khādyaṭapākika*, *sāndhivigrahika*, *kumārāmātya* and *mahādaṇḍanāyaka*. Besides Allahabad Pillar Inscription, the Maharauli Iron Pillar Inscription of Candra, the Mandasor Inscription of Kumāragupta I and Bandhuvarman, which were composed by the Vatsabhaṭṭi, the Junāgaḍh Inscription of Skandagupta may be safely treated as *kāvya*.

Teachers were highly honoured in this age. Mathurā Pillar Inscription of the time of Candragupta II states that Uditācārya, the desciple of Upamita-Vimala and the grand-disciple of Kapila. Vimala erected (*pratiṣṭāpitam*) two images of his teachers, i.e., Upamita and Kapila in, perhaps, two shrines to make prominent the fame of his teachers. The Kahaum Stone Pillar Inscription of Skandagupta dated AD 460 refers to one Madra who was full of affection and regards for brāhmaṇas, preceptors and ascetics (*dvijaguruyatiṣu prāyaśaḥ pr̥timān yaḥ*). Thus it is proved that respect was shown to by installing statues in specially made shrines. The Sārnāth Stone Inscription points out the superior position of a teacher even compared to the parents. It records that one Buddhist *bhikṣu*, Harigupta, was erecting an image of the Buddha (*kāritā pratimā śātuḥ*); he first worshipped his *guru* and then his mother and finally his father. This type of veneration show the respective importance of the superiors. Sacred Buddhist texts were worshipped in shrines.

It may be inferred from some evidences that the *Padma*, *Bhaviṣya* and *Brahmā Purāṇa*s must have been well-known to the people of those days.

The watches of the day and night was evidently calculated by the device of the well-known water-clock. In the Harāha Inscription of

Īśānavarman, dated 551, it is stated that "the victorious one (Īśānavarman) whose watches can only be determined by means of the water-clock (*nāḍikā*) as if it were at night, the world being encompassed in darkness and bewildered as to the beginning, the middle or the end of the day. . . ." In the Wāle Inscription of the Maitraka ruler Guhasena, dated AD 566-7, the reference to *ghaṭa* is found. The term *ghaṭa* indicates probably the vessel employed to keep the water by the trickling of which the passing of time was recorded. An allusion to *ghaṭikāsthāna* most probably where the *ghaṭikā*s were measured, is made in the famous Talguṇḍa Inscription of the Kadamba ruler Śāntivarman, dated AD 450. It is possible that in the temples, and *maṭha*s the water-clock was usually kept. It was evident that to set this water-clock it was necessary to be a good mechanic. So this type of training was imparted to students in this age. In this context it is informed that Mayuraśarma "desiring to be proficient in Pravacana, entered into all religious centres (*ghaṭikā*) and became a quick debator or disputant".[53] In Nālandā water-clock was kept by 'the imperial order'.[54]

Contemporary epigraphs furnish details about the Hindu calendar. The Khoh Copper Plate Grant, the Gayā Copper Plate Grant, Kahaum Stone Pillar Inscription of Skandagupta, etc. recorded the name of the month. The calculation of Hindu calendar was prevalent is evident.

Vihāras served the purpose of residential college as well as collective education. Sāñcī Stone Inscription of Candragupta II, dated AD 412, records the name of a great *vihāra* Kākanādaboṭa (ancient name of Sāñcī). Here lived the members of the Buddhist community whose organs of sense are subdued by the virtues of good character, religious meditation and wide wisdom.[55] The Gunaigaḍh Inscrption records that

---

53. *pravacanaṁnikhila-ghaṭikāṁ viveś-āśutārkukaḥ* — *Epigraphia Carnatica*, VII, p. 113, text, p. 269

54. *JRAS*, XIII (New Series), p. 571: *Two Chinese Buddhist Inscriptions*

55. *Sel. Ins.*, p. 475, II, 3-4.

one Buddhist *saṁgha* was housed in a *vihāra* called *āśrama-vihāra*, which was dedicated to the Avalokiteśvara. The Pahārpur Copper-Plate Inscription, dated AD 479, speaks of the Nirgrantha Śramaṇācārya Guhanandin who resided in a *vihāra* at Vaṭa-Gohali accompanied by his disciples and grand-disciples.

The Tālaguṇḍā Stone Pillar Inscription records that in a *gurukula*, a preceptor's family was to be served, and a Vedic recension was studied; these could lead one to attain perfection in holiness (*gurukulāni samyag ārādhya śākhām adhītyāpi yatnataḥ brahmasiddhi*). So it can be proved that the *gurukula* system was in vogue in the Gupta age. Royal patronage was bestowed on the educational institutions. So it may be assumed that the *vihāras*, *ghaṭikās*, *gurukulas* were patronised by the *ghaṭikā*, like *vihāra*, appears to be another establishment for the people devoted to religious and learned discourses. It appears to be something like a college. The stone pillar inscription of Talguṇḍa, written at the time of Śāntivarman (AD 455-70), records that Mayuraśarman, who wås the best of the brāhmaṇas (*dvijottama*) and was endowed with learning, good character and purity (*śrauta-sīla-śaucādyalaṁ-kr̥taḥ*), went with his teacher Vīraśarman to the Pallava capital Kāñcī (*yaḥ prayaye pallavendrapurīm guruṇā samaṁ vīraśarmanā*) and was admitted to a *ghaṭikā*, as an earnest student, to acquire knowledge in all the religious scriptures (*adhijigāmsuḥ pravacanaṁ nikhilām ghatikām viveśāsu tarkkukaḥ*).[56]

The Udayagiri Cave Inscription, dated AD 445,[57] of the reign of Kumāragupta I mentions the constructions of an image of Jineśvara Pārśva. The Kahaum Stone Pillar Inscription of the time of Skandagupta records endowment in favour of Jainism.[58] Jaina *vihāras* were as familiar as the Brāhmaṇical.

According to the *Kalpa Sūtra*, there were six schools of thought (*gaṇas*) with their respective branches (*śākhās*) each of which separated

---

56. Manabendu Banerjee, *Historical and Social . . . Gupta Inscription*. Talgunda Pillar Inscription, pp. 128-34.
57. Udayagiri Cave Inscription, *Ibid.*, pp. 62-4.
58. Kahaum Stone Pillar Inscription, *Ibid.*, pp. 144-7.

in course of time into its own family (*kula*). Nāgabhūtikiya *kula* is the only identifiable reference in the records.[59]

From the Udayagiri cave Inscription we learn that the chief of the Jaina institutions was called the *ācārya*. The Mathurā Stone Pillar Inscription dated AD 443, records the consecration of an image by a person belonged to Koṭṭiya Gana and the Vidyādharī *śākhā*.[60] It may be noted that the *śākhā* as well as the *gaṇa* of the *ācārya* were recorded in the inscriptions. The Kahaum Stone Pillar Inscription records a donation to the Jaina *maṭha* by four generations of people. It may be safely concluded that Kahaum was probably a centre of Jainism. Thus Jaina education kept its flow uninterrupted in India for a long time. The Pahārpur Copper-Plate Inscription of the year AD 479 refers to a *maṭha* at Vaṭa Gohali presided over by a succession of Nirgrantha monks.[61] A grant of the reign of Kākusthavarmā[62] and one of the inscriptions of Mṛgeśavarmā[63]relates the gift of land for the welfare. This gift was more or less of the character of *agrahāra* dedicated to Hindu brāhmaṇa. These gifts of land from the State emblemed the Jaina monks to carry on their feasts and religious observances.

Sāñcī continued to be a great centre of Buddhism. An inscription[64] dated AD 412 records the gift of a village to the Āryasaṁgha of Kākanādaboṭa *vihāra* (Sāñcī) and also of 25 *dīnāras*, by the interest of which was to feed five *bhikṣus* and lighting each evening a lamp. Sāranāth was another centre of Buddhism and noted for the two famous images of the Buddha bearing insciptions of the time of Kumāragupta II and Buddhagupta. The Buddha is here called Śāstā. He is also called Sugata.[65]

---

59. *Epigraphia Indica,* I, No. XIV, p. 391.
60. Fleet, *CII*, III (61), pp. 259-60.
61. *Ep. Ind.*, XX, p. 62.
62. *IA*, VII, pp. 34-5.
63. *Ibid.*, VI, p. 25.
64. *CII*, No. 5.
65. *CII*, No. 52.

It is stated by the Chinese pilgrims that monastery which was known as the Mahābodhi monastery was erected by the king of Ceylon with the approval of Mahā Śrī Rāja of India. Two inscriptions found at Bodh Gayā may help us to corroborate the statements. Both of them refer to the name of *mahānāma*. The number one is dated in the year 269 enumerates the erection of the Bauddha *vihāra*.[66] The second one which is undated states same fact.[67]

Candragupta II appointed men to high offices irrespective of caste and creed. His military general Āmrakārddeva was possibly a Buddhist and the role played by him for the progress of Buddhism was remarkable. The Sāñcī Stone Inscription related this fact.[68]

There are two other inscriptions which give useful information relating to the flourishing condition of Buddhism during Candragupta II's time. The first inscription, found near a small ruined temple close to the south gate of the railing of the great temple of Bodh Gayā, records the dedication of the image of Bodhisattva.[69] The second inscription records the dedication to the universal congregation.[70] A stone inscription of Mandasor bears testimony to the establishment of a Buddhist monument at Mandasor.[71] An inscription, dated AD 448, found at Mankwar in the Allahabad distirict records the installation of an image

---

66. *āmradvīpādhivāsī pṛthukula-jaladhi-tasya śiṣyo mahīyān laṅkā-dvīpa-prasūtaḥ para-hita-nirataḥ san mahānāmā-rāmātenochchair-vvo(bho) dhimaṇḍe śaṣīkar-dhavalaḥ sarvvato maṇḍapeṇa . . . .*

— *IA*, XV, 1886, pp. 358-9

67. *om deye-dharmmo-yam śākya-bhikṣoḥ āmradvīpa-vāsisthavira-mahānāmasya yadatra puṇyam tad-bhāvatu sarvva-sat-vānam-anuttara-jñān-āvāptaye stu'*

— *IA*, XV, 1886, p 369

68. *EI*, XXI, 1931-2, pp. 1-9.

69. *ARASI*, II, 1922-3, p. 169.

70. *EI*, XVI, 1921-2, p. 15.

71. *IHQ*, XXXII, No. I. 1956, pp. 200-01.

of Buddha by Bhikkhu Buddhamitra.[72] K.P. Pāṭhak and Rādhā Kumud Mookerji have identified Bhikkhu Buddhamitra of the inscription with Buddhamitra, the teacher of Vasubandhu.[73]

The Sārnāth Buddhist Stone Image Inscription of Kumaragupta II, dated AD 473-4, proves the predominance of Buddhist education.[74] Another inscription of the Buddha image may indicate the erection of this image by king Kumāragupta.[75] Another inscription, found at Sārnāth, describes the installation of the image of the Buddha by Bhikṣu Harigupta.[76]

The Sārnāth Buddhist image inscription of Budhagupta supports the patronage of Budhagupta.[77] Another inscription on a detached pedestal of an image of the Buddha was discovered at Sārnāth.

All the inscriptions, described above, give vivid picture of Buddhist activities and learning in the Gupta age.

The Gunaigarh Inscription[78] refers to the Buddhist Avaivarttika *saṁgha* of the Mahāyāna sect.

The Gupta inscriptions record numerous instances of building and temple constructions as well as erections and installations of images. These records will help to fathom the exquisitive beauty of the Gupta arts.

The Lāṭa distirct (*lāṭaviṣaya*) was made beautiful with temples, assembly halls and *vihāras* (*devakulasabhāvihāraramayāni*), the house of the city of Daśapura were of bright whiteness and of high altitude (*atyarthaśuklānyadhikonnatām*), the rows of storeyed mansions were

72. *CII*, III, pp. 45-7.
73. *IA*, XLI, 1912, p. 244.
74. *ARASI*, 1914-15, p. 124.
75. *IHQ*, XXXII, No. I, 1956, pp. 188-9.
76. *CII*, III, p. 2.
77. *ARASI*, 1914-15, pp. 124-5.
78. *IHQ*, 1930, pp. 53-60.

comparable to the rows of aerial chariots (*vimāna-mālāsadr̥śāṇī*).[79] A temple of Kārttikeya was furnished with a gateway having flight of steps, a charitable alms-house and a firm and excellent lofty pillar (*sthiravarasthambhocchaya*).[80] Skandagupta caused to construct a group of temples (*devaniketamaṇḍalam*).[81] From the Junāgaḍh Inscription of Skandagupta,[82] a reservoir entitled Sudarśana which was originally constructed during the Maurya period was described. In the time of Skandagupta, as its embankment burst owing to continuous rain, the engineers repaired it within two months and implementing proper masonry (*samyagghaṭitopalena*) reconstructed the embankment. The lenght of the embankment was 100 cubits (*āyāmato hasta-śatam*), breadth of 68 cubits (*vistarataḥ ṣaṣṭir athāpi cāṣṭaṁ*), and seven man's height (i.e., about 40 feet). This description of the embankment proves the advanced skill of the then engineers. As the Sun temple was partly dilapidated, it had been repaired again by skilled artisans (*bhānumato gr̥ham saṁskāritam idaṁ bhūyaḥ*). These skilled engineers and artisans must have some technical training in those days. The technical training education centre may be proved with other informations. Science of architecture and iconography was also highly in advanced stage. Various images, such as those of Śiva, mother goddess, Varāha,[83] Jaina *tīrthaṁkaras*, Buddha[84] speak on the advancement of art. The art of architecture and sculpture was mastered by a class of inquisite people.

The inscriptions of the Gupta age prove that the art of writing was cultivated by the skilled artisans. There were various scripts such as Brāhmī and Kharoṣṭhī. The art of engraving letters in the stone or copper or other metals was also in a highly advanced stage. The

---

79. *CII*, III, pp. 81f.
80. *Ibid*., p. 43.
81. *Ibid*., p. 49.
82. *Ibid*., pp. 58f.
83. *Ibid*., p. 159.
84. *Ibid*., p. 46.

inscriptions had passed through several ages, and they speak themselves of the culture and feelings of the Gupta age as well as the skill that the artists possessed of that age.

Copying of manuscripts was one of the important activities of the Buddhist students.[85]

Reference to education in the coins of the Gupta age is very scarce. Only a coin of Samācāradeva of later Gupta age bears the idol of Sarasvatī which proves the high estimation for education in the Gupta age.

---

85. Bandell — *Catalogue of Buddhist Sanskrit Manuscripts in the University Library,* Cambridge, p. 101.
— *JASB* (Numismatic Supplement), IV, p. 105

6

Conclusion

General Trend of Education in Gupta India and its Legacy in the Educational System Prevalent in Modern Age

PHILOSOPHY of education would cover the nature of discipline. According to *Webster's New World Dictionary* discipline means (1) a branch of knowledge of learning, (2) training that develops self-control, character, or orderliness and efficiency. Ancient Indian Education as a discipline denotes the second meaning.[1]

Philosophy of education is one of many branches of social ethics. On the other hand, social ethics applies to moral philosophy or ethics of various societies. Moral philosophy establishes knowledge of the end of man and of the species of kinds of act by which he may reach the end. Man is a social being and needs the cooperation of other men to achieve the conditions of life appropriate to him and to reach his final end. That part of moral philosophy which directs the individual person to his end was called 'monastics' by Aristotle and St. Thomas. Schematically

1. Webster, *New World Dictionary*, New york, 1956.

arranged, the classification would appear like this.[2]

Some knowledge of certain educational discipline is necessary for the scientific construction of a philosophy of education. The most basic of these is the experimental and philosophical psychologies of learning. The former deals with such topics as readiness to learn, the rate of learning, the transfer of learning; the latter would consider principally the human cognitive powers and their iteration in the learning process. The Brāhmaṇic education prescribed *upanayana* for the three echelons of higher social class. This marks the readiness of the mind to acquire knowledge. The rate of learning was taken into consideration in the monitorial system of education. The transmittance of knowledge to the student from the teacher was the main factor in ancient Indian education. Since philosophy of education is part of social ethics, it is concerned with human acts.[3]

Sometimes education is used in the sense of that lifelong process of development which is identical with the course of a human life itself. In this significance the end of education is the same as the end of life itself, and the philosophy of education becomes identical with that aspect of moral philosophy. But in this discussion education specifically though

---

2.

	Moral Theology	Monastics (Individual Ethics)	Philosophy of the State + Politics.
			Philosophy of the economy
Moral Science			Philosophy of primary and secondary groups+
	Moral Philosophy (Ethics)	Social Ethics	Sociology
			Philosophy of education+ some educational discipline.

— Herbert Johnston, *A Philosophy of Education,* New York, 1963, p. 13.

3. *Ibid.*, p. 14.

not exclusively refers to formal education.[4]

If a man is considered a rational and responsible being, capable of achieving truth and directing his own life, his education will take one direction. Man starts with the concrete, particular things of the physical universe, but does not end there. From these things, he draws general universal knowledge which is abstract knowledge. Ancient educators of India fixed the aim of education as the attainment of Brahmā or final bliss.[5]

The human achievement points to human capabilities unknown to the other animals, to intellectual and moral capacities that cry out for the development which is education. Language is one of the examples. Animals make sounds for expressing emotions. Whereas *homo-sapiens* use language to signify ideas and their relations; their concepts and judgements are expressed in terms and propositions, and their language has a formal grammar and syntax. This indicates an intellectual grasp not only of abstract concepts or ideas but of their connection in a larger whole whose parts are no longer isolated.[6]

In realm of language the capacity to produce and appreciate literature marks man as unique in the animal world. In drama, novel, lyric, epic the great writers have caught something of the constant and universal in human nature and human life and have expressed it in concrete and telling terms. Thus history came into existence. Science involves an attempt to get behind the surface phenomena and to identify and understand an intelligible casual pattern in human affairs. In such useful arts (viz. carpentry and tailoring) men show an ability. In fine arts as painting and sculpture and the dance, a further reach of intelligence is manifested. Ancient Indian education flourished and touched all the fields which is a manifestation of intellectual side of the human being.[7]

---

4. *A Philosophy of Education*, p. 22.
5. *Ibid.*, pp. 27f.
6. *Ibid.*, p. 34.
7. *Ibid.*, pp. 31f.

Human education develops human power. Direct specific end of the school or any type of institution is a natural one, worthy of pursuit for itself with its own means: and also that the end of the school is not the same as the end of life. The institution cannot wisely ignore the end of life. In Western countries the church-related schools provide for the regular practice of religion on the part of its students. This usually looked after by the provision of opportunities for assistance at daily man, reception of the sacraments, and a generally religious atmosphere. The church-related school can furnish instruction in sacred doctrine as the most important of its intellectual functions. The secular school cannot make the same provisions. Even here there will inevitably by some degree of moral influence on the student, though it is indirect and informal. The goal can be achieved directly through the experiences which the student has in the school and demands that are made on him, and which can lead to the further development of preservance, honesty, justice, courage and most of the other moral virtues. In ancient Indian perspective the institutions conducted by the Hindus, Jainas, Buddhists are religion-based. The religious atmosphere was the essential feature of these institutions. From morning to night the life of the student was tuned with the various aspects of religion. In ancient India religion or *dharma* has been used and utilised in its broadest sense. So the air of the country in Gupta age was imbibed with religion. Moral training was directly provided in the educational institutions. The ancient educators are of opinion that moral education was the first and foremost thing to be taught to the promising future citizens. So every minute thing was planned with the specific aim. Hence character building was the main features.[8]

In Western country educators also realise that inculcation of social awareness and some of the social graces amongst the students is specifically humane; precisely it is because the educand has intellectual knowledge and moral responsibility. Man is naturally a social animal, not in the way that ants or bees are social but in a peculiar social milieu. To become better men and to lead more humane lives everyone needs

8. *A Philosophy of Education*, p. 36.

the experience of living socially. Societies will be more or less successful to the degree that those members develop the knowledge and the willingness that will enable them to cooperate in achieving the goals of those societies. The school can play an effective part in such development, both inside and outside the classrooms.[9]

Though men evolved from animals, yet they are animals of a unique sort, they have certain physical powers that also deserve development. Such motor skills are obviously indispensable for any real intellectual achievement. The motor activity appears very early in infancy. It represents the first effort of the child towards self-realisation through self-help in an unconscious fashion. Physical training of any kind, whether aimed at participation in organized sports or not, is an admirable thing, for it is better to have a healthy body that not to have one. This view is propounded by the Western educators. On the other hand the Indian counterparts of them had included the physical training in the activities of the students throughout the day that it was very nicely set-up and intermingled. They had imbibed some duty along with the physical exercise. That helped the student in character building with the exercise of motor activities.[10]

The modern educators recognize two factors in education (1) internal and (2) external. The internal factors denotes all the congenital tendencies and innate capacities. The potentialities of the child are the internal factors. These determine the future possiblities. As the teacher cannot there in the child potentially the external factors is the child's environment. This includes the social heritage through which the suggestion and imitation operates on him and tends to shape his language, manners, customs and beliefs. It also denotes the influence which are consciously and deliberately designed for him by the adult members of the society. These external influences determine the amount and direction of his development.[11]

---

9. *A Philosophy of Education*, p. 59.
10. *Ibid.*, p. 62.
11. N.N. Mazumder, *Education in Ancient India*, Calcutta, 1932, pp. 80f.

The early teachers of the Gupta period took into consideration the tastes and innate tendencies of the individual. They took care to evaluate the internal factor of the student in planning of his career. They also took serious consideration to the external factors. They did not depend on the environment of the house in which they lived. They foresaw the far-reaching effect of the second factor also on the child in his education. As soon as the mind of the child began to form the child was transferred to the house of the preceptor. The child was settled in an atmosphere where he could breathe freely moral health and strength and which was most favourable to the development of a spiritual life which concerned the Indians of that age more than else. The school environment which was peaceful and calm and imbibed with the air of disciplined, orderly and pure life which formed the external factor ideally. The principle underlying the system that was planned by the ancient educators is the same which enthuses the modern educators to advocate the system of residential universities. Moreover as the student lived in the house of his preceptor as one of his family members he felt there, the atmosphere of his own home. Thus the ancient residential system was free from most of the defects and artificialities of modern boarding schools and residential universities. It is noteworthy that the idea of the residential system was conceived and realized in India long before it was planned in the outside world.[12]

It is a curious fact that cruelty appears as a special trait in the child at a certain stage of its development. It runs to take pleasure in giving pains to others, specially to birds and insects. We can cite from *Triṣaṣṭiśalākā Puruṣa-carita* — "The royal boys, surpassing the Vāyukumāras in speed, caught birds, pleasure-parrots, peacocks, etc."[13] The cruelty trait i.e love of viloence and lawlessness is sometimes transformed into a criminal tendency. We find in the *Jātaka* stories that the one prince planned to murder even his preceptor as revenge. Over and above the dark traits in childhood, the fighting instinct or

12. *Education in Ancient India*, p. 81.
13. Hemacandra — *Triṣaṣtiśalākā Puruṣacarita,* tr. by Helen M. Johnson, Vol. II, p. 67.

pungency also characterises this period. We have on record in the Buddhist literature how the cruelty trait in Girika, manifested in his boyhood, developed into a criminal trait in his adolescence. Thus Girika, a weaver by caste was cruel to insects and in youth he even killed his parents.[14] Youth is not only characterised by full physical vigour but also by love for adventure, when they out of adventurous spirit roam far and near. Religious trait is also manifest in some young adolescence.[15] The adolescent girls are timid, bashful[16] and weak though possessed of noble heart.

Social traits are developed in man in his adolescence. The restlessness is given away to sobriety during this period. The fair sex in their adolescence learn manners and etiquette and social in their dealings with others. This sociability is common to males and females alike in their adolescence. So it can be found that in *Abhijñāna-śākuntalam*. Śakuntalā, Anasūyā and Priyaṁvadā were entrusted for receiving guests and they performed their duty accordingly. Cool temparament, modesty, sweet-voice and courtesy — these traits in the young ladies earn for them universal respect and admiration. Young women are conscious of their self-respect. The intelligence of the growing child grows gradually when individual difference with reference to intelligence became perceptible in adolescence.[17]

Natural virtues are those which man develops and practises in order to perfect the human nature. Our last end is beyond the reach of the nature if it is left unaided. Hence it needs to be strengthened.[18] The intellectual virtues are those which enable us to know what is true and

14. *Legends of Indian Buddhism,* tr. by Winifred Stephens, pp. 31-2.
15. *Lalitavistara*, tr. by Rajendralal Mitra, pp. 192-4.
16. Harṣadeva — *Nāgānanda,* tr. by V.R. Nerukar, Acts I and IV, pp. 6, 36.
17. Debendra Chandra Dasgupta, *Educalional Psychology of the Ancient Hindus,* Calcutta: University of Calcutta, 1942.
18. St. Thomas, *Summa Theologiae,* p. 51.

to know how to do and to make things. The good habits which perfect human powers so that men can do what is right, to perform the actions that will lead us to those ends which we actually have, including our last end are called moral virtues.[19] Ancient Indian educators arranged to teach moral virtues side by side with the teaching of other subjects. Moral discipline which is outcome of moral discipline is first and foremost postulate of the ancient Indian education.

From the sayings, injunctions and maxims of the Buddha the educational views of Buddha can be understood. According to Buddha, every individual is simultaneously a member of the family, of the society and of the state. Education of every individual should have an eye to the tripartite duties. Every student should be taught the paramount importance of obedience to parents. This is the first hand training in moral discipline. From the family he should rise to the conception of society which is a collection of individuals. The individual must sacrifice his individuality for the common interest. This indicates self-sacrifice, self-surrender. From society he is to rise to conception of the state which is combination of many societies. The interest of the state demands higher virtues of philanthropy, devotion, civil and military service. A true ideal of education should bear all these postulates in view. Education should cultivate virtue. Buddha's notion of education bear resemblance with the view of Socrates who also believed virtue to be a teachable thing.[20]

Buddha advised to practice virtue, follow the duties righteously, be not cruel and to care elders. He call people in good living.[21] He has mentioned individual and the family, state is implied in it. The difficulties, the trials, and the discipline of the family are of great educative value even in the field of religion. Nobody can be expected to

---

19. (Sister) Mary William Hollenbach, *The Nature of the Intellectual and Moral Virtues and their Various Relationships,* (Notre Dame: Unpublished dissertation, 1959).
20. D.C. Dasgupta, "Lord Buddha and His Educational Psychology", in *Prabuddha Bhārat,* 1940, pp. 80f.
21. *The Jātaka Stories,* Vol. IV, tr. by Rouse, p. 110.

be successful in the pursuit of religious truth without undergoing the discipline involved in discharging his duties as member of a family. Buddha was as reformer who attached importance to the purely physical and hygienic factor in the matter of proper education leading to the higher life of spiritual truth. He has said, "To live in the world is also a part, through endless ages to have the cares of wife and child, without interval of rest looking forward to and anticipating future happiness with interval of sorrow, this is difficult."[22]

According to Kālidāsa infancy, adolescence and senescence are the three distinct periods of human life. Thus infancy is the most suitable period for education, youth for household duties and senescence for the anchorite life.[23]

It is interesting to note that the theory of Kālidāsa on 'infant education' under the fostering care of the mother is practically identical with those of Comenius, Rousseau, Pestalozzi, Froebel.

The family should continue to function as an educational centre up to the completion of the fourth birthday.

Kālidāsa holds the senses to be the gates of knowledge, the children should receive teaching in the rudiments of arithmetic through the senses from their environments.

The children should learn through 'trial and error' method through sense-perception. In *Kumārasaṁbhavam* it is found that Kārttikeya, the son of Lord Śiva, learns his calculation in this way—'sometimes the son of Maheśa used to sit upon the lap of his father in a fit of childish desire to display beauty, and he used to count the teeth of the serpent round his father's head — "one, nine, two, ten, five and seven" .[24] In *Śākuntalam*, Sarvadamana, the son of Śakuntalā violently open the mouth of a cub to count its teeth.[25] This view is also supported by

---

22. *Dhammapada*, tr. by Beal, p. 124.
23. *Raghu*, I.8.
24. *Kumārasambhavam,* XI.45.
25. *Abhijñānaśākuntalam,* VII.88.

Pestalozzi. Pestalozzi advocated a similar method of learning through concrete situations, in his famous Leonard and Gertrude:[26] She taught them to count the number of steps from one end of the room to the of other; two of the rows of five panes each, in one of the windows, gave her an opportunity to unfold the decimal relations of numbers. She also made them count their threads while spinning, and the number of turns on the reel when they wound the yarn into skeins. Above all, in every occupation of life she taught them an accurate and intelligent observation, of common objects and forces of nature.

Education at home is followed by primary education at school, which leads to higher education. Each grade of institution is appropriate to the psychological development of the student. Writing preceded reading and general information preceded writing.

Buddha as an educationist is quite modern in view. It is interesting that he was dead against cramming. Education must train the intellect and must not indulge in memory work. True education must penetrate from the surface to greater depths. It must go into the core of the subject. The advice of Buddha may be followed by modern teacher and student. "Many deluded men learn the doctrine in all its different branches and having so learnt this doctrine, they do not go to enquire easily into its meaning, and not reaching to its meaning, they fail to attain insight. Lacking in wisdom, they learn the doctrine only with a view to quoting texts for the sake of advantage in argument.... In the self-same way, discipline, may a foolish deluded man learns the doctrines only that he may argue and dispute about them, never enquiring into their real meaning."[27]

Michael De Montaigne condemns the practice of mere studpid cramming which prevailed. Cramming was also prevalent in Europe in mediaeval period. "We only toil and labour to stuff the memory, and in

---

26. Pestalozzi, *Leonard and Gartrde*, tr. by Evoe Channing, pp. 130-1.

27. *Majjhimanikāya*, pp. 167-8.

the meantime leave the conscience and the understanding void and like birds who fly abroad to forege for grain and bring it home in thier beak without tasting it themselves, to feed their young, so our pedants go picking knowledge here and there out of several authors, and hold it at their tongue's end, only to distribute it amongst their pupils. And here I cannot but smile to think how I have paid off myself in showing the foppery of this kind of learning, who myself am so manifest an example, for do I not perform the same thing almost throughout this whole book? I go here and there, culling out of several books the sentences that best please me, not to keep them (for I have no memory to retain them in), but to transplant them into this; were, to say the truth, they are no more mine than in their first places. We are, I conceive, knowing only in present knowledge, and not all in what is past, no more than in that which is to come. But the worst of it is, their scholars and pupils are no better nourished by it than themselves: it makes no deeper impression upon them than on the other, but passes from hand to hand, only to make a show, to be tolerable company, and to tell pretty stories, like a counterfeit coin, of no other use or value but as counters to reckon with, or set up at cards."

"They have learned to speak with others, not with themselves."

"We take other man's knowledge and opinions upon truth, and that is all; wherein we should make them our own, we are in this very like him who, having need of fire, went to a neighbour's house to fetch it; and finding a very good one there, sat down to carry any with him home."[28]

According to Buddha personality is one of the main factors of education. Atmosphere of receptibility of new ideas and new truths in a child must be created. "For at the close of such discourse, as respects the indications of concentration in the former, I settle and steady each person his mind, repose it, bring it one and unify it, and thus I do."

Buddhists always preach the law with reference to the disposition

---

28. Michael De Montaigne, *Essays*, tr. by C. Cotton. pp. 54-5.

of mind of each individual. "The teacher preached the law on that day, he had regard to Machapāla's predisposition."[29] Buddha in his policy of education had taken recourse to apperception method. Herbert Spencer propagated this apperception method. According to this theory, the student should take nothing on authority. The student should learn nothing to be taken as granted. The duty of the teacher is to reflect and consider the lesson is to learnt with reference to previous experience of the student. "For this will teach him to making comparisons and giving reasons, all the continuous practice of comparing and reasoning on his part will enable me to impart learning to him."[30] Buddha preferred teaching through comparisons which help to develop inner reasoning power. Buddha laid special emphasis on the objective method of instruction through stories and parables. One of the brethren had a pet viper. Buddha forbade him to trust it. But he did not pay any heed. This man went out for two or three days and after returning tried to give food to the viper and was bitten by the viper and died. Budha advised to learn the lesson from this man.

The curriculum of the Jaina education includes academic subjects along with art courses. The curricula of the Jaina takes care of 'g' and 's' factors. The Vedic, the Buddhistic and the Jaina systems took care of the first factor or general native abilities as well as the specific abilities such as art courses. These two types of intelligence were known to the ancient Jainas, which have been proposed by Spearman in modern time.

Kālidāsa also realized the necessity of adoption of education to the quality and the intelligence of the student as well as graded development. Kṣatriya scholars were imparted higher education after the initiation ceremony by eminent scholars versed in the different branches of learning. "When Raghu reaches his eleventh year, the great savants taught him various branches of learning with great care, and the versatile, people, more than justified their care by attaining brilliant

---

29. *Dhammapada Commentary*, Part III, p. 225.
30. *The Jātaka Stories*, Vol. I, tr. by Chalmers, p. 272.

proficiency in all these subjects."[31]

The liberal education of the princes aimed at qualifying them for the elevated positions of rulers of the State. The curriculum of the study includes four principal branches of learning — the science of *āṇvikṣikī* or philosophy, the science of *trayī* or the three Vedas, the science of *vārtā* or trade (including commerce, agriculture and veterinary), the science of *daṇḍa* or 'politics'.[32] Plato combined kingship with philosophy. The liberal curriculum helped to achieve success in ruling. Besides this four-fold subjects of study, prince Raghu, putting on the deer skin, learnt from his father Dilīpa, who was expert in archery, the science of military tactics. Here the prince's learning military science took place under the direct supervision and guidance of powerful and competent military leaders of practical experience.

Kālidāsa believes in the innate ideas of students in the matter of education. While describing proficiency of Sudarśana[33] and Pārvātī[34] Kālidāsa refers to the inherent power of grasping subjects.

The princes depicted by Kālidāsa, received training in fine arts, music, painting. Music plays an important role. Vālmīki teaches music to Lava and Kuśa: "As the princes grew older the sage initiated them into the mysteries of the science of archery and when they arrived at the age of puberty, he taught them *Rāmāyaṇa*" composed by himself.[35] Drawing is also an important item of education. In the *Raghuvaṁśa*[36] and *Śākuntalam*[37] proof of efficiency of kings can be found.

In coins of Samudragupta, he was seen as playing lute and described as emperor of poets. It proves the education based on academic subjects

---

31. *Raghu*, III.29.
32. *Ibid.*, III.30.
33. *Ibid.*, XVIII.50.
34. *Kumārasambhavam*, I.80.
35. *Raghu*, XV.33.
36. *Ibid.*, XIX.19.
37. *Śākuntalam,* VI.80-1.

along with fine arts of the emperor.

In modern education system, art as work permitted with the play attitude. Indeed the work inside and outside school needs to be infused with the spirit of play and art. Therefore art as work is a humanising part of education.[38]

The scheme of education of Kālidāsa combines the theory with practice, knowledge with application.[39]

Intelligence grows and develops gradually with years reach perfection in adolescence.[40] It remains latent in an infant, it is only in youth it manifests itself. The Buddhist source supports the view.

Buddha had a healthy sense of the dignity of labour. Buddhistic education as well as Hindu education embraces physical education along with other subjects. This proves that the modern outlook was prevalent among the ancient Indians.[41]

The distinctive feature of Buddhistic Benedictive rule was insistence upon manual labour of some kind. Chastity as well as obedience was special feature of the students.

It is noteworthy that Buddha attached great importance to games along with manual arts. The candidate for the spiritual order had to be thoroughly trained in manual, physical and moral discipline as an essential factor before training. The laity must be trained. "This boy, with the growth and devclopment of his faculties, takes part in all sorts of games, sports appropriate to youth such as ploughing with toy ploughs, playing tip cat, toycarts and by bows and arrows."[42]

---

38. John S. Brubacher, *Modern Philosophies of Education,* 4th edn., Bombay, McGraw Hill, 1962.
39. Kunhan C. Rāja, — *Kālidāsa*, p. 184.
40. D.N. Dasgupta, *Educational Psychology of Ancient Hindus,* p. 116.
41. Henry Clarke Warren, *Buddhism in Translations,* pp. 255-6.
42. *Majjhimanikāya*, Vol. I, tr. by Bhikkhu Silacara, p. 182.

The great Moravian scholar, preacher and educationist, John Amos Comenius holds same view regarding this matter. It may be quoted: "It will be of immense use, if the amusements that are provided to relax the strain on the minds of the scholars be of such a kind as to lay stress on the more serious side of life, in order that a definite impression may be made on them even in their hours of recreation. For instance they may be given tools, allowed to imitate the different handicrafts, by playing at farming, at politics, at being soldiers or architects, etc."[43]

In Nalanda University an outsider student has to undergo a strict admission tests. This method can be compared with Rashdall's saying "any process of enquiry into the candidate's fitness as well as direct testing of his scholastic attainment".

Grammar was one of the compulsory subjects of study for the ancient Indians of Gupta age. According to Newman, the grammar has taught by the educationists of Europe and India to teach method, order, principle, system of rule and science.[44]

In spite of unsympathetic attitude of Buddha[45] towards the entry of women into the Buddhist order, once they were taken in, he made arrangement for their education and discipline by a competent teacher whether male or female.[46]

Buddha meant religious education to be universal. It was open not only to the regular female members of the order but also to other and lay women.

Ānanda was assigned the duty of reciting the ordinance to the

---

43. John Amos Comenious, *The Great Didactic,* tr. by M.W. Keatings, p. 179.
44. Newman, *Preface*, xix.
45. *The Sacred Books of the East,* Vol. XX, edited by Macdonell, pp. 325-6, 328.
46. *Ibid.*, pp. 334, 351.

queens, the consort of Prasenadi, king of Kośala.[47] The court school of king resembles the palace school at the court of Charlemagne (767-814). The great teacher Alcuin, like Ānanda was assigned the task of teaching the members of the royal family in the rudiments of instruction in AD 781.[48]

Kālidāsa felt the necessity of female education. He had a sound systematic conception. His girls received a training suited to their suitable environment. The advice of Kaṅva to Śakuntalā was worth mentioning.[49] Wife had to play the role of a counsellor, friend and student of fine arts to her husband.[50]

The knowledge of psychology of Kālidāsa has been revealed in his works. The maternal instinct of the adolescent girls revealed themselves not only in their attitude to plants[51] but also in their attitude to domesticated animals.[52]

That Śakuntalā and her friends could read can be guessed from the following verse: "The two friends slowly read the name engraved on the ring presented by the king and looked into each other's face."[53] That they could also write is proved from a writing of a love-letter to Duṣyanta by Śakuntalā.[54] In the *Kumārasaṁbhavam*[55] and *Vikramorvaśīyam,*[56] the scenes of writing love-letters is depicted. This establishes the fact that the females of India during the time of Kālidāsa could read and write.

47. *Dhammapada*, IV, tr. by Burlingame, p. 58.
48. E.P. Cubberley, *The History of Edcuation,* p. 141.
49. *Śākuntalam*, IV.
50. *Raghu*, VIII.67.
51. *Śākuntalam*, I.47, IV.80.
52. *Ibid.*, IV.104.
53. *Ibid.*, I.121.
54. *Ibid.*, III.41.
55. *Kumāra*, I.7.
56. *Vikramorvaśī,* II.93.

The heroines of Kālidāsa knew arithmetic and could count. Duṣyanta suggested Śakuntalā to count each day an alphabet of his name in his wedding ring.[57]

The female education embraced history and literature: 'Anasūyā: "Hallo Śakuntalā, we do not understand a jot of love-affairs. But as far as we can gather from literature and hearsay you seem to be terribly afflicted with love".'[58]

The curricula of female education embraced fine arts — drawing, music and dancing. Kālidāsa prescribes these courses of study in the *Kumārasaṁbhavam*[59] and *Mālavikāgnimitram*.[60]

Kālidāsa believed in individual capacity to cope with the subject. Instruction in literary subjects and fine arts must have been adjusted to the capacities of the students and they must be mentally and physically qualified to achieve success (*Mālavikā*, I.14).[61]

Social efficiency has been set-up as the aim of education from time immemorial. Hindu religious students received at school practical training in the study of the Vedas, in performing sacrifices and in every other duty in connection with. He received education and training in the various sciences and fine and mechanical arts. In the Hindu system of the Gupta age, the life outside was reproduced in miniature in the school—this fact is propounded by Dewey of Chicago. It can be said that the pupil was made fit for 'a practical, successful, efficient, useful and happy life of action'.

The moral purpose dominated the school life of ancient Indians. The teacher took the greatest possible care to train the will of his

---

57. *Śākuntalam*, VI.68.
58. *Ibid.*, III.10.
59. *Kumāra*, V.58.
60. *Mālavikāgnimitra*, I.14, I.31.
61. D.C. Dasgupta, "Educational Ideas in Kālidāsa's India", *Prabbudha Bharat*, 1942, pp. 181f.

disciple. Through attendance on the precept or, the student taught self-abnegation, patience, endurance, loyalty and devotion. The system helped the boy to form habits of courtesy and giving expression to the ideas of harmonious and virtuous conduct of life.

This training was in accordance with the views of modern educators. Kirkpatrick[62] is of opinion that as the child is in capable of forming abstract religious conceptions, the training during this period "should be of the heart rather than of the head and perhaps even more of the hand, i.e., a training in doing, or, in other words, taking part in religious forms."

Hindu student received a thorough training of self-control and self-sacrifice for the good of the world. It is the training which was in marked contrast with the modern secular education.

The precepts were not only taught but reduced to practice. This made the system more practical and effective. The teacher in the Indian education system authenticated and illustrated in his own life the model of ideas. The teacher-pupil relationship was erected not on any economic ties but on friendship and affection.

The system of education prevalent in the Gupta age is emphasised in a democratic society, viz., that education should be as far as practicable free and compulsory.

The educators of the Gupta age urged that religion, industry and temperance should mark their system of education.

The co-education was not rare in the ancient India. The custom is similar to the modern days has been proved.

The extension of education was not rare can be proved from the stories of the *Jātakas*. The preceptor used to come to his student to examine his advancement of learning after intervals of time.

The popularity of listening to the Purāṇas and great Epics proves the existence of non-formal education.

---

62. Kirkpatrick, *Fundamentals of Child Study*.

Rabindranāth Tagore has set up the ideals of *gurukula* system and teaching in the atmosphere of nature in Viśvabhāratī situated in Śāntiniketan.

The ancient Indians of Gupta age realised the importance of library. In Nālandā, there was nine-storeyed building called Ratnodadhi where the library was located and it was considered to be the largest in India. The books of library were classified and arranged according to the subject.[63]

The observatory of Nālandā proves the existence of modern scientific observations.

So it can be proved that, the then society of the Gupta age had a sound education philosophy which was simultaneously practical, comprehensive and suited to the varying educational needs of both sexes; it had taken into consideration the limitations of human nature. The educational scheme was not an utopia, devoid of touch with reality. The educational system was based on experience and observation. It is curious enough that this system anticipated some of the fundamentals of the educational theories of the great educators of modern times.

63. S.C. Das, *Universities in Ancient India.*

Glossary

Adhvaryū: Any officiating priest, technically distinguished from Hotṛ, Udgātṛ and *Bramhan*. His duty was "to measure the ground, build the altar, prepare sacrificial vessels, to fetch wood and water, light the fire, bring the animal and immolute it, and while doing this to repeat the *Yajurveda*".

Agadatantra: The science of antidotes; one of the eight parts of medical science, i.e., *Āyurveda*.

Ālīdha: A particular attitude in shooting, the right knee being advanced and the left leg retracted.

Animā: The superhuman power of becoming as small as an atom; one of the 8 powers of *siddhis* of Śiva.

Anuṣaṅga: A word or words repeated from the context to supply an ellipsis. In Nyāya philosophy it denotes connecting together the *upanaya* or application and *nigamana* or conclusion by the use of the pronoun *idaṁ*.

Āṇvikṣikī: Logic, logical philosophy. It is a name of Nyāya philosophy.

Āpta: (1) A word of received acceptation and established by usage only.

(2) The Vedas or Śruti, a word of authority. It is applied to Smṛtis, *itihāsa*-s and Purāṇas also, which are considered as authoritative evidence.

Āramika: A gardener.

Aṅga: A supplementary or auxiliary portion, supplement of the Vedas or a symbolical expression for the number six (derived from the six Vedāṅgas).

Aṅgulī: A finger, the names of the five fingers are *aṅguṣṭha* (thumb), *tarjanī* (forefinger), *madhyamā* (middle finger), *anāmikā* (ring-finger) and *kaniṣṭhā* is equal to 8 barley-corns, 12 *aṅgula*'s making a *vitasti* or span, and 24 *aṅgula*'s making a *hasta* or Cubit.

Arthāpatti: An inference from cicrumstances, presumption, implication, one of the five sources of knowledge or modes of proof, according to the *mīmāṁsaka*-s.

Āṣāḍha: Name of a Hindu month (corresponding to June and July).

Aśleṣā: An expiatory ceremony performed on account of the birth of a child under the *aśleṣā*.

Āśleṣā: The 9th *nakṣatra* or lunar mansion containing five stars.

Ayana: The Sun's passage, north and south of the equator. The period of duration of this passage, i.e., half year, the time from the solstice to another.

Āyurveda: The science of health or medicine, counted as a sacred science and regarded as supplement of the *Atharvaveda*.

Brahmacārī: A religious student, a brāhmaṇa in the first order of his life, who continues to live with his spiritual guide from the investiture with sacred thread and performs the duties pertaining to his order till he settles in life.

Brahmavādinī: The lady who teaches or expounds the Vedas.

Chanda: Metrical science, prosody. It is regarded as one of the six Vedāṅgas or auxiliaries to the Vedas.

Daitya: A son of Diti, A *rākṣasa*, demon.

Daṇda: The staff given to a twice-born man at the time of investiture with the sacred thread.

Daṇḍanīti: The system of civil and military administration, the science of politics.

Dhanuḥ: A measure of length equal to four *hasta*-s.

Dvija: (1) A man of the first three castes of the Hindus (a brāhmaṇa, kṣatriya or vaiśya).

(2) A brāhmaṇa over whom the *saṁskāras* or purificatory rites are performed.

Gaura-sarṣapa: White mustard. It is considered as a kind of weight.

Gavyūti: A measure of length nearly equal to two miles or one *krośa*.

Godāna: A ceremony of tonsure of cutting the hair. It is performed with the side-hair of a youth of 16 or 18 years when he has attained puberty and shortly before his marriage.

Hasta: The fore-arm, cubit, a measure of length. It is equal to twenty-four *aṅgula*s or about eighteen inches, being the distance between the elbow and tip of the middle finger.

Hetvartha: The logical reason, the reason for an inference, middle term which forms the second member of the five-membered syllogism.

Homa: One of the five deity *yajña*s, to be performed by a brāhmaṇa, called *devayajña*. *Homa* is offering oblations of gods by throwing clarified butter into the consecrated fire.

Īśitva: Superiority, greatness, one of the eight *siddhi*-s or attributes of Śiva.

Jyotiṣa: One of the six Vedāṅgas. Astronomy, astrology: the science of the course of the heavenly bodies and divisions of time resting thereon.

Kalpa: One of the six Vedāṅgas, i.e., that which lays down the ritual and prescribes rules for ceremonial and sacrificial acts.

Kaupīna: A small piece of cloth worn over the privities.

Krośa: A measure of distance equal to one-fourth of a *yojana*.

Laghimā: The supernatural power of assuming excessive lightness at will, one of the eight *siddhi*s.

Likṣā: A very minute measure of weight (said to be equal to 4 or 8 *trasareṇu*-s).

Lokāyata: Materialism, atheism. The materialistic philosophy propounded by Cārvāka.

Maṇḍala: A division of the *R̥gveda* is divided into 10 *maṇḍala*-s or eight *aṣṭaka*-s.

Manvantara: The period or age of a Manu. This period comprises 4,320,000 human years of 1/14 th day of Brahmā, the fourteen *manvantaras* making up one whole day; each of these fourteen periods is supposed to be presided over by its own Manu.

Mekhalā: The girdle worn by the first three castes.

Mūla: The nineteenth luner mansion containing eleven stars.

Muñja: (1) A sort of rush or grass of which the girdle of a brāhmaṇa should be made.

(2) The sacred cord or girdle itself.

Naimiṣāraṇya: A sacred forest celebrated as the residence of certain sages to whom Sauti related the *Mahābhārata*.

Nakṣatra-Puruṣa: In (Astronomy). The figure of a man's body on the limbs of which are shown the various asterism.

Nāmakaraṇa: The ceremony of naming a child after birth.

Nibandha: A literary composition or treatise work.

Nimeṣa: Twinkling of the eye, a moment, etc.

Nirukta: It contains glossarial explanation of obscure words, specially those occurring in the Vedas. It is one of the six Vedāṅgas.

Niyama: In Yoga philosophy, it is restraint of the mind, the second of the eight principal steps of meditation.

Padārtha: A category or predicament, the number of such categories, according to the Vaiśeṣikas is seven, twenty-five while according to Yogas it is twenty-seven and the number is two according to the Vedāntins.

Pāradas: A barbarous tribe.

Prahelikā: A riddle, an enigma.

Prākāmya: Irresistible will, considered as one of the eight attributes, or, *siddhi*-s of Śiva or the Supreme Being.

Prakriyā: An introductory chapter of a work.

Pramāṇa: A mode of proof, a means of arriving at correct knowledge. The Naiyāyikas recognize only four kinds: *pratyakṣa*, *anumāna*, *upamāna* and *śabda*. Vedāntins: *anupalabdhi* and *arthāpatti*; while the Sāṁkhyas admit *pratyakṣa*, *anumāna* and *śabda* only.

Prāpti: The power of obtaining anything, i.e., one of the eight *siddhi*-s.

Pratisarga: Secondary creation as by the agents of one Supreme Being.

Punarvasu: The seventh lunar mansion consisting of two or four stars.

Puṣyā: The eighth lunar mansion consisting of three stars.

Rāja-sarṣapa: Black mustard.

Sabhāsada: A member of an assembly of meeting.

Sadyavadhūḥ: Newly-married.

Śaiva: One of the three principal hindu sects, which is related to the God Śiva.

Śakas: Of a particular tribe or race of people.

Śākta: Worshipper of Śakti. The Śāktas are generally worshippers of Durgā representing the female personification of divine energy, and the ritual enjoined to them is of two kinds, the pure of right-hand ritual *dakṣiṇācāra* and impure or left-hand ritual, i.e., *vāmācāra*.

Samidh: An oblation to fuel or firewood.

Sammitīya: Of equal measure, extent or value, equal, similar like.

Saṁskāra: A purificatory rite, a secred rite or ceremony. Manu mentions *saṁskāra*-s; some writers increase the number to sixteen.

Sāṁkhya: One of the six systems of Hindu philosophy, attributed to the sage Kapila. This philosophy is so called because it enumerates twentyfive *tattva*-s of true principles; and its chief object is to effect the final emancipation of the twentyfifth *tattva*; i.e., the *puruṣa* or soul, from the bonds of this worldly existence the fetters of phenomenal creation by conveying a corect knowledge of the twenty-four other *tattva*-s and by properly discriminating the whole universe as a development of an inanimate principle called *prakṛti*, while the *puruṣa* is altogether passive and simply a looker on. It does not admit god as the creator and controller of Universe.

Sarga: The creation of the world.

Sarṣapa: Mustard. A small measure of weight.

Sarvāstivādin: The doctrine that all things are real. One of the four divisions of the Vaibhāṣika system of Buddhism.

Saura: The religious sect adherent to worshipping of the Sun.

Śikṣā: One of the six Vedāṅgas. The Science which teaches the proper pronunciation of words and laws of euphony.

Snātaka: A brāhmaṇa who has performed the ceremony of ablution which has to be performed on his finishing of his first *āśrama* which is of a *brahmcārin*.

Śrāddha: A funeral rite or ceremony performed in honour of the departed spirits of dead relatives. It is of three kinds *nitya*, *naimittika* and *kāmya*.

Śrotriya: Proficient in the Veda. A learned brāhmaṇa who is well-versed in sacred learning.

Sthaviravādin: Propounder of ancient views.

Svātī: The star Arcturus, considered as forming the fifteenth lunar asterism.

Tarka: The science of Logic. A system of doctrine found on pure reasoning or free thinking, a philosophical system, particularly one of the six principal Hindu philosophy.

Trayī: The three Vedas taken collectively i.e. *Ṛg*, *Yajur* and *Sāmaveda*.

Uddeśa: (In Philosophy) The enunciation of a thing by its name which is to further discussed and explained.

Upādhyāya: (1) A teacher or preceptor in general.

(2) A sub-teacher who instructs for wages only in a part of the Veda and is inferior to an *ācārya*.

Upakurvānaka: A brāhmaṇa in a state of pupilage or *brahmacārin*, who wishes to pass on to the state of a house-holder or *gṛhastha*.

Upanayana: The ceremony by which the boy is invested with the sacred thread or initiated into studies.

Upaniṣad: Knowledge derived from sitting at the feet of the preceptor; but according to Indian authorities it means to destroy ignorance by revealing the supreme spirit and cutting off the bonds of worldly existence. Later the term denotes certain mystical writing attached to the brāhmaṇas, the chief aim of which is to ascertain the secret meaning of the Vedas.

Upasaṁhāra: Summing up, winding up, conclusion.

Upavīta: The sacred thread worn by the first three classes of the Hindus.

Upodghāta: (1) An introduction, a preface.

(2) An example, an opposite argument or illustration.

Vaiṣṇava: One of the three important modern Hindu sects. This religious sect worships Viṣṇu. Other two sects are Śaiva and Śākta.

Vājinīrājana: A kind of military and religious ceremony performed by kings or generals of armies in the month of Āśvina before they took the field. It was a purification of the king's horses by means of sacred *mantra*-s.

Vaṁśa: A race, family, dynasty or lineage.

Vārtā: Agriculture, the occupation of a vaiśya.

Vedāṅga: From derivative meaning it means a member of the Veda. It denotes certain classes of works regarded as auxiliary to the Vedas and designed to aid in the correct pronunciation and interpretation of the text of the Veda and the right employment of the *mantras* in ceremonials. The Vedāṅgas are six in number: (1) Śikṣā, (2) Kalpa, (3) Nirukta, (4) Vyākaraṇa, (5) Jyotiṣa, (6) Chanda.

Vidyāsthāna: A branch of knowledge.

Vihāra: A Jaina or Buddhist temple, convent, monastery.

Vijñānavādin: The theory of knowledge. The doctrine was taught by Buddha.

Yama: Self-control. Any great moral or religious duty or observance. The Yamas are usually said to be ten, but their names are given differently. According to Yoga philosophy, it is the first of the eight *aṅga*-s or means of attaining Yoga.

Yava: (1) A measure of length to 1/6th or 1/8th of an *aṅgula*.

(2) A barley-corn or the weight of a barley-corn.

Yavanas: A Greek or an Ionian. In broader sense it denotes any foreigners or barbarian.

Yoga: The system of philosophy established by Patañjali, which is considered to be second division of the Sāṁkhya philosophy, but is practically reckoned as a separate system. The chief aim of the Yoga philosophy is to teach the means by which the human soul may be completely united with the Supreme Spirit and thus secure absolution; and deep abstract meditation is laid down as the chief means of securing this end, elaborate rules being given for the proper practice of Yoga or concentration of mind.

Yojana: A measure of distance equal to four *krośa*s or eight or nine miles.

Bibliography

Sanskrit Works

Aitareya Brāhmaṇa, ed. by Th. Aufrecht, Bonn, 1879.

Āpastamba Dharmasūtra, ed. by R. Halasyanatha Sastrin, Kumbhakonam, 1895, tr. by George Bühler (Sacred Books of the East Series, II, pt. I), reprint edn., Varanasi, 1986.

Āpastamba Gṛhyasūtra, tr. by Herman Oldenberg, S.B.E. Series, vol. XXIX, reprint edn., Varanasi, 1981.

Āpastamba Śrauta Sūtra, ed. by R. Garbe, Calcutta, 1882-1902 (B.I.), ed. by Chinnaswami Śāstrī, with commentary by Dhūrtasvāmī, Baroda, 1955.

Apte, Vāman Śivarām, *Practical Sanskrit-English Dictionary*, 4th rev. edn., Delhi: 1985.

Āryabhaṭa, *Āryabhaṭīya*, ed. with Eng. tr. by Kripa Sankar Sukla in collaboration with K.V. Śarmā, New Delhi, 1976, with the commentary of Bhāskara and Somesvara, ed. by Kṛpā Śaṅkar Śukla, New Delhi, 1976, with the commentary of Suryadeva Yajvan, ed. by K.V. Sarma, New Delhi, 1976.

Āryamañjuśrī Mūla Kalpa, ed. by T. Ganapati Sastri, Trivandrum, 1925, ed. by K.P. Jayswal, Patna, 1934.

Atharvavedasaṁhitā, ed. by W.D. Whitney, New Haven, 1881.

Bāṇabhatta, *Harṣacarita*, ed. by K.P. Parab, 5th edn., Bombay, 1925; tr. by E.B. Cowell, London, 1897.

———, *Kādambarī*, ed. by P. Peterson, Bombay, 1900.

ed. by A.A.M. Sharpe, Leuvern, (n.d.).

tr. by M.R. Kale, Bombay, 1925.

Baudhāyana Dharmasūtra, ed. by L. Srinivasacharya, Mysore, 1907; ed. by George Bühler (Sacred Books of the East Series, II. pt. I) reprint edn., Varanasi, 1986.

Bhagavat Dutta, *Vedic Kosa*, Lahore, 1926.

Bhāgavata Purāṇa, ed. with Eng. tr. by Mahendra Nath Chatterjee, Calcutta, 1985; ed. by Pancanana Tarkaratna, Calcutta, 1908; tr. by G.V. Tagare, Delhi, 1979.

Bhāravi, *Kirātārjunīyam*, ed. by M.R. Kale, Varanasi, 1988.

Bhartṛhari, *Śatakatraya*, ed. by D.D. Kosambi, Bombay, 1946.

Bhāsa, *Pañcarātra*, ed. by T. Ganapati Sastri, Trivandrum, 1917.

Bṛhaspati, *Dharmasūtra*, ed. by Manmatha Nath Dutta, Calcutta, 1908; tr. by George Bühlar (S.B.E Series, XXXIII).

Buddhacarita, ed. by E.B. Cowell, Oxford, 1893.

Candeśvara Thakkur, *Rājnīti Ratnākara*, ed. by K.P. Jayaswal, Patna, 1924.

Deva, Rādhākanta, *Śabdakalpadruma* (5 Vols.), Calcutta, 1986-92.

Devana Bhaṭṭa, *Smṛticandrikā* (5 Vols.), ed. by L. Srinivāsācarya, Delhi, 1988.

Dharmaśāstrasaṁgraha (2 Vols.), ed. by Vachaspati Upadhyaya, Delhi, 1982.

Diṅnāga, *Kundamālā*, ed. by Kali Kumar Datta, Calcutta, 1946.

Dvivedī, *Kālidāsa: Mānavaśilpī Mahākavi*, Sagar, 1973.

Eighteen Principal Upaniṣads, ed. by V.P. Limaye and R.D. Vadekar, Poona, 1958.

Gautama Dharmasūtra, ed. with commentary by Hari Narayan Apte, Puna, 1910, tr. by George Bühler. S.B.E. XXXIII.

Kālidāsa, *Abhijñāna Śākuntalam*, ed. by Dilip Kumar Kanjilal, Calcutta, 1988; ed. by Subodh Chandra Paul 2nd, rev. edn., Delhi, 1985; ed. by Jībānanda Vidyāsāgara, 5th edn., Calcutta, 1914. ed. by M.R. Kale, 10th edn., Delhi, 1969.

———, *Kālidāsa Granthāvalī*, ed. by Revaprasad Dvivedi, Varanasi, 1976.

———, *Kālidāsa-Sūktiśatakam*, ed. by Kunja Govinda Gosvāmī, Calcutta, 1958.

———, *Kumārasambhavam*, ed. by Premchandra Tarkavagisa, Calcutta, 1861, ed. by Gurunath Vidyanidhi, Calcutta, 1970.

———, *Mālavikāgnimitram*, ed. by Sankar Pandurang Parab, 2nd edn., Bombay, 1889.

———, *Meghadūtam*, ed. by Kasinath Bapu Pathak, 2nd edn., Pune, 1916.

———, *Meghadūta*, ed. by Vasudeva Laksman Pansikar, 13th edn.,

Bombay, 1929.

——, *Raghuvaṁśa*, ed. by Premchandra Tarkavagisa, Calcutta, 1861, 1929.

——, *Raghuvaṁśa*, ed. by Kāśīnāth Pandurang Parab.

——, *Ṛtusaṁhāra*, ed. by N. B. Godabole, Bombay 1885.

——, *Vikramorvaśīyam*, Calcutta, 1830; ed. by Sankar Pandurang Pandit, 2nd edn., Bombay, 1889.

Kāmandaka, *Nītisāra*, ed. by Ganapati Sastri, Trivandrum, 1912; ed. by Rajendra Lala Mitra, rev. by Sisir Kumar Mitra, Calcutta, 1982 (B.I. 309).

Kaumudī-mahotsavam, ed. by Ramakrishna Kavi and S.K. Ramanatha Sastri, Madras, 1929.

Kauṭilīyam Arthaśāstram, ed. by Raghunath Singh (2 vols.), Varanasi, 1982, ed. by R.P. Kangle, Bombay, 1972.

Kumāradāsa, *Jānakīharaṇam*, ed. by S. Purnavitana, C.E. Godakumbure, Ceylon, 1967; tr. by Vrajmohan Vyas, Allahabad, 1966.

Kūrma Purāṇam, ed. by Pancanan Tarkaratna, Calcutta, 1925.

Lalitavistara, tr, by Rajendra Lala Mitra, Calcutta.

Mahābhāratam, ed. by Pancanan Tarkaratna, Calcutta, 1904-1908, ed. by V.S. Sukhthankar, Pune, 1933-59.

Mahendravikrama-Varman, *Mattavilāsaprahasanam*, ed. by Kapiladeva Giri, Varanasi, 1966.

Mānava-Dharmaśāstram, ed. by Ganganath Jha, Calcutta, 1932; tr. by George Bühler, Oxford, 1886.

Manuṭikāsaṁgraha, ed. by Julius Jolly, Calcutta, 1986 (B.I., 104).

Mārkaṇḍeya Purāṇam, ed. by Pañcānan Tarkaratna, 4th edn., Calcutta, 1910; tr. by F.E. Pargitar, Calcutta, 1904 (B.I. series).

Matsya Purāṇam, ed. by Pañcānana Tarkaratna, Calcutta, 1910; tr. by Talukdar of Oudh, Allahabad, 1916-17 (*Sacred Books of the Hindus*).

Nārada Smṛti, ed. by Julius Jolly, Calcutta, 1885.

Pāṇini, *Aṣṭādhyāyī*, ed. by Śriśacandra Vasu (2 Vols) reprint edn. Varanasi, 1980.

Patañjali, *Mahābhāṣyam*, ed. by Śivadatta, Bombay, 1912.

Parāśara Dharma Saṁhitā, ed. by Krishnakamal Bhattacharjee, Calcutta, 1887 (B.I. Series).

Rāmāyaṇam, ed. by P.C. Ray, Calcutta, 1881-2.

Subandhu, *Vāsavadattām*, ed. by Fitzedward Hall, Calcutta, 1859 (B.I. Series); *Vāsavadattām*, ed. by Śaṅkara Deva Śāstrī, Varanasi, 1954.

Suśruta, *Suśrutasaṁhitā*, ed. by Jadavji Trikamji Acarya, 2nd rev. edn., Bombay, 1931.

Varāha Purāṇam, ed. by Hrisikesa Śāstrī, Calcutta, 1893.

Vāyu Purāṇam, ed. by R.L. Mitra, Calcutta, 1880.

Viśākhadatta, *Mudrārākṣasam*, ed. by K.T. Telang, Bombay, 1884; ed. with tr. by K.H. Dhruva, Pune, 1923.

Viṣṇu Purāṇam, ed. by Pancanana Tarkaratna, Calcutta, 1925.

———, tr. by H.H. Wilson, Delhi, 1982.

———, tr. by Manmatha Nath Datta, Varanasi, 1972.

Viṣṇudharmottara Purāṇam, ed. by Khemraj Srikrishnadas, Bombay, 1912.

Yājñavalkyasmṛti, ed. by Vāsudev Lakṣman Paṅśīkar, 3rd edn., Bombay, 1926; tr, by Manmatha Nath Dutta, (3 vols), Calcutta, 1896-1909.

Pāli, Prākṛt and Hindi Works

Agarwal, V.S., *Harṣacarita; ek samskritika adhyayan*, Patna, 1953.

———, *Kādambarī: ek samskritika adhyayan*, Patna, 1953.

Aṅguttara Nikāya, London, 1885-1910.

Āyārāṁga Sūtra, Oxford, 1882.

Bṛhatkalpasūtra, Bhavanagar, 1936.

Buddhaghoṣācārya, *Visuddhimagga*, ed. by Henry Clarke Warren, Rev. by D. Kosambi, Delhi, 1989.

Cullavagga, ed. by Dines Anderson and Helmer Smith, reprint edn., London, 1984.

Dhammapada, ed. by H.C. Norman, London, 1870.

Dīghanikāya (3 vols.) ed. by T.W. Rhys Davids and J. Estin Carpenter, reprint edn., London, 1975-82.

Hemacandra Acarya, *Prabandhacintāmaṇi*, tr. by C.H. Tawney.

Jaina Sūtras, tr. by Herman Jacobi, Oxford, 1884.

Jātaka — ed. by V. Fousboll, London, 1879; tr. by E.B. Cowell, London, 1905.

Kalpasūtra, tr. by Kasturī Chand Lalwani, Delhi, 1979.

Kathākośa, tr. by C.H. Tawney, ed. by Hiralal Jain, London, 1969.

Kathāvatthu, ed. by Arnold C. Taylor, London, 1979.

Kundakundācārya, *Pravacasasāra*, tr. by A.N. Upadhye.

Mahāvagga, ed. by Dines Anderson and Hermer Smith, reprint edn. London. 1984.

Mahāvastu, tr. by J.J. Jones, London, 1949.

Majjhimanikāya, ed. by J.H. Woods and D. Kosambi, London, 1976-9.

Milindapañho, ed. by Dvarikā Nāth Śāstrī, Varanasi, 1970.

Niryāvalīya, ed. by S. Warren, Amsterdam, 1879.

Pātimokkhasūtra, ed. by R.D. Vadekar, Poona, 1939.

Pravarasena, *Setubandha*, Delhi, 1982.

Puggalapannati, ed. by George Landsberg and Mrs. Rhys Davids, reprinted London, 1972.

Saṁyutta Nikāya, London, 1889-94, tr. by Mrs. Rhys Davids, London, 1952-6.

Suttanipāta, ed. by Dines Anderson, reprint edn. London, 1984.

Uvasagadasāo, tr. by Rudolf A.F. Hoernle, Calcutta, 1888 (B.I. Series).

English works

Agarwala, V.S., *India as Known to Pāṇini*, Lucknow, 1962.

Aiyangar, K.V.R., *Some Aspects of the Hindu View of Life According to Dharmaśāstra*.

Allan, John, *Catalogue of the Coins of the Gupta Dynasties and Śaśāṅka*, London, 1914.

Altekar, A.S., *The Position of Women in Hindu Civilisation*, Varanasi, 1938;

———, *Education in Ancient India*, Varanasi, 1956.

Ānand, Shanta, *Kṣatriyas in Ancient India*, Delhi, 1985.

Apte, D.G., *Universities in Ancient India*.

Banerjee, Dr. Manabendu, *Historical and Social Interpretation of the Gupta Inscription*, Calcutta, 1989.

———, R.D., *The Age of the Imperial Guptas*, Varanasi, 1933.

———, Śāstrī, A.P., *Sources of Indian History*, Patna, 1941.

Barua, Beni Madhab, *Aśoka and His Inscription*, Calcutta, 1953.

Basak, R.G., *Aśokan Inscriptions*, Calcutta, 1959.

———, The *History of North Eastern India*, Calcutta, 1965.

Basham, A.L., *History and Doctrine of the Ajivikas*, London, 1951.

———, *The Wonder that was India,* Calcutta, 1985.

Bendall, Cecil, *Catalogue of Buddhist Sanskrit Manuscripts in the University Library*, Cambridge, 1883.

Bhandarkar, R.G., *Early History of the Deccan*, 2nd edn., New Delhi, 1979.

Bhāratīya Vidyā Bhavan, *History and Culture of the India*, Bombay, 1954.

Bose, Phanindra Nath, *Indian Teachers of Buddhist Universities*, Madras, 1923.

Brubacher, John S., Modern Philosophies of Education, Bombay, 1962.

Chakravartī, Haripada, *India as Reflected in the Inscription of the Gupta Period*, Delhi, 1978.

Chanda, Ratna, *Kumāradāsa: A Study*, Calcutta, 1990.

Chatterjee, Sudhakar, *Early History of North India*, Calcutta, 1968.

———, *Social Life in Ancient India,* Calcutta, 1965.

Chide, V. Gordon, *The Aryans*, London, 1926.

Comenius, John Amos, *The Great Didactic*, tr. by M.H. Kaetings.

Cunningham, A., *Coins of Ancient India From the Earliest times to the Seventh Century*, London, 1891.

Dandekar, D.B., *Selection From Sanskrit Inscriptions*, New Delhi, 1977.

Dasgupta, Debendra Chandra, *Educational Psychology of the Ancient Hindus*, Calcutta, 1942.

———, *Jaina System of Education*, Calcutta, 1942.

Das, S.C., *Universities in Ancient India.*

Das, S.K., Education Systems of the Ancient Hindus, Calcutta, 1930.

Davids, Rhys, *Buddhist India.*

De, G.D., *Significance and Importance of Jatakas*, Calcutta, 1951.

Deüssen, Paul, *The Philosophy of the Upaniṣads*, Edinburgh, 1919.

Dey, Sitanath, *Indian Life in the Śukla-Yajurveda*, Calcutta, 1985.

Dutta, Ramesh Chandra, *Ancient India* (2000 BC-AD 800), New edn., Delhi, 1980.

Fa-Hien, *Travels of Fa-Hien*, tr. by H.A. Giles, London, 1956.

Fick, *Social Organisations in North-East India in Buddha's time.*

Fleet, John Faithful, *Corpus Inscription Indicarum*, Varanasi, 1970.

Froebal, F.W.A., *Pedagogics of the Kindergarten*, tr, by Josephine Jarvis, New York, 1905.

Ghosal, U.N., *A History of Hindu Public Life*, Calcutta, 1945.

Ghosh, Aurobindo, *Kālidāsa*, Pondicherry, 1964.

Gyānī, S.D., *Agni Purāṇa: A Study*, Varanasi, 1964.

Hazra, Kanai Lal, *Buddhism in India as Described by the Chinese Pilgrim* (AD 399-689), Delhi, 1983.

———, *Royal Patronage to Buddhism in Ancient India*, Delhi, 1984.

Hazra, R.C., *Studies in the Puranic Records on Hindu Rites and Customs*, Dacca, 1940.

———, *Studies in the Upapurāṇas*, Calcutta, 1958.

Hiuen Tsang, *Buddhist Records of the Western World*, tr. by Samuel Beal, 1906.

Hopkins, E.W., *Ethics of India*, London, 1925.

Hwui Li, *Shaman — The Life of Hiuen Tsang*, tr. by Samuel Beal, London, 1911.

I-tsing, *A Record of the Buddhist Religion*, tr. by J. Takakusu, Oxford, 1896.

Jain, J.C., *Life in Ancient India as Depicted in the Jain Canons*, Bombay, 1947.

Jolly, Julius, *Hindu Law and Custom*, tr. by Baṭakrishna Ghosh, Calcutta, 1928.

Jayaswal, K.P., *An Imperial History of India*, Lahore, 1934.

———, *Hindu Polity*, Calcutta, 1924.

Jha, Chakradhar, *History and Sources of Law in Ancient India*, Delhi, 1987.

Johnston, Herbert, *A Philosophy of Education*, New York, 1963.

Kane, P.V., *History of Dharmaśāstra*, Poona, 1930-58.

Karambelkar, V.W., *The Atharvavedic Civilisation: Its Place in the Indo-Aryan Culture*, Nagpur, 1959.

Keay, F.E., *Indian Education in Ancient and Later Times*, 2nd edn., Oxford, 1942.

Kabilsingh, Chatsumaru, *A Comparative Study of Bhikkuni Patimokkha*, Varanasi, 1984.

Kirkpatrick, W.H., *Froebel's Kindergarten Principles Criticically Examined*, New York, 1916.

Kneller, George, F., *Introduction to the Philosophy of Education*, 2nd edn., New York, 1971.

Law, B.C., *Early Indian Monasteries*, Bangalore, 1958.

———, *India as Described in Early Texts of Buddhism and Jainism*, London, 1941.

Maity, Sachindra Kumar, *The Imperial Guptas and Their Times* AD *300-550*), Delhi, 1975.

Majumder, R.C., *Ancient India*, Delhi, 1974.

Majumder Ramesh Chandra and A.S. Altekar, *The Vākāṭaka Gupta Age*, Varanasi, 1954.

Majumder, R.C. & Pusalkar, A.D., *The History and Culture of the Indian People*, Bombay, 1951-60.

Mankad, D.R., *Pauranic Chronology*, Gujarat, 1951.

Mazumder, N.N., *Education in Ancient India*, Calcutta, 1932.

McCrindle, J.W., *Ancient India as Described by Megasthenes and Arrian*, Calcutta, 1926.

Mitra, Veda, *India of Dharmaśāstra*, Delhi, 1965.

Monroe, Paul, *A Brief Course in the History of Education*, London, 1949.

Montessori, M., *The Montessori Method.*

Mookherjee, Radha Kumud, *Ancient Indian Education*, London, 1947.

———, *Gupta Empire*, Delhi, 1973.

Mukherjee, B.N., *Kuṣāṇas and the Deccan*, Calcutta, 1968.

———, Radhakamal, *A History of Indian Civilisation*, Bombay, 1956.

———, *Culture and Art of India*, London, 1959.

Newman, John Henry, *The Idea of a University*, 1910.

———, *Select Discourses From the Idea of a University*, Cambridge, 1931.

Pargitar, F.E., *Ancient Indian Historical Tradition*, reprint edn., Patna, 1972.

———, *The Purāṇa Text of Dynasties of the Kali Age*, London, 1913.

Patil, D.R., *Cultural History From the Vāyu Purāṇa*, Poona, 1946.

Pestalozzi, Henrich, *Leonard and Gertrude*, 1781.

———, *How Gertrude Teaches Her Children*, tr. by Lucy, 1801.

Puri, Brij Nath, *India in the Time of Patañjali*, Bombay, 1967.

Pusalkar, A.D., *Studies in the Epics and Puranas*, Bombay, 1951.

Radhakrishnan, S., *The Hindu View of Life*, London, 1926.

Raja, Kunhan C., *Kālidāsa*, Waltair, 1956.

Rasdall, Hastings, *Universities of Europe in the Middle Age*, Oxford, 1895.

Ramesh, K.V., *Indian Epigraphy* (Vol. I)., Delhi, 1984.

Renou, Louis, *Vedic India*, Calcutta, 1957.

Ross, James, S., *Groundwork of Education Theory*, London, 1964.

Roy Choudhury, H.C., *Political History of Ancient India*, Calcutta, 1972.

———, *Studies in Indian Antiquities*, Calcutta, 1958.

Rukmani, T.S., *A Cultural Study of the Bhāgavata Purāṇa*, Varanasi, 1970.

Rusk, Robert, R., *The Doctrines of Great Education*, London, 1952.

Saletore, Rajaram Narayan, *Life in the Gupta Age*, Bombay, 1943.

Sankalia, H.D., *The University of Nalanda*, Madras, 1934.

Samaddar, J.N., *The Glories of Magadha*, 2nd edn., Patna, 1927.

Sarkar, S.C., *Educational Ideas and Institutions in Ancient India*, Patna, 1979.

Sen, S.P., *Sources of History of India* (5 vols.), Calcutta, 1978.

Singh, Nisha, *The Origin and Development of Buddhist Monastic Education in India*, Delhi, 1997.

Singh, Sushil Kumar, *Cultural History of Northern India (AD 550-650)*, Delhi, 1986.

Sircar, D.C., *Select Inscriptions*, Vol. I, Calcutta, 1965.

Smart, W.M., *Text Book on Spherical Astronomy*, Cambridge, 1923.

Smith, V.A., *Early History of India*, Allahabad, 1880.

Tripathi, R.P., *Studies in Political and Socio-economic History of Early India*, Allahabad, 1981.

Tripathi, R.S., *History of Ancient India*, 2nd edn., Varanasi, 1960.

Tucci, Giuseppe, *Dialogue of the Buddha* (Sacred Books of the Buddhists), Oxford, 1899. 1921.

Webster, *New world Dictionary*, New York, 1956.

Journals

Annals of Bhandarkar Oriental Research Institute.

Annual Report of the Archaeological Survey of India.

Epigraphia Indica.

Indian Antiquary.
Indian Historical Quarterly.
Journal Asiatique.
Journal of Andhra Historical Research Society.
Journal of the Assam Research Society.
Journal of Bihar and Orissa Research Society.
Journal of Bombay Branch of Royal Asiatic Society.
Journal of Department of Letters, Calcutta University.
Journal of Oriental Research Institute, Pune.
Journal of the Pali Text Society.
Journal of Proceedings of Asiatic Society of Bengal.
Journal of Royal Asiatic Society, Great Britain and Ireland.
Prabuddha Bharat, RMIC, Calcutta.
Proceedings of All India Oriental Conference, Pune.
Proceedings of Indian Historical Congress.

Index